BEACON
BIBLE
EXPOSITIONS

BEACON BIBLE EXPOSITIONS

1. Matthew
2. Mark
3. Luke
4. John
5. Acts
* 6. Romans
7. Corinthians
8. Galatians, Ephesians
9. Philippians, Colossians, Philemon
10. Thessalonians, Timothy, Titus
11. Hebrews, James, Peter
12. John, Jude, Revelation

BEACON BIBLE EXPOSITIONS

VOLUME 6

ROMANS

by

WILLIAM M. GREATHOUSE

Editors
WILLIAM M. GREATHOUSE
WILLARD H. TAYLOR

BEACON HILL PRESS OF KANSAS CITY
Kansas City, Missouri

Library of Congress Catalog Card No. 74-78052
Printed in the United States of America
ISBN: 0-8341-0317-6

Permission to quote from the following copyrighted versions of the Bible is acknowledged with appreciation:

The Holy Bible, New International Version (NIV), copyright © 1973 by New York Bible Society International.

The *Revised Standard Version of the Bible* (RSV), copyrighted 1946 and 1952.

The *New American Standard Bible* (NASB), copyright © The Lockman Foundation, 1960, 1962, 1963, 1968, 1971.

The New English Bible (NEB), © The Delegates of the Oxford University Press and the Syndics of the Cambridge University Press, 1961, 1970.

The Bible: A New Translation, by James Moffatt. Copyright 1954 by James Moffatt. By permission of Harper and Row, Publishers, Inc.

Today's English Version of the New Testament (TEV). Copyright © American Bible Society, 1966.

The New Testament in Modern English, copyright © by J. B. Phillips, 1958. Used by permission of the Macmillan Co.

Contents

Editors' Preface

No Christian preacher or teacher has been more aware of the creating and sustaining power of the Word of God than the Apostle Paul. As a stratagem in his missionary endeavors, he sought out synagogues in the major cities where he knew Jews would gather to hear the Old Testament. No doubt he calculated that he would be invited to expound the Scriptures and so he would have a golden opportunity to preach Christ. That peripatetic preacher was confident that valid Christian experience and living could not be enjoyed apart from the Word of God, whether preached or written. To the Thessalonians he wrote: "And we also thank God constantly for this, that when you received the word of God which you heard from us, you accepted it not as the word of men but as what it really is, the word of God, which is at work in you believers" (1 Thess. 2:13, RSV). Strong Christians, and more broadly, strong churches, are born of, and nurtured on, authentic and winsome exposition of the Bible.

Beacon Bible Expositions provide a systematic, devotional Bible study program for laymen and a fresh, homiletical resource for preachers. All the benefits of the best biblical scholarship are found in them, but nontechnical language is used in the composition. A determined effort is made to relate the clarified truth to life today. The writers, Wesleyan in theological perspective, seek to interpret the gospel, pointing to the Living Word, Christ, who is the primary Subject of all scripture, the Mediator of redemption, and the Norm of Christian living.

The publication of this series is a prayerful invitation to both laymen and ministers to set out on a lifelong, systematic study of the Bible. Hopefully these studies will supply the initial impetus.

—William M. Greathouse and
William H. Taylor, *Editors*

Topical Outline of Romans

Introduction and Theme (1:1-17)

- The Gospel of God (1:1-6)
- Called Saints (1:7)
- The Missionary Task (1:8-15)
- The Gospel of Christ (1:16-17)

The Wrath and the Righteousness of God (1:18—5:11)

- The Wrath of God (1:18-25)
- The Sin of Mankind (1:26-32)
- God's Righteous Judgment (2:1-16)
- God's Law and True Worship (2:17-29)
- God's Faithfulness and Man's Unfaithfulness (3:1-8)
- The Guilt of the World (3:9-20)
- The Gospel of Justification (3:21-26)
- Light from the Cross (3:27-31)
- The Example of Abraham's Faith (4:1-12)
- Justification by Faith Alone (4:13-15)
- The Nature of Faith (4:16-25)
- New Life in Christ (5:1-11)

God's Eternal Purpose in Christ (5:12—11:36)

- Christ and Adam (5:12-21)
- The New You (6:1-14)
- The Holy Life (6:15-23)
- The Freedom of the Gospel (7:1-25)
- Life in the Spirit (8:1-11)
- Holiness by the Spirit (8:12-17)
- The Hope of Glory (8:18-27)
- If God Be for Us! (8:28-39)
- The Majesty of God's Ways (9:1-29)
- The Sin of Unbelief (9:30—10:21)
- The Salvation of Israel (11:1-36)

Practical Applications (12:1—16:27)

- Your Spiritual Worship (12:1-2)
- Being the Body of Christ (12:3-8)
- The Power of Christian Love (12:9-21)
- The Power of Christian Hope (13:1-14)
- Weak and Strong Christians (14:1—15:13)
- The Christian Mission (15:14-33)
- A Glimpse of a Real Church (16:1-27)

Introduction

Martin Luther regarded the Epistle to the Romans as "the purest gospel, which surely deserves the honour that a Christian man should not merely know it by heart word for word, but that he should be occupied with it as the daily bread of his soul." And Bishop Nygren claims that "what the gospel is, what the content of the Christian faith is, one learns to know in the Epistle to the Romans as in no other place in the New Testament."[1]

Throughout Christian history this Epistle has in a peculiar way furnished the impulse for spiritual renewal. When the Church has drifted away from the gospel, a deep study of Romans has repeatedly been the means by which the loss has been recovered.

One summer day in the year 386 the brilliant Augustine, professor of rhetoric at Milan, sat weeping in the garden of his friend Alypius. Having fled North Africa and the prayers of his godly mother, Monica, he had come to Milan, where under the preaching of Bishop Ambrose he had been brought to deep conviction of sin. As he sat that day in the garden, almost persuaded to break with his sinful past, he heard voices of children at play: "Take up and read! Take up and read!" Receiving this as the voice of God, he picked up the scroll which lay at his friend's side and let his eyes rest on the words: "Not in rioting and drunkenness, not in chambering and wantonness, not in strife and envying. But put ye on the Lord Jesus Christ, and make not provision for the flesh, to fulfil the lusts thereof" (13:13-14). "No further would I read," he tells us, "nor needed I; for instantly at the end of the sentence, by a light as it were of serenity infused into my heart, all the darkness of doubt vanished away." Augustine's conversion set in motion spiritual forces which continue to this day.

In November, 1515, Martin Luther, Augustinian monk and doctor of sacred theology at the University of Wittenberg, began his lectures on Romans. As he prepared his expositions he came to see more and more clearly Paul's doctrine of justification. He wrote:

> Certainly I had been possessed by an unusually ardent desire to understand Paul in his Epistle to the Romans. Nevertheless, in spite of the ardour of my heart I was hindered by the unique word in the first chapter: "The righteousness of God revealed in it." I hated that word "the righteousness of God," because in accordance with the usage and custom of the doctors I had been taught to understand it philosophically as meaning, as they put it, the formal and active righteousness according to which God is righteous and punishes sinners and the unjust. . . . Day and night I tried to meditate on the significance of these words. . . . Then, finally, God had mercy on me, and I began to understand that the righteousness of God is that righteousness whereby, through grace and sheer mercy, he justifies us by faith. Thereupon I felt as though I had been reborn altogether and had entered Paradise."[2]

We all know the consequences of this new insight given to Martin Luther.

Under the date of May 24, 1738, John Wesley notes in his *Journal:* "In the evening I went very unwillingly to a society on Aldersgate Street, where one was reading from Luther's Preface to the Epistle to the Romans. About a quarter before nine, while he was describing the change which God works in the heart through faith in Christ, I felt my heart strangely warmed. I felt I did trust in Christ, Christ alone for salvation: and an assurance was given me that he had taken away *my* sins, even *mine,* and saved *me* from the law of sin and death."[3] That was the decisive event which launched the evangelical revival of the eighteenth century.

We have no way of telling what may happen in any person's life and ministry who really gives himself to a study of this Epistle. What happened to Augustine, Luther, and Wesley turned the tide of Western civilization. On a smaller scale things similar may happen to us if we will let the gospel in this Epistle come alive in our minds and spirits by the power of the Spirit.

Preaching from Romans

No preacher or student of the Christian faith can afford to be indifferent to the book which has so profoundly fashioned the life and thought of the Church. Nevertheless, when the average person turns to Romans he generally finds many things hard to understand. Christians nowadays show no particular eagerness to read Romans, much less to make it "the daily bread of their souls." They are reluctant to give themselves to the hard work necessary to understand this theological treatise. On what grounds, then, can we insist that they make the effort to master this brief but important book?

Most preachers are content to deal with texts and passages scattered throughout the Epistle, without attempting an overview for themselves, or a series of sermons that would open up the book to their people. Many great passages are thus overlooked or deliberately bypassed. The practice of random preaching from Romans, however, deserves more serious criticism than that of incompleteness. Even the glowing passages, when they are wrenched from their context, fail to yield their full truth. Only when a congregation is led patiently through the entire Epistle do preacher and people come to sense the splendor and power of Paul's gospel.

This series of expositions is intended simply to suggest one way of preaching through Romans. They presuppose the prior work of exegesis which may be found in my treatment of Romans in *Beacon Bible Commentary* or in many fine commentaries suggested in the bibliography.

To preach from Romans one must first discover its true message and then address that message to the contemporary situation. Romans is always pertinent to the human situation because its truth transcends temporal and cultural boundaries. It is not addressed to one age but to all ages; it speaks to the problems and needs which are common to men at any time and under all conditions. To immerse oneself in Romans is to realize that we are not so remote from our first-century ancestors as we sometimes think, and to discover that the gospel is both timely and timeless.

With P. T. Forsyth we believe: "The Epistles are Christ himself interpreting his finished work through men in whom not they lived but Christ in them. Christ in the Apostles interpreted his finished work as truly in his lifetime he interpreted his unfinished work."[4] If this is true of the Epistles in general, how eminently true is it of Romans! In these pages we are led by one who has "the mind of Christ" (1 Cor. 2:16) to view Christ's finished work through eyes illumined and purified by the Holy Spirit, so that we can view it in its whole historical context, beginning with the justification of Abraham and climaxing with the salvation of all Israel at the end. As A. M. Hunter says, Romans is the master key to the gospel of God in Christ.

The Message of Romans

The theme of Romans is the righteousness of God (1: 16-17). This is a dynamic biblical idea which comes from such Old Testament passages as Ps. 71:15-16; 98:2; Isa. 45:21-25; 46:13; 51:5.[5] This righteousness is primarily God's saving action in history, which comes to its culminating exhibition in the death of Christ as the world's Sin Offering. In the cross of Christ, God justifies himself as God and vindicates His holiness while at the same time He offers His saving mercy to all who believe in Jesus (3:21-26).

The purpose of Romans is to declare that true righteousness is the free gift of God to men who have faith in Christ. In the apostle's day many of God's people found this hard to believe; for them righteousness was a work to be performed under the law, a meritorious achievement. But we make a grave mistake if we assume that such legalism is dead. "Basically, the legalist is the self-made man; and legalism is the attempt to run our own lives and earn our own salvation—to be good without God."[6] Obviously, this is not a sin peculiar to the Pharisees; it is the tendency of all religion. And whenever it appears, Paul's gospel in Romans is the sword of the Spirit to destroy it.

The first major division of the Epistle (1:18—3:20) is basic to the development of Paul's gospel. Men have no claim on God's favor; the whole race of unbelieving men exist under the wrath of God—all men in general, because they have turned from the Creator to the creature and have thereby become morally depraved; the Jews in particular, because they have misconceived and disobeyed the higher revelation of God in the law. Before God, "there is none righteous, no, not one" (3:10).

At 3:21, Paul takes up his main theme he so boldly set forth in 1:16-17. He has demonstrated the utter failure of man to win by his own achievement or merit a rightness with God. *But now in Christ a new day has dawned.* God himself in the person of His Son has broken the impasse and provided a righteousness of His own as a free gift to be received by faith. While the gospel reveals a "righteousness apart from the law," this divine righteousness is "witnessed to by the law (Abraham, ch. 4) and the prophets (Hab. 2:4; quoted in 1:17)." Thus while the revelation of God's righteousness is new in one sense, in yet another it is but the climactic manifestation of the way He has always saved men of faith.

After setting forth the *wrath* of God in the first section of Romans (1:18—3:20) and the *righteousness* of God in the second (3:21—5:11), Paul next relates these two themes to their original points of departure, Adam and Christ (5:12-

21). Adam and Christ are more than historic persons; they represent two orders of humanity. Adam is the first man *and* mankind under the dominion of sin and the sentence of death; Christ is the "new man," the "last Adam," *and* the new humanity freed from sin and through grace reigning in righteousness to eternal life.

How does Christ bring about this new humanity freed from sin? In 6:1—8:39 we find the answer to this question. Basically, Paul's position is that the man who is righteous before God through faith is also sanctified by God. The converted man has died to sin and been raised to newness of life by the Spirit (6:1-11). Reckoning himself to be thus dead to sin and alive to God in Christ, he is now called upon to yield himself to God in an act of consecration for the true sanctification where his body becomes the temple of the Holy Spirit (6:12-23).

The new man has not only died to sin, he also has died to the law as a means of his salvation (7:1-6). The law was given to fallen man to reveal to him the utter depravity of his heart and to reduce him to the point of self-despair where he calls upon Christ, who alone can sanctify (7:7-25). The law cannot sanctify. But what the law could never do, God has done through the incarnation and death of His Son: He has destroyed sin in the flesh and opened the floodgates of the sanctifying Spirit, who lifts us out of the flesh into himself (8:1-17).

Nevertheless, as glorious as it is, life in the Spirit is not yet consummated. Our existence as Spirit-indwelt and Spirit-empowered believers is still an existence "between the times"—viz., between Pentecost and the Parousia. It is therefore an existence marked by suffering, infirmities, and incompleteness. But it is an existence also of hope. The Spirit of adoption who now witnesses to us is the Spirit of the Christ, who is yet to return and glorify us with himself, at the same time redeeming the whole creation which now groans with us in travail. Thus we have been saved in hope, the hope of glory. God's sovereign purpose marches on to its grand consummation, and meanwhile nothing can separate us from the love of God in Christ (8:18-39).

After giving us this majestic overview of God's eternal purpose in Christ, Paul shows us how that purpose has been working itself out in history (9:1—11:36). Despite the unbelief of ancient Israel, God's sovereign purpose moves forward in the affairs of men. Rather than defeating God's purpose, the crucifixion of Christ made it possible for Him to break open the treasures of His grace to the Gentile world. The Israel which has always been constituted by faith in God's promise has now been enlarged to encompass believing Gentiles. Moreover, God has not forgotten His ancient people. His gifts and callings are without repentance. In a word of pure prophecy Paul lifts the veil and introduces us into the mystery of Israel's final restoration. "And so all Israel shall be saved" (11:26). With this vision before his eyes, Paul bursts into a doxology to the infinite wisdom and goodness of God.

Paul has now concluded his doctrinal statement. Beginning at chapter 12 he makes an appeal to his readers to present their bodies living sacrifices to God and to be utterly transformed by the mind of Christ. He sees love as the key to the Christian ethic, love in the body of Christ and love in society. Love is the one thing needful. And hope: "For now is our salvation nearer than when we [first] believed." Chapters 12 through 15 are rich in guidance to the Christian community. The moving appeal in chapter 14 for Christian understanding and tolerance, climaxing in 15:1-13 with a call to Christlikeness, is one of the great ethical passages of the New Testament. In 15:14-33 we find a powerful sermon on the Christian mission in the world, and finally in chapter 16 a picture of a real local church.

This, in essence, is the extraordinary Epistle which Paul wrote to the Roman church. Surprisingly inclusive, clearly outlined, dealing on every page with vital, searching truth, divinely wise and intensely practical, it has no companion and no equal among religious writings of its kind. But it is more than a great religious masterpiece; it is the gospel which is the power of God to salvation to everyone who believes.

Place and Date of Writing

In none of Paul's other letters are the place and time of writing so clearly indicated in the letter itself as in the case of Romans. In 15:19-32 the apostle makes it clear that he is nearing the culmination of his ministry in the East. He has preached the gospel "from Jerusalem, and round about unto Illyricum," and goes on to say that he feels he has completed his mission to that vast region. Now he plans to go to Spain, and since Rome is already evangelized, to visit the Roman church on the way. But first he must perform a special task at Jerusalem. For some time he has been engaged in gathering a collection among the churches of Macedonia and Greece for "the poor saints which are at Jerusalem." That offering is now virtually complete, and Paul is awaiting only the opportunity of delivering it.

Since, in 1 Cor. 16:3-4, Paul indicates he plans to end his work on the collection in Corinth and to depart from that city to Jerusalem, and since at the time of writing 2 Corinthians (see 9:3-5) he is carrying out that plan and is on his way to Corinth, it is reasonable to suppose that he wrote Romans in Corinth. This position finds further support in the fact that the Epistle was delivered by the deaconess Phoebe, who was from Cenchrea, the eastern port of Corinth (16:1). This would have been the apostle's last visit to that city, since it was in Jerusalem just after this that his long imprisonment began (cf. Acts 20:2-3). The letter was dictated to a certain Tertius (16:22).

Scholars have been unable to establish with any degree of certainty the exact time of this final visit to Corinth. The date depends upon the entire chronology of Paul's ministry which one adopts. The earliest date suggested is January—March, A.D. 53; and the latest, January—March in 59. A date of A.D. 57 or 58 is most probable.

Introduction and Theme
Rom. 1:1-17

ROMANS 1

The Gospel of God

Romans 1:1-6

1 Paul, a servant of Jesus Christ, called to be an apostle, separated unto the gospel of God,
2 (Which he had promised afore by his prophets in the holy scriptures,)
3 Concerning his Son Jesus Christ our Lord, which was made of the seed of David according to the flesh;
4 And declared to be the Son of God with power, according to the spirit of holiness, by the resurrection from the dead:
5 By whom we have received grace and apostleship, for obedience to the faith among all nations, for his name:
6 Among whom are ye also the called of Jesus Christ:

In the opening sentence of Romans we find a play on words. The adjective translated *separated* is from the same root as *Pharisee.* As a youth Saul had made himself a Pharisee, a separatist for God's law; by His call and commission God had made Paul a separatist for the gospel.

The gospel of God, or simply "God's gospel," is an attractive phrase too. The proclamation of Jesus Christ is God's good news for mankind. We are sometimes inclined to complain bitterly, "Look what the world's come to!" But if we really believe the gospel, we will gladly announce, "Look what's come to the world!"

But what is the *gospel of God?* It concerns *his Son Jesus Christ*—His incarnation, death, resurrection, and glorification. Everything focuses in Jesus Christ, who is himself the world's Best News.

With a stroke of genius Paul's first word about Jesus is the recitation of an early Palestinian creed (3-4) well known among the Romans. This creed he weaves into his introduction, to reassure his readers that the gospel he preaches is the gospel they themselves have received and believe. But, first, Paul reaches back into God's ancient purposes and declares that the gospel concerning God's Son was—

1. *Promised in Holy Scripture* (2). God preached and promised this gospel in the Old Testament (Gal. 3:8). Certainly the apostle had not always known this. As a Jewish rabbi he had read the scriptures with a veil over his eyes (2 Cor. 3:14). It was not until Christ confronted him on the Damascus Road and removed that veil (2 Cor. 3:15-18) that Paul was given to see the true meaning of the Old Testament, namely, that it is first and foremost a book of promise pointing toward Christ. Christ is the King of scripture (Luther). Everything God did in ancient times—calling Abraham, delivering the people from Egypt and settling them in Canaan, sending prophets to them, judging them, and then restoring them after the Exile—all these acts of God were but preparatory to that Event of all events, Jesus Christ, in whom God's act and God's being are one.

2. *Proclaimed in Creed* (3-4). Throughout Paul's letters we find the gospel summarized in bits of verse, song, and creed. One of these creeds Paul now quotes. Notice how this balanced couplet focuses on the two interrelated events which constitute the gospel: the incarnation and the resurrection of the Son of God.

First, the Incarnation. The Son of God *was descended from David according to the flesh* (RSV). *Flesh* stands for man in the totality of his existence. The Son of God became man.

"Forasmuch then as the children are partakers of flesh

and blood, he also himself likewise took part of the same; that through death he might destroy him that had the power of death, that is, the devil; and deliver them who through fear of death were in their lifetime subject to bondage" (Heb. 2:14-15). Again, here in Romans: "For what the law could not do, in that it was weak through the flesh, God sending his own Son in the likeness of sinful flesh, and for sin, condemned sin in the flesh" (8:3).

Identification unlimited. Total involvement. "The Son of God became what we are, that we might become what He is" (Irenaeus). He became flesh, that we might receive the Spirit. He was made "sin for us," that we might be made righteous and holy. He died, that we might live.

Jesus Christ is *God's Son*—He partakes of the Father's very being as God; Jesus Christ is *man*—He partakes of our being as sinful mortals. We must never be guilty of cutting off Jacob's ladder at either end. "God was in Christ." But this Christ was one of us, bone of our bone, flesh of our flesh, our true Elder Brother. And it was all for us. He was made "sin for us" (2 Cor. 5:21). "The miracle of the Incarnation," P. T. Forsyth claims, "is not the Word made flesh, but the Holy made sin for us."

Perhaps we may modify Forsyth's sentence to read, "The miracle of the Incarnation is *not merely* that the Word was made flesh." That truth is precious:

Without reluctance,
Flesh and blood His substance,
My God and Saviour came,
And Jesus was His name.

This gives Him understanding and sympathy. We need this succor. But we need more—we must have redemption from sin and death. That is what Forsyth is getting at. Bethlehem was but the gateway to Calvary. The cradle found fulfillment in the Cross. He was born to die. He "loved me, and gave himself for me" (Gal. 2:20).

Secondly, the Resurrection. The New Testament does not stop with the Incarnation. The incarnate Son of God, who offered up himself on our behalf, has been *designated Son of God in power according to the Spirit of holiness by his resurrection from the dead* (RSV). He was delivered up for our offenses, but He was raised again for our justification, sanctification, and redemption (4:25; cf. 1 Cor. 1:30).

Two things must be said about the Resurrection. For one thing, if God had not raised Jesus from the dead, His death would have been no more efficacious than that of Socrates. The Resurrection was God's Amen to Jesus—the validation of His death as the world's Sin Offering.

But the Resurrection was more. As this brief creed says it, by raising Him from the dead God installed Jesus as *Son of God in power.* As Peter announced in his Pentecostal sermon, "Let all the house of Israel know assuredly, that God hath made that same Jesus, whom ye have crucified, both Lord and Christ" (Acts 2:36). God has vindicated His Son, making Him Lord of the Church.

Furthermore, as the glorified Christ, He bestows upon the Church the sanctifying Spirit. "Therefore being by the right hand of God exalted, and having received of the Father the promise of the Holy Ghost, he hath shed forth this, which ye now see and hear" (Acts 2:33). This was Peter's announcement to the people of Jerusalem. It is also the gospel announcement to us. "For if, when we were enemies, we were reconciled to God by the death of his Son, much more, being reconciled, we shall be saved by his life" (5:10)—His risen life as the exalted Lord. As our risen Lord, He stands in the presence of the Father for us. As our risen Lord, He ever lives to make intercession for us. As our risen Lord, he floods our hearts with the love of God, through the Spirit He gives us (5:5).

But this is not all. "We are saved by hope" (8:24)—in the joyous expectation that God will send His Son back to finalize His kingdom and consummate our salvation.

3. *Published Among All Nations* (5-6). From the glorified Christ, Paul had *received grace and apostleship to bring about the obedience of faith . . . among all nations* (RSV). God's ultimate purpose is unmistakable: "That at the name of Jesus every knee should bow . . . and that every tongue should confess that Jesus Christ is Lord, to the glory of God the Father" (Phil. 2:10-11).

By the preaching of the gospel this purpose is now being effected in grace. *The obedience of faith* which the gospel accomplishes may be understood as the faith-obedience which penitently surrenders to Christ and confesses Him as Lord (10:8-13). But there is also *the obedience that comes from faith* (NIV); for through the gift of the Spirit, the gospel makes it possible for "the just requirement of the law" to be "fulfilled in us" (8:4, RSV).

Not all men believe the gospel. Nevertheless, in God's own time the proclamation shall be sounded: "The kingdoms of this world are become the kingdoms of our Lord, and of his Christ; and he shall reign for ever and ever" (Rev. 11:15). This is the coming of God's kingdom in judgment.

The commission of the Church is to bring as many as possible to the present acknowledgment of Jesus Christ as Lord, so that in that final day they shall join with all the redeemed in crowning Him the triumphant Lord of the universe.

He is Lord; He is Lord;
He is risen from the dead,
And He is Lord.
Ev'ry knee shall bow,
Ev'ry tongue confess
That Jesus Christ is Lord.

Called Saints

Romans 1:7

7 To all that be in Rome, beloved of God, called to be saints: Grace to you and peace from God our Father, and the Lord Jesus Christ.

The Romans are addressed as those who, *beloved of God,* are *called to be saints.* Paul is *klētos apostolos,* literally "a called apostle" (1)—not a so-called apostle but one whose apostleship is real, from God and not himself (cf. Gal. 1:1). The Roman Christians are *klētois hagiois,* literally "called saints"—real saints by virtue of God's call, to which they had responded in penitent faith and obedience.

1. First, this is a *corporate* holiness. *Saints* is always plural (except one reference to "every saint," Phil. 4:21). As "the assembly of the called-out ones" *(ecclesia)* the Church is "holy." Holiness is a social reality; it characterizes the people of God or the body of Christ as a corporate entity. We have been called into a fellowship of believers, "the household of God" (Eph. 2:19).

Holiness is not something we individually achieve; it is a gift we receive as we respond obediently to God's grace in Christ. Responding to God's call, we enter into covenant relationship with Him and His redeemed people, the Blood-washed and Spirit-indwelt ones.

2. Secondly, this is a *relational* holiness. God alone is holy; He stands over against all He has created as the Holy One. Persons and things are "holy" only as they are separated for special relationship to Him. In the Old Testament, the Sabbath, the Temple, the tithe were "holy." The Church is thus "holy." We have been separated from the world and sin for God's possession and use (1 Pet. 2:9-10). We are not our own; we have been bought with a price (1 Cor. 6:19); we are *called to belong to Jesus Christ* (6, NIV); we are "sanctified in Christ Jesus" (1 Cor. 1:1), and in Christ we belong to God. "[We] are Christ's; and Christ is God's" (1 Cor. 3:23, RSV).

Holiness then is basically relational: we are holy only as we are "in Christ" and "abide" or "remain" in Him and He in us (John 15:1-8). Then, and only then, we become "partakers of his holiness" (Heb. 12:10).

3. Finally, this is an *ethical* holiness. As moral beings we cannot belong to God without being, to the utmost of our

obedience, like Him. "As he who called you is holy, be holy yourselves in all your conduct; since it is written, 'You shall be holy, for I am holy'" (1 Pet. 1:15-16, RSV).

a. Faith in Christ initiates this holiness. Paul will remind these Romans that, as baptized believers, they have died with Christ and been raised with Him to new life in the Spirit—where sin's reign has ceased (6:1-11).

b. But he will go on to urge them to "yield" (6:13) or "present" (12:1) themselves to God in an act of consecration "for sanctification" (6:19, RSV) in a yet deeper and more pervasive sense. He prays for another church: "May God himself, the God of peace, sanctify you through and through" (1 Thess. 5:23, NIV).

c. Those who are thus sanctified "through and through" (in spirit, soul, and body), however, have simply begun to realize the full meaning of true sanctification; for in the highest sense sanctification involves a continuous growth in Christlikeness (2 Cor. 3:18; Rom. 12:2). From this perspective the true saints still "fall short of the glory of God" (3:23, RSV) and confess with Paul, "Not that I have already attained, or am already perfected" (Phil. 3:12, John Wesley).

Finish then Thy new creation;
Pure and spotless let us be.
May we see Thy great salvation,
Perfectly restored in Thee!
Changed from glory into glory,
Till in heaven we take our place,
Till we cast our crowns before Thee,
Lost in wonder, love, and praise.
—Charles Wesley

The Missionary Task

Romans 1:8-15

8 First, I thank my God through Jesus Christ for you all, that your faith is spoken of throughout the whole world.
9 For God is my witness, whom I serve with my spirit in the gospel of

his Son, that without ceasing I make mention of you always in my
prayers;
10 Making request, if by any means now at length I might have a
prosperous journey by the will of God to come unto you.
11 For I long to see you, that I may impart unto you some spiritual
gift, to the end ye may be established;
12 That is, that I may be comforted together with you by the mutual
faith both of you and me.
13 Now I would not have you ignorant, brethren, that oftentimes I
purposed to come unto you, (but was let hitherto,) that I might have
some fruit among you also, even as among other Gentiles.
14 I am debtor both to the Greeks, and to the Barbarians; both to the
wise, and to the unwise.
15 So, as much as in me is, I am ready to preach the gospel to you
that are at Rome also.

Here we have a look into the mind and heart of the Church's greatest missionary. *Apostle* also means "missionary"—the first term derives from the Greek, the other from Latin. A missionary, like the apostle, is one who knows himself "called" and "sent" to preach the gospel of God's Son to those who have not heard. In this sense every God-called preacher is a missionary of Christ, wherever the commission may send him.

1. First, we see *the missionary spirit* (8-12). Like Paul, the Christian missionary is embued, empowered, and impelled by the Spirit, to bear witness to Christ (Acts 1:8). This is what Paul means when he writes, *God is my witness, whom I serve with my spirit in the gospel of his Son.* Spiritual service is ministry in the Spirit. To prepare Paul for his ministry God sent Ananias to him with the word, "Brother Saul, the Lord—Jesus, who appeared to you on the road as you were coming here—has sent me so that you may see again and be filled with the Holy Spirit" (Acts 9:17, NIV).

This "charisma" of the Spirit was also Paul's burden for the Romans (11). Not only must missionaries be Spirit-filled; the Church must also. The fact that Paul was genuinely humble in sharing his concern (12) is actually the clearest indication that he *was* Spirit-filled (see 1 Corinthians 13).

2. We are permitted to see here also *the missionary obedience* (13). One who is truly sent of God is sensitive to

God's providences and obedient to God's directives. At times he is "forbidden by the Holy Spirit" (RSV) to speak the word at a certain place, only to be redirected to another assignment (cf. Acts 16:6-10). So Paul had been prevented from going to Rome with his message. When he finally reached the Imperial City, it was in chains. But, said John Calvin, any journey is prosperous which is within God's will.

Obedience to God's guidance means instant readiness to walk through open doors with the assurance that God will be with us, and also a patient spirit which does not chafe when God closes the doors and says, "Wait."

3. Finally, *the missionary compulsion* throbs here (14-15). One who is truly set apart and sent by God feels himself under obligation to every man "to give him the gospel in the same measure . . . [he has] received it" (Phineas F. Bresee). So he is *eager* to share the good news of Christ anywhere God may lead.

Jesus, confirm my heart's desire
To work, and speak, and think for Thee;
Still let me guard the holy fire,
And still stir up Thy gift in me.

Ready for all Thy perfect will,
My acts of faith and love repeat,
Till death Thy endless mercies seal,
And make the sacrifice complete.

—Charles Wesley

The Gospel of Christ

Romans 1:16-17

16 For I am not ashamed of the gospel of Christ: for it is the power of God unto salvation to every one that believeth; to the Jew first, and also to the Greek.
17 For therein is the righteousness of God revealed from faith to faith: as it is written, The just shall live by faith.

Shortly after the last world war a German pastor was being shown through the notorious concentration camp at

Belsen. Passing through the chambers of unspeakable horror, he reached a point where he could go no further. Stopping in his tracks, he burst into tears and cried, "I am ashamed of my country!"

The man's confession of shame showed him to be a true patriot, for it was a kind of cleansing flame. It proved to be an expression of a spreading fire of contrition which eventually purged the conscience of a great nation.[1]

Yet, while a man may be ashamed of his country and be a true patriot, no one can be ashamed of the gospel and be a true Christian. To be truly Christian is to say with Paul, *I am not ashamed of the gospel.*

Paul's confession is actually a figure of speech which means, "I am proud of the gospel." He glories in the gospel and counts it a high honor to proclaim it. But his rejoicing arises from no reliance upon his own resources, or his eloquence, or anything else like that (cf. 1 Cor. 2:1-5). His confidence is solely in the gospel itself, for—

1. *The gospel is the power of God.* Notice exactly what the apostle says: not that the gospel *has* power, but that it *is* power. The gospel itself is God's unique, incomparable power at work. Paul chooses the word *dunamis* rather than *energeia.* His accent is upon the Source of the gospel's power rather than its process.

God is the Source of our salvation, but He saves through the word of the Cross. Through the proclamation of Christ crucified God's power is released. "For the word of the cross is folly to those who are perishing, but to us who are being saved it is the power of God" (1 Cor. 1:18, RSV). "The gospel," P. T. Forsyth says, "is not a statement, nor a doctrine nor a scheme nor a promise. It is an act of power, an act of redemption, an eternal, perennial act of God in Christ."[2] *The gospel IS the power of God.* "When you received the word of God which you heard from us," Paul wrote the Thessalonians, "you accepted it not as the word of men but as what it really is, the word of God, which is at work in you believers" (1 Thess. 2:13, RSV).

The message which turned the world upside down was the heralding of Christ's death for us. When Paul's Galatian converts were lapsing from the gospel to the law, he wrote them scorchingly: "You foolish Galatians! Who has bewitched you? Before your very eyes Jesus Christ was clearly portrayed as crucified. I would like to learn just one thing from you: Did you receive the Spirit by observing the law, or by believing what you heard? Are you so foolish? After beginning with the Spirit, are you now trying to attain perfection by human effort?" (Gal. 3:1-3, NIV).

Several things stand out here. The Christian message is a graphic portrayal of Christ's crucifixion. This message received by faith brings justification and the release of the Spirit. This power of the Spirit is the very essence of Christian existence. The message of Christ announced and believed justifies, sanctifies, and perfects.

2. *The gospel, therefore, brings God's salvation.* Salvation *(sōtēria)* means "deliverance," both in the negative sense of rescuing from sin and wrath and also in the positive sense of imparting the sanctifying Spirit and bestowing eternal life. It means healing, holiness, wholeness.

This salvation has its beginnings in prevenient grace (in the awakening and conviction of sin which attends preaching). Salvation proper occurs at the moment of saving faith, along with justification (pardon, acceptance) and regeneration (new life in the Spirit). Justification and the new birth occur simultaneously; together they constitute the gateway to a life of holy love. In his sermon "Working Out Our Own Salvation," Wesley has given us a classic summation of Christian salvation:

> All experience as well as Scripture, show that this salvation is both instantaneous and gradual. It begins the movement we are justified, in a holy, humble, gentle love of God and man. It gradually increases from the moment we are justified, till at another instant the heart is cleansed from all sin and filled with the pure love of God and man. But even that love increases more and more till we "grow up in all things into him who is the

Head;" till we attain "the measure of the stature of the fulness of Christ."[3]

The salvation which *begins* as justification and new birth becomes full salvation in entire sanctification; it becomes final salvation in glorification. I can therefore say scripturally, "I have been saved" (Eph. 2:8-9; 1 Cor. 15:2; 2 Tim. 1:9); "I am being saved" (1 Cor. 1:18, NIV; Phil. 2:12-13); and, "I shall be saved" (5:9; 13:10; 1 Pet. 1:3-5).

The final goal of New Testament salvation, however, is the return of Christ and our glorification with Him. In the strictest sense we are in the process of being saved. But through the gift of the Spirit we have an anticipatory enjoyment of salvation—true deliverance from sin and a present knowledge of God through Christ: the "earnest" and "firstfruits" of the glory which shall be ours when Christ returns to redeem our bodies and take us to himself forever (Rom. 8:22-24; 2 Cor. 1:22; Eph. 1:13-14).

It is in this comprehensive sense that *the gospel . . . is the power of God unto salvation.* We are "confident of this, that he who began a good work in . . . [us] will carry it on to completion until the day of Christ" (Phil. 1:6, NIV), "if . . . [we] continue in the faith grounded and settled, and . . . [are] not moved away from the hope of the gospel" (Col. 1:23).

3. *Finally, the gospel reveals God's righteousness.* The gospel is God's power to salvation because in the gospel *the righteousness of God [is] revealed* (17).

It was the discovery of the scriptural meaning of this phrase which ushered Martin Luther through "the gates of Paradise." He says:

> Day and night I tried to meditate upon the significance of these words: "the righteousness of God revealed in it, as it is written, The righteous shall live by faith." Then, finally, God had mercy on me, and I began to understand that the righteousness of God is that righteousness, whereby, through grace and sheer mercy, he justifies us by faith. . . . Thereupon I felt as though I had been reborn altogether and had entered Paradise. In the

same moment the face of the whole of Scripture became apparent to me.[4]

The light had begun to filter into Luther's mind earlier as he lectured from the Psalms. There we find this sentence: "The Lord hath made known his *salvation:* his *righteousness* hath he revealed in the sight of the heathen" (Ps. 98:2, mg.). The idea of God's righteousness as His justifying mercy comes straight out of the Old Testament. In Isaiah we read, "My *righteousness* is near; my *salvation* is gone forth" (51:5; cf. Ps. 71:12-16; 98:1-3, 9; Isa. 45: 21-25). In the two quotations above "righteousness" and "salvation" are parallel expressions. God's righteousness is His saving activity. It is God justifying, sanctifying, and finally glorifying those who put their trust in "Christ Jesus, who has become for us wisdom from God—that is, our righteousness, holiness and redemption" (1 Cor. 1:30, NIV).

Our salvation has as its foundation, in its forefront, *the righteousness of God*—not first His love, but His "righteousness." Love is there, but love which vindicates justice and produces holiness in us. Throughout the Epistle we encounter this phrase, *the righteousness of God,* but it is 3:25-26 which gives us the key. In 2:5 it is His judgment upon the finally impenitent. In 3:5 it is His fidelity to His promises. In chapter 3, however, it is "the culminating exhibition of the divine resentment against sin" (Sanday and Headlam), making it possible for God to remain just while He justifies the person who puts his trust in Jesus. In the death of Christ, God's righteousness becomes His saving mercy extended to all who believe.

Furthermore, "The Cross that satisfies God sanctifies man" (P. T. Forsyth). The righteousness of God is "authentic goodness wrought into the existence of man as God's own glorious achievement," Frank Staggs insists. "Jesus came to give not only a new standing, acceptance, but also new life, a new kind of existence."[5] "He hath made him to be sin for us, who knew no sin; that we might be made the righteousness of God in him" (2 Cor. 5:21). The righteousness *of* God becomes therefore a righteousness *from* God (Phil. 3:9). As the disobedience of the first Adam made men actually sinners, the obedience of the Last Adam makes men actually righteous (5:19-21). Staggs comments further:

> The crux of the matter is that in salvation God brings about real righteousness in man, not mere forensic righteousness. God accepts sinners, but he does not accept sin, just as a physician accepts sick people, but does not make peace with sickness. The whole point is to bring about cure, not to count well one who is not well.[6]

The righteousness is ours on the simple condition of faith—*by faith from first to last, just as it is written: "The righteous will live by faith"* (1:17, NIV). This saving faith is *trust*—"trust with a strong element of obedience in it" (A. M. Hunter; cf. 1:5). It is an open-eyed, obedient resting in Christ's death and resurrection *for us* (cf. Gal. 2:20*b*).

John Wesley, in his sermon "Salvation by Faith," has given a beautiful and comprehensive definition of saving faith:

> Christian faith is not only an assent to the whole gospel of Christ, but also a full reliance on the blood of Christ: a trust in the merits of His life, death, and resurrection; a recumbency upon Him as our atonement and life, as *given for us* and *living in us;* and in consequence hereof, a closing with Him, and cleaving to Him, as our "wisdom, righteousness, sanctification, and redemption," or, in one word, our salvation.[7]

The Wrath and the Righteousness of God
Rom. 1:18—5:11

The Wrath of God

Romans 1:18-25

18 For the wrath of God is revealed from heaven against all ungodliness and unrighteousness of men, who hold the truth in unrighteousness;
19 Because that which may be known of God is manifest in them; for God hath shewed it unto them.
20 For the invisible things of him from the creation of the world are clearly seen, being understood by the things that are made, even his eternal power and Godhead; so that they are without excuse:
21 Because that, when they knew God, they glorified him not as God, neither were thankful; but became vain in their imaginations, and their foolish heart was darkened.
22 Professing themselves to be wise, they became fools,
23 And changed the glory of the uncorruptible God into an image made like to corruptible man, and to birds, and fourfooted beasts, and creeping things.
24 Wherefore God also gave them up to uncleanness through the lusts of their own hearts, to dishonour their own bodies between themselves:
25 Who changed the truth of God into a lie, and worshipped and served the creature more than the Creator, who is blessed for ever. Amen.

Modern thought about God has been so sentimentalized we find it difficult to speak of His wrath. But wrath—the judgment of the Holy One upon sin in every form—is an essential part of the biblical picture of God. Man's fallen condition is an existence under *the wrath of God* which is *revealed from heaven.*

A. M. Hunter speaks of God's wrath as "his holy love reacting against evil—the 'adverse wind' of the divine will blowing against the sinner, not only on the Judgment Day, but now, and resulting in the degeneration and abasement of the sinner."[1]

Because God is God, His wrath is a terrible reality. But wrath is not hate. "Hate opposes love; wrath is the form love takes with those who oppose it. Hate is unjust; wrath is just. Hate seeks to destroy; wrath forgives," Burton Throckmorton observes. "So when Paul says that the wrath of God is being disclosed along with His righteousness, he is saying that God is offering acquittal, but that those who refuse to accept it are condemned."[2]

1. Consider, first, the *reality* of God's wrath (18). *The wrath of God is revealed from heaven,* just as His righteousness. The repetition of the verb shows this double revelation. As the righteousness of God means the whole situation in which man exists when he is right with God, so the wrath of God means his total situation where he has turned away from the Creator. The God who reveals himself as saving mercy to those who believe also reveals himself as wrath to those who refuse to acknowledge His claims and who spurn His love.

Every human being without exception stands in an indissoluble relationship to God. This is what distinguishes man as man: he exists always responsible before God. Consequently everyone experiences either God's righteousness or God's wrath—His love or His displeasure, His favor or His judgment. "In Christ," says Luther, "'God is love.' Outside Christ, 'Our God is a consuming fire.'"

2. Furthermore, we are told the *reason* for God's wrath (19-23). It is because fallen man refuses to acknowledge God. *That which may be known of God is manifest* both *to* man in creation and *in* him by the Spirit. The creation itself bespeaks an eternal and divine Creator. As John Macquarrie has written,

> Let us suppose—*per impossibile*—that the time had come when the sciences had answered all possible questions within their competence, and all the gaps had been closed, so that there was no place left for the so-called "God of the gaps." There would still be a question which

> no science can answer and which, indeed, no science claims competence to entertain: "Why a world at all, rather than just nothing?" The question might be framed even more specifically: "Why an ordered world, capable of being rendered intelligible to the intelligences which it has itself brought forth, rather than an unknowing and unknown chaos?" These are questions which no science either entertains or answers, but they are questions which man cannot renounce unless he is prepared to renounce what is most distinctively human in him.[3]

Through the created universe God is seeking to engage man in dialogue with himself. To be human is to experience what Rudolph Otto calls "the holy," that immediate awareness of God which cannot be explained or rationalized. Man stands under God's wrath because he suppresses the truth of God.

Man refuses to acknowledge God because he does not want God to rule over him. In the pride of his heart he prefers to be his own god. "Every man would like to be God if it were possible," Bertrand Russell says; "and some few refuse to admit the impossibility!" More seriously, as Jean Paul Sartre writes, "Since there is no God, it is the chief project of man to become God." This is what the Bible calls the Fall: "basically a venture into autonomy" (Leonard Verduin). Paul has a word for such folly: *When they knew God, they glorified him not as God, neither were thankful; but became vain in their imaginations, and their foolish heart was darkened. Professing themselves to be wise, they became fools* (21-22).

As Jesus said, "This is the judgment, that light has come into the world, and men loved darkness rather than light, because their deeds were evil" (John 3:19, RSV). Man's problem is not ignorance but sin. Until we repent, therefore, we are doomed to blindness—and ultimately to hell.

3. Finally, the *result* of God's wrath is shown (24-25). When we refuse to "let God be God" and do not acknowledge Him, He abandons us to our vicious impulses. Three

times in this chapter we read the terrible sentence, *God gave them up* (24, 26, 28). This is the nemesis of sin: God gives us over to the consequences of our folly and selfishness.

"What else could God do if He respects the freedom given man from the beginning?" Frank Staggs asks. The lost, says C. S. Lewis in *The Problem of Pain,* "enjoy forever the horrible freedom they have demanded, and are therefore self-enslaved." The final retribution of hell is to be abandoned forever to ourselves!

Aldous Huxley, himself an out-and-out unbeliever, was honest enough to recognize the emptiness of what the world calls freedom. In *Eyeless in Gaza* he makes one of his characters say, "Freedom's a marvellous name. . . . You think that, if you call imprisonment true freedom, people will be attracted to the prison. And the worst of it is, you're quite right. The name counts more with most people than the thing."

Emptiness is the awful fate awaiting those who refuse God. Since nothing really has any meaning, there can be no hope, no joy. D. H. Lawrence, the modern prophet of sex, realized with horror what such emptiness means. His poetry repeats the terrible sensation:

It is a fearful thing to fall into the hands of the living God
But it is a much more fearful thing to fall out of them.

And still . . . man can break away, and fall from the hands of God
into himself alone, down the godless plunge of the abyss,
a god-lost creature turning upon himself
in the long, long fall, revolving upon himself
in the endless writhe of the last, the last self-knowledge
which he can never reach till he touch the bottom of the abyss

which he can never touch, for the abyss is bottomless.

So it wriggles its way even further down, further down
at last in sheer horror of not being able to leave off
knowing itself, knowing itself apart from God, falling.

The Sin of Mankind

Romans 1:26-32

26 For this cause God gave them up unto vile affections: for even their women did change the natural use into that which is against nature:
27 And likewise also the men, leaving the natural use of the woman, burned in their lust one toward another; men with men working that which is unseemly, and receiving in themselves that recompence of their error which was meet.
28 And even as they did not like to retain God in their knowledge, God gave them over to a reprobate mind, to do those things which are not convenient;
29 Being filled with all unrighteousness, fornication, wickedness, covetousness, maliciousness; full of envy, murder, debate, deceit, malignity; whisperers,
30 Backbiters, haters of God, despiteful, proud, boasters, inventors of evil things, disobedient to parents,
31 Without understanding, covenant breakers, without natural affection, implacable, unmerciful:
32 Who knowing the judgment of God, that they which commit such things are worthy of death, not only do the same, but have pleasure in them that do them.

This scripture is as contemporary as today's edition of the *London Times* or the *Kansas City Star*. It presents a frank and unblushing account of lesbianism, homosexuality, sexual permissiveness, violence, social strife, and crimes against humanity. Paul concludes by lamenting that these wicked practices and lawless acts were not only being practiced but actually applauded.

Of course this is a portrayal of pagan Roman society. Suetonius' *Lives of Emperors* reveals how widespread were such sins in the highest circles of the empire. Of Julius Caesar, regarded as one of history's greatest men, he reports, "He was every woman's man and every man's woman." Tiberius and Nero were even worse. Nero murdered his own mother, Agrippina, with the conniving of the pagan moralist Seneca!

Yet to limit this to a depiction of pagan Rome is to miss in it God's word to us. Paul's intention goes deep. He is pointing out that man has sunk into sin because he has turned away from his Creator to self-idolatry. He has exchanged the glory of God for the shame of creature-worship. *For this cause God gave them up unto vile affections: for even their women did change the natural use into that which is against nature* (26). Man has fallen into sin because he has fallen away from God.

Calvin Coolidge was a man of few words. Upon his returning from a church service his wife asked, "What was the pastor's sermon about?" "Sin," the president answered. "What did he say?" she continued. "He's against it," was his reply.

Too often this is as far as our sermons go. But with Paul we must expose sin for the blasphemous thing it really is: finite man's attempt to dethrone God and enthrone himself!

1. First of all, then, we see here *sin in root.* All man's sins, vices, and crimes spring from one common source: his refusal to acknowledge, honor, and worship God. Man's fall was his prideful unwillingness, in Luther's words, to "let God be God." Millard Reed has coined a phrase for this: "man's delusion of self-omnipotence."

Because man himself would be god, his foolish heart is darkened, and in his blindness he creates idolatrous "religion": a way of worship which permits him to express the sinful idolatry of his depraved heart.

Such "religion" itself becomes the spawning ground for immorality and perversion. Man's religious history is not one of evolution but of degeneration. Sin first corrupted man's relation to God; from this alienation came lust and illicit desire. Deprived of God's life, man immediately became depraved.

"There is only one sin," claims William Temple, "and it is characteristic of the whole world. It is self-will which prefers 'my' way to God's—which puts 'me' in the center where only God is in place." "And," John Wesley observes, "where the last end is changed, there can be no real goodness." With God dethroned and self at the center, all life is corrupted.

Sin is essentially self-sovereignty. Falling for Satan's lie, man has denied his creaturehood in his decision to define for himself what is "good" and what is "evil." F. F. Bruce points out that Paul's account here is deliberately stated in terms of the Genesis version of Adam's fall. Casting the pair out of the Garden, God said: "Behold, the man has become like one of us, knowing good and evil" (Gen. 3:22, RSV). Rejecting God's definition of good (responsible obedience to the Creator), Adam and Eve created their own ethical system (defining good and evil in terms of what *they* believed and wished). This dethroning of God and enthroning of self is the quintessence of sin.

2. Secondly, here we see *sin in fruit.* Man's original sin is his "ungodliness," but perversion of faith issues immediately in perversion of life: "unrighteousness" (see 1:18). Deprivation becomes depravation.

a. D. R. Davies, in *Down Peacock's Feathers,* has observed that rebellion against God has created a moral vacuum. "And nature abhors a moral as well as a physical vacuum," says Davies.

> That vacuum must be filled, if not by God, then by the devil of self. All the lusts and excesses of human behaviour are attempts to satisfy "that aching void the world can never fill." Man, as a result of his Fall from Divine Grace, is cursed by an infinite craving.[4]

It is this curse upon man—sensuality and its vile brood of perversions, vices, and crimes—which Paul delineates in the closing part of this chapter. *God gave them up.* This solemn phrase, thrice repeated, explains the moral consequences of revolt and alienation from God.

The calculated risk God took in making man in His own image was that man might abuse his freedom. God could have prevented the Fall only by making man a robot. But if man was to be created in the divine image, he must be free—even to destroy himself. Parents take this risk when they choose to have a child. For God or man, personal existence has its built-in risks; and God himself chose those risks. God gave them up, then, to themselves, to their own deliberate choices.

b. God gave them up to sexual perversions (24-27). Sex is one of God's most sacred and beautiful gifts to mankind (Gen. 1:27-31). But when man turns from God to the worship of sex, this sacred urge explodes and destroys his humanity. Man turns out to be just a "male" or a "female." But he goes further and perverts his sexuality into homosexual expression. "Seeking to become God, man becomes biology. Falling short of wholeness, man becomes a fraction, a fragment, a torso."[5] In the worship of sex man sinks beneath the beast!

c. God gave them up to social vices that destroy the human family (28-32). Cut off from God, man cuts himself off from not only his own authentic self but also from his fellowman. Adam and Eve break their relationship with God, then they accuse one another, and next Cain kills Abel. This is the story of man's self-ruin.

d. Verse 28 is a play on words: Because they did not *see fit* to acknowledge God, God gave them up to an *unfit* mind. In rejecting the knowledge of God man debased his own reason and distorted the whole of his life.

e. For a picture of the corruption that plagues man in his stupid self-idolatry this passage is unexcelled. Swinburne composed a "Hymn to Man":

Glory to Man in highest!
For Man is the master of things.

Master of things! No, man is the groveling slave of his base passions and instincts. The prodigal son swaggering down the road to Vanity Fair imagines himself free, but he is the bellhop of his own desires. "No man is more a slave than he who thinks himself free without really being so" (Goethe).

God takes our freedom with such seriousness that he permits a man to self-destruct if he so chooses.

f. What hope then for man? That like the prodigal he may "come to himself" and return to the Father. The gospel is this: *Christ has come to our far country, to lead us back home to God.* In Paul's words, "God was in Christ, reconciling the world unto himself, not imputing their trespasses unto them. . . . For he hath made him to be sin for us, who knew no sin; that we might be made the righteousness of God in him" (2 Cor. 5:19, 21).

Hark! the gospel news is sounding,
Christ has suffered on the tree;
Streams of mercy are abounding,
Grace for all is rich and free,
Now, poor sinner,
Come to Him who died for thee.
—H. Bourne

ROMANS 2

God's Righteous Judgment

Romans 2:1-16

1 Therefore thou art inexcusable, O man, whosoever thou art that judgest: for wherein thou judgest another, thou condemnest thyself; for thou that judgest doest the same things.
2 But we are sure that the judgment of God is according to truth against them which commit such things.
3 And thinkest thou this, O man, that judgest them which do such things, and doest the same, that thou shalt escape the judgment of God?
4 Or despisest thou the riches of his goodness and forbearance and longsuffering; not knowing that the goodness of God leadeth thee to repentance?
5 But after thy hardness and impenitent heart treasurest up unto thyself wrath against the day of wrath and revelation of the righteous judgment of God;
6 Who will render to every man according to his deeds:
7 To them who by patient continuance in well doing seek for glory and honour and immortality, eternal life:
8 But unto them that are contentious, and do not obey the truth, but obey unrighteousness, indignation and wrath,

9 Tribulation and anguish, upon every soul of man that doeth evil, of the Jew first, and also of the Gentile;
10 But glory, honour, and peace, to every man that worketh good, to the Jew first, and also to the Gentile:
11 For there is no respect of persons with God.
12 For as many as have sinned without law shall also perish without law: and as many as have sinned in the law shall be judged by the law;
13 (For not the hearers of the law are just before God, but the doers of the law shall be justified.
14 For when the Gentiles, which have not the law, do by nature the things contained in the law, these, having not the law, are a law unto themselves:
15 Which shew the work of the law written in their hearts, their conscience also bearing witness, and their thoughts the mean while accusing or else excusing one another;)
16 In the day when God shall judge the secrets of men by Jesus Christ according to my gospel.

Therefore you have no excuse, O man, whoever you are, when you judge another; for in passing judgment upon him you condemn yourself, because you, the judge, are doing the very same things (1, RSV).

God's judgment exposes every human being.

Paul here imagines an objector protesting: "Surely you aren't classing me with the riffraff you have just described?" "Yes," Paul replies, "for in pronouncing judgment on others and excusing yourself you have usurped God's judgment throne. You have put yourself in the place of God, which is the root of all other sins."

After hearing Dr. R. A. Torrey preach from the text "For all have sinned, and come short of the glory of God" (3:23), a lordly, cultured man exploded to the preacher, "You anger me with your charge that I am a sinner like everyone else. I'm no church member, it is true, but I am a decent husband and father; I am an honorable citizen and upright man. What sin do you charge *me* with?"

"I charge you with treason against high heaven!" Torrey retorted.

Some weeks later the evangelist was preaching in Australia. After his sermon the same man came forward, but this time in a broken spirit. As he clasped Torrey's hand he said, "Kneel down with me, brother! Never again will you charge me with treason against God." He was converted and transformed.

If we understand Paul's gospel we have only one choice—to bow before God and submit to His righteous judgment. The apostle says three things about that judgment: it is *according to truth* (2-5); it is *according to* our *deeds* (6-11); it is *according to* the *gospel* (12-16).

1. First, God's righteous judgment is *according to the truth.* God's word to Samuel upon His rejection of Saul is apropos: "The Lord sees not as man sees; man looks on the outward appearance, but the Lord looks on the heart" (1 Sam. 16:7, RSV). We can deceive man, but God is not mocked.

God, who judges our hearts, knows how "desperately wicked" they are. "I the Lord search the heart, I try the reins, even to give every man according to his ways, and according to the fruit of his doings" (Jer. 17:9-10). God desires "truth in the inward parts" (Ps. 51:6). Only the heart He has purified can bear the scrutiny of His holiness (cf. Acts 15:8-9).

We must not be deceived into smug self-complacency because God's judgment is restrained by His forbearance and goodness. His perfect knowledge is now the handmaid of His love.

The light of Thy redeeming love,
Like sunbeams darted from above,
Doth all my sins display,
Countless as dancing motes, and small,
Shall chase them all away.

—Charles Wesley

This revelation of His judgment mingled with mercy moves us to pray, "Search me, O God, and know my heart" (Ps. 139:23-24). "If we walk in the light" of His holy revealings and "confess" our sin (acknowledge the sin He sees), "the blood of Jesus Christ his Son cleanseth us from all sin" (1 John 1:7-10).

But to reject this true self-knowledge *after* our *hardness and impenitent heart* is to treasure up to ourselves *wrath against the day of wrath and revelation of the righteous judgment of God.*

2. Secondly, God's righteous judgment is *according to our deeds.* Special privileges disappear before the tribunal of divine justice. Ultimately it will be a question, for each one of us, of "true righteousness and holiness" (Eph. 4:24, RSV).

This is not a contradiction of Paul's doctrine of justification by faith alone. But it is a warning against permitting the gospel of grace to lapse into an antinomianism which confuses liberty with license (see 3:8; 6:1-2; Gal. 5:13-16).

"Do we then make void the law through faith? God forbid: yea, we establish the law" (3:31). *Patient continuance in well doing* (7), however, must not be confused with "the deeds of the law" (in 3:20). The latter is a way of self-salvation by law-works. True salvation is the way of justification where faith works by love (cf. Gal. 5:5-6). Salvation is by faith alone, but faith is never alone. True faith always evidences itself by *patient continuance in well doing;* otherwise it is not saving faith.

Well doing is a sincere response to God's grace, given to us freely "apart from law" (3:21, RSV). Abraham was justified before God, by faith, 430 years before the law was given (4:1-3; Gal. 3:5-6, 16-17). Old Testament saints were thus righteous before God during the era of the law (Ps. 32:1-2; quoted by Paul, 4:6-8). Gentiles who have never heard of Christ may thus respond to God's Spirit and be accepted on the day of judgment. When Peter stood before Cornelius and his household, he said, "Of a truth I perceive that God is no respecter of persons: but in every nation he that feareth him, and worketh righteousness, is accepted with him" (Acts 10:34-35). "There is not a damned sinner," John Wesley believed, "who, *if he had done well,* would not be in Paradise." "Shall not the Judge of all the earth do right?" (Gen. 18:25).

3. Finally, God's righteous judgment is *according to the gospel.* And what is the judgment note in Paul's gospel? This, that God judges according to the light we have been given. "Whatever the law says it speaks to those who are under the law" (3:19, RSV). Gentiles who do not have the law will be judged according to how they respond to *the law written in their hearts.* Paul's word *conscience* was a common word among his contemporaries. John Wesley prefers "prevenient grace," since God is secretly working in every person's heart. Admittedly, this inward light is not as bright as the gospel's. However, God does not give just enough light to some to damn them but not enough to save them. Nothing in the passage supports any conclusion except that man is responsible only within the limits of his ability to respond. He is responsible for the light he has. Men are not condemned for limited light but for the rejection of that light.

Such fairness of judgment on God's part in no way relieves the Church of its responsibility to "send the light" of the gospel to those in pagan darkness. As Spurgeon is reported to have said, it is not a question of whether a heathen can be saved without hearing the gospel but rather, Can the Church be saved if it does not obey Christ's commission? Although the possibility of a heathen's being saved through prevenient grace cannot be denied on gospel grounds, the probability (because of original sin) is so slight as to lessen in no way the urgency of preaching Christ to all men.

Let us remember Paul's real point here: *GOD [not you or I] shall judge the secrets of men.* "Every one of us shall give account of himself to God" (14:12). Let us not therefore fall into the snare of judging others. Paul's gospel will not permit a judgmental spirit. Rather, it calls upon me to put *myself* under God's righteous judgment in Christ. Only as I live under this judgment at the Cross do I enjoy His favor and salvation. My only hope is to "win Christ, and be found in him, not having mine own righteousness, which is of the law, but that which is through the faith of Christ, the righteousness which is of God by faith" (Phil. 3:8-9).

My hope is built on nothing less
Than Jesus' blood and righteousness.
I dare not trust the sweetest frame,
But wholly lean on Jesus' name.

On Christ, the solid Rock, I stand;
All other ground is sinking sand.

—EDWARD MOTE

God's Law and True Worship

Romans 2:17-29

17 Behold, thou art called a Jew, and restest in the law, and makest thy boast of God,
18 And knowest his will, and approvest the things that are more excellent, being instructed out of the law;
19 And art confident that thou thyself art a guide of the blind, a light of them which are in darkness,
20 An instructor of the foolish, a teacher of babes, which hast the form of knowledge and of the truth in the law.
21 Thou therefore which teachest another, teachest thou not thyself? thou that preachest a man should not steal, dost thou steal?
22 Thou that sayest a man should not commit adultery, dost thou commit adultery? thou that abhorrest idols, dost thou commit sacrilege?
23 Thou that makest thy boast of the law, through breaking the law dishonourest thou God?
24 For the name of God is blasphemed among the Gentiles through you, as it is written.
25 For circumcision verily profiteth, if thou keep the law: but if thou be a breaker of the law, thy circumcision is made uncircumcision.
26 Therefore if the uncircumcision keep the righteousness of the law, shall not his uncircumcision be counted for circumcision?
27 And shall not uncircumcision which is by nature, if it fulfil the law, judge thee, who by the letter and circumcision dost transgress the law?
28 For he is not a Jew, which is one outwardly; neither is that circumcision, which is outward in the flesh:
29 But he is a Jew, which is one inwardly; and circumcision is that of the heart, in the spirit, and not in the letter; whose praise is not of men, but of God.

"You bear the honored name of Jew," Paul says; "your possession of the law gives you confidence; you glory in the fact that you worship the true and living God and understand His will. Do you not realize that privilege brings responsibility?"

In order to transfer this to our situation, just change "Jew" to *Christian* and place *gospel* instead of "law." For Jesus said, "Do not think that I have come to abolish the Law or the Prophets; I have not come to abolish them but to fulfill them" (Matt. 5:17, NIV).

It is true, the law *as the mediator of salvation* has been abolished. "Christ is the end of the law for righteousness to every one that believeth" (10:4). Christ himself has fulfilled the law, and by His death has brought the legal dispensation to its conclusion (7:1-6); He is now revealed as the "one mediator between God and men" (1 Tim. 2:5). But the law *as the expression of the divine will* remains forever valid. "Do we then make void the law through faith?" Paul will soon answer: "God forbid; yea, we establish the law" (3:31). Christ's obedience unto death makes possible the law's being fulfilled in us (8:1-4).

Recognizing, therefore, that the law remains valid in the gospel dispensation as the expression of God's will for His children (7:12), we understand the apostle to be saying three things in this passage:

(1) Knowing God's will is insufficient to save us (17-24);

(2) Doing God's will is required (25-26);

(3) Fulfilling God's will is promised (27-29).

1. *Knowing God's will is insufficient to save us.* Those who perceive clearly that the gospel is not legalism are tempted to conclude falsely that gospel freedom means license (Gal. 5:13). Freedom, however, must be properly understood, not as the right to do as I please but as the power to do as I ought. Freedom is the ability to fulfill God's will—and His will is that we shall obey Him in love. To know God's will and not obey it is spiritually fatal. "Shall we sin, because we are not under law, but under grace? God forbid. Know ye not, that to whom ye yield yourselves servants to obey, his servants ye are to whom ye obey; whether of sin unto death, or of obedience unto righteousness?" (6:15-16). The gospel does not cancel the moral law; it reinforces it (Matt. 5:17-43).

Paul clearly echoes Jesus in the Sermon on the Mount as he poses the searching questions in vv. 21-23:

You who preach against stealing, do you steal (NIV)—by being less than honest in your dealings with others? by withholding from God tithes and offerings (Mal. 3:8-9)? by not rendering Him the worship and service which is His due?

You who say that people should not commit adultery, do you commit adultery (NIV)—by cherishing lustful desires? by inward infidelity to your marriage vows? by spiritual infidelity to Christ?

You who abhor idols (NIV)—do you know that idolatry is really a matter of the heart—that the worship of any creature is a violation of the second commandment?

You who brag about the law, do you dishonor God by breaking the law? (NIV).

2. *Doing God's will is required.* Paul and James have sometimes been made to contradict each other with respect to faith and works. But Paul is surely advocating in this passage what James calls for when he writes, "Be ye doers of the word, and not hearers only, deceiving your own selves" (Jas. 1:22).

Paul reminds these converted Jews of Rome that *circumcision has value if you observe the law* (NIV). On the other hand, *If those who are not circumcised keep the law's requirements, will they not be regarded as though they were circumcised?* (NIV). To *keep the law* is clearly not an outward but an inward matter. It does not mean carrying out the detailed precepts of the Torah, but fulfilling the relation of covenant love. "For in Jesus Christ neither circumcision availeth any thing, nor uncircumcision; but faith which worketh by love" (Gal. 5:6).

"Master, which is the great commandment in the law?" a lawyer asked Jesus. "Jesus said unto him, Thou shalt love the Lord thy God with all thy heart, and with all thy soul, and with all thy mind. This is the first and great commandment. And the second is like unto it, Thou shalt love thy neighbour as thyself. *On these two commandments hang all the law and the prophets"* (Matt. 22:36-40). Paul echoes this later in Romans when he writes, "Love is the fulfilling of the law" (see 13:8-10).

"The whole law under which we now are," Wesley writes in *A Plain Account of Christian Perfection,* "is fulfilled by love (Rom. xiii.9, 10). Faith working or animated by love is all that God now requires of man. . . .

"How is 'love the end of the commandment'? (1 Tim. i.5)" Wesley then asks.

"It is the end of every commandment of God. It is the point aimed at by the whole and every part of the Christian institution. The foundation is faith, purifying the heart; and the end love, preserving a good conscience."[6]

3. *Fulfilling God's will is promised.* The law, even though it is subject to misunderstanding and perversion, is nevertheless a good and holy gift of God (7:12). It points to the true relation between God and man and between man and man; it also witnesses to the righteousness of God by which we are justified by grace "apart from law" (3:21-24, RSV).

Furthermore, the law promises inward sanctification: "And the Lord thy God will circumcise thine heart, and the heart of thy seed, to love the Lord thy God with all thine heart, and with all thy soul, that thou mayest live" (Deut. 30:6). It is this remarkable promise which illuminates Paul's reference to *circumcision of the heart, by the Spirit* (29, NIV). What the Torah promises is freely given to Christian believers. This is one of the most definitive promises of entire sanctification in the Bible. The fulfillment of this promise constitutes the very essence of Paul's gospel:

> There is therefore now no condemnation for those who are in Christ Jesus. For the law of the Spirit of life in Christ Jesus has set me free from the law of sin and death. For God has done what the law, weakened by the flesh, could not do: sending his own Son in the likeness of sinful flesh and for sin, he condemned sin in the flesh, *in order that the just requirement of the law might be*

fulfilled in us, who walk not according to the flesh but according to the Spirit (8:1-4, RSV, italics added).

Oh, that in me the sacred fire
Might now begin to glow,
Burn up the dross of base desire,
And make the mountains flow!

Refining Fire, go through my heart,
Illuminate my soul;
Scatter Thy life through every part,
And sanctify the whole!
—Charles Wesley

ROMANS 3

God's Faithfulness and Man's Unfaithfulness

Romans 3:1-8

1 What advantage then hath the Jew? or what profit is there of circumcision?
2 Much every way: chiefly, because that unto them were committed the oracles of God.
3 For what if some did not believe? shall their unbelief make the faith of God without effect?
4 God forbid: yea, let God be true, but every man a liar; as it is written, That thou mightest be justified in thy sayings, and mightest overcome when thou art judged.
5 But if our unrighteousness commend the righteousness of God, what shall we say? Is God unrighteous who taketh vengeance? (I speak as a man)
6 God forbid: for then how shall God judge the world?
7 For if the truth of God hath more abounded through my lie unto his glory; why yet am I also judged as a sinner?
8 And not rather, (as we be slanderously reported, and as some affirm that we say,) Let us do evil, that good may come? whose damnation is just.

Paul now imagines a critic of his gospel breaking into his argument and objecting, "Well, now, if it is being a Jew inwardly that counts, if it is 'the circumcision of the heart' that matters, what advantage is there in belonging to the Jewish nation and being physically circumcised?"

A modern objector might take a different tack. He might ask Paul, "If Christianity is a spiritual affair, a matter of the heart and of love, why then the Church with its sacraments? What advantage is there in baptism and church membership? And what need does one have for the written Word when God's law is inscribed in our hearts by the Spirit?"

And he might continue (as some have indeed done, v. 8): "If salvation by the law is impossible, if *our* unrighteousness brings out *God's* righteousness, as your gospel seems to say, how can God justly punish us for sin? If salvation is by grace alone, thus magnifying God's goodness, let us do evil that good may come!"

It is true, Paul's gospel of grace tends to raise these very questions when it is faithfully proclaimed. In fact, if such questions are *not* raised at times, one wonders if the true gospel is being preached. As Wesley often said, the truth is "within a hair's breadth" of antinomianism. Nevertheless, that hair's breadth is absolutely crucial, as this passage clearly shows.

The problem of God's faithfulness and man's unfaithfulness is the issue. Do these cancel out each other? *By no means!* (RSV), Paul answers.

1. First, God's faithfulness is *not annulled* by man's unfaithfulness (1-2). "If we believe not, yet he abideth faithful: he cannot deny himself" (2 Tim. 2:13).

a. God's faithfulness is witnessed to by the Church. "The church exists because God willed it to exist." It stands as a monument to God's faithfulness. The faithlessness of God's people down through the millennia has not defeated God's purposes or cancelled out His faithfulness. God has preserved the Church despite its obtuseness and apostasy. Why? Because He is "the faithful God" (see Deut. 7:6-9). The order of reception of persons into one Protestant church begins, "Dearly beloved, the Church is of God, and will be preserved unto the end of time."

b. God's faithfulness is also attested to by the sacraments of baptism (6:1-11; Col. 2:11-14) and the Lord's Supper (1 Cor. 11:23-26). These are more than ordinances or rites; they are even more than signs. The sacraments are *seals* which attest the faithfulness of God to perform what He has promised. They are forms of preaching the gospel—concrete, objective assurance that, in Christ, God is for us. The sacraments objectify God's redemption and become true channels of grace to those who receive them in true faith.

c. God's faithfulness is divinely certified in *the oracles of God* (2), *the very words of God* (NIV), in Holy Scripture. In these oracles are given to us "exceeding great and precious promises, that by these . . . [we] might be partakers of the divine nature" (2 Pet. 1:4). The Scriptures assure us of God's faithfulness to freely justify us (1 John 1:9—2:3), to truly sanctify us (1 Thess. 5:23-24), to preserve us in the time of temptation and trial (1 Cor. 10:13), and to consummate our salvation (1 Cor. 1:8-9).

2. Moreover, God's faithfulness is *brought out* by man's faithlessness (3-4).

Ancient Israel was faithless to her divine trust; she rejected the prophets and finally the Crucified, and so was rejected by God as His chosen servant. But Israel's stumbling over a crucified Messiah became the occasion for a fresh display of God's faithfulness. God would not be without a people, so He grafted into Israel's stock believing Jews and Gentiles, who now constitute the new Israel of the Christian Church. (This in brief is the meaning of cc. 9—11.) So *Israel's faithlessness* brought out *God's faithfulness* in a more striking display of His righteousness.

Now, shall our unfaith nullify God's fidelity? *By no means! Let God be true though every man be false, as it is written,* "That thou mayest be justified in thy words, and prevail when thou art judged" (4, RSV).

The apostle's usage of the word "justified" here anticipates what he is to say about justification later in this chapter. God justified himself, as well as making available justification to believing sinners, in the death of Christ. "God presented him as a sacrifice of atonement. . . . He did this to demonstrate his justice, because in his forbearance he had left the sins committed beforehand unpunished—he did it to demonstrate his justice at the present time, so as to be just and the one who justifies the man who has faith in Jesus" (25-26, NIV).

Christ's death is the disclosure of God's righteous judgment upon sin. Before Calvary men might have misconstrued God's mercy as mere forbearance, Paul admits. But no more. God has vindicated himself as the just God by presenting Christ "as a sacrifice of atonement." As our Representative, Jesus has stood where *we* should have stood and has died, the Innocent for the guilty, the Holy for the sinful, to demonstrate God's justice at the present time.

Our faithlessness, therefore, rather than nullifying God's faithfulness and righteousness, has *manifested* it. Our unfaith became the occasion not only of God's justifying himself, but also of His justifying *us*. We now know Him "to be just *and* the one who justifies the man who has faith in Jesus."

3. However, God's faithfulness may be *presumed on* by man's unfaithfulness (5-9).

God made himself supremely vulnerable in the Cross. He put himself before us in such humble, self-giving love that it is possible for us to pervert His truth into our lie! It is possible to make His sacrifice for sin an excuse for sinning.

So we hear the critic raising his third objection: If man's sin commends God's righteousness, why then should the sinner be condemned? All Paul answers at the moment is *If that were so, how could God judge the world?* (NIV).

The objection is carried further. Some had actually

reported Paul as saying, *Let us do evil that good may result!* (NIV). Paul's answer is terse but unmistakable: *Whose damnation is just.*

Those who thus pervert God's sacrificial love in Christ stand self-condemned. Their moral obtuseness is so evident they cannot be seeking God's truth; they are *presuming upon* God's faithfulness. Although God's truth is always within a knife's edge of error, the gospel of justification "by faith apart from works of law" (3:28, RSV) can never be twisted into an imputed or "as if" righteousness.

If my "faith" does not produce the good works of fidelity to God and love toward my fellowman, it is not faith but presumption. True faith creates within us a passion to be holy as He is holy (1 Pet. 1:16). "By faith we eagerly await through the Spirit the righteousness [glorification and final justification] for which we hope. For in Christ Jesus . . . the only thing that counts is faith expressing itself through love" (Gal. 5:5-6, NIV).

So, "The foundation of God standeth sure, having this seal, The Lord knoweth them that are his. And, Let every one that nameth the name of Christ depart from iniquity" (2 Tim. 2:19). To forget or deny this, even through some theory of the atonement which claims to glorify Christ, is not to remember that God *shall . . . judge the world* (6).

But, if "the wages of sin is death, . . . the gift of God is eternal life through Jesus Christ our Lord" (6:23).

The Guilt of the World

Romans 3:9-20

9 What then? are we better than they? No, in no wise: for we have before proved both Jews and Gentiles, that they are all under sin;
10 As it is written, There is none righteous, no, not one:
11 There is none that understandeth, there is none that seeketh after God.
12 They are all gone out of the way, they are together become unprofitable; there is none that doeth good, no, not one.
13 Their throat is an open sepulchre; with their tongues they have used deceit; the poison of asps is under their lips:
14 Whose mouth is full of cursing and bitterness:
15 Their feet are swift to shed blood:

16 Destruction and misery are in their ways:
17 And the way of peace have they not known:
18 There is no fear of God before their eyes.
19 Now we know that what things soever the law saith, it saith to them who are under the law: that every mouth may be stopped, and all the world may become guilty before God.
20 Therefore by the deeds of the law there shall no flesh be justified in his sight: for by the law is the knowledge of sin.

As God's prosecuting attorney, the apostle now presents his final arguments and rests his case against the human family.

By way of introduction he raises two questions. *What then?* he asks first, meaning, *What shall we conclude then?* (NIV). Paul is summing up his argument. Oddly, the second question may be translated either, *Are we any better?* (NIV); or, "Are we any worse?" Or it may be rendered, "Do we put forward anything in our defense?" (The problem arises from the uncertainty of the voice of the Greek verb.)

But, however the question is translated, the point is unmistakable: Before God's bar of perfect justice no one has any advantages over any other. *We have before proved both Jews and Gentiles,* declares Paul, *that they are all under sin* (9)—both its guilt and its power.

God's prosecutor then proceeds by selecting a series of scriptural indictments which cover a wide range of human depravity, to show that, from whatever aspect humanity may be viewed, the verdict of scripture is one of universal sin and guilt.

To feel the force of Paul's argument, however, we first must see—

1. *The Perspective of the Law.* Paul's doctrine of total depravity makes sense only when we understand that he is describing man's condition *before God.*

He is not denying that fallen man has many natural gifts or that he performs many noble deeds (cf. 5:7). Paul rather means that in God's presence man has no goodness to plead; there he can only confess his sin and guilt. It is before God, not before society, that unregenerate man is utterly helpless and undone.

Fallen man has not completely forfeited the natural image of God (personhood), but he has effaced the moral image. He has turned from the Creator to the creature, thus distorting completely the meaning of his existence. The substitution of self-government for the lordship of God spells total depravity and corruption. Our good capacities have been twisted from their true fulfillment in obedience to God's design and have been prostituted for false ends.

As fallen creatures, we are still able to conceive and perform creative social acts, but actions judged "good" by society or even the external law of God (cf. Phil. 3:6) are religiously corrupt when they issue from a heart "alienated from the life of God" (Eph. 4:18). Such works are not "good works" in God's sight because they do not spring from a living relationship with Him. Our relationship to God is determinative of all else. "Whatsoever is not of faith is sin" (14:23); so that even morally good acts, performed by men who do not love God, are sinful (cf. Matt. 7:16-20).

John Wesley has written clearly at this point. Notice carefully his analysis:

> The unrenewed will is wholly perverse, in reference to the end of man. Man is a merely dependent being; having no existence or goodness originally from himself; but all he has is from God, as the first cause and spring of all perfection, natural and moral. . . .
>
> And thus man was created looking directly to God, as his last end; but falling into sin, he fell off from God, and turned into himself. Now, this infers a total apostasy and corruption in man; for where the last end is changed, there can be no real goodness. And this is the case of all men in their natural state: They seek not God, but themselves. Hence though many fair shreds of morality are among them, yet "there is none that doeth good, no, not one." For though some of them "run well," they are still off the way; they never aim at the right

> mark. Whithersoever they move, they cannot move beyond the circle of self. They seek themselves, they act from themselves; their natural, civil, and religious actions, from whatever spring they come, do all run into, and meet in, this dead sea.[7]

Such is Paul's perspective throughout this lengthy indictment of mankind (1:18—3:20). Since man has turned from his true End, *"None is righteous, no, not one"* (RSV)—before God, who made man for himself. Even fallen man's good deeds performed to gain God's favor are an abomination in His sight (see Matt. 7:21-23).

2. *The Pronouncement of the Law* (10-18). Paul now strings together a group of scriptures, mostly from the psalms, to prove his point that none is righteous before God. Sin is so universal as to admit no single exception. He proves:

a. Sin in human character (10-12)
b. Sin in human speech (13-14)
c. Sin in human conduct (15-17)

He concludes by showing the cause of all sin: "There is no fear of God before their eyes" (18). Man is sinful because he has lost his creaturely reverence for God.

As it is essential first to grasp that Paul is demonstrating the guilt of mankind before God and not before society, we must now see that he (like Wesley in the quote above) is describing *fallen man apart from the grace of God.* Unregenerate man, left entirely to himself, seeks only himself. This is the meaning of his sin. "None is righteous . . . no one understands, no one seeks for God. All have turned aside" (RSV).

Here is the reason sinful man cannot save himself. He has torn himself from his orbit in God's love and is now a wandering star. Forces beyond his own control hurl him farther into outer space. If he is ever to be saved, God himself must come close and draw man back into the circle of His gracious love. With this in mind, we see how futile are man's puny efforts to save himself. He is headed in the wrong direction, and he has no power of himself to reverse his course into the outer darkness!

3. *The Purpose of the Law.* We are now prepared to hear Paul's final statement as he rests his case: "Now we know that whatever the law says it speaks to those who are under the law, so that every mouth may be stopped, and the whole world may be held accountable to God. For no human being will be justified in his sight by works of the law, since through the law comes knowledge of sin" (19-20, RSV).

The purpose of the law is, first, to stop all cavil. Anyone who proposes to place himself before God on the grounds of his own supposed righteousness stands self-condemned and speechless. The function of God's law is to reveal to us our sin and guilt before God; *through the law comes knowledge of sin.* The law is God's mirror; it shows us our sin but it has no power to forgive and cleanse. When it has brought me to the place where I cry out, "God be merciful to me a sinner," it has performed its primary task.

But the law has an ultimate purpose: to bring me to Christ, the only Saviour (Gal. 3:24). It shows me my wounds and my sickness, that I may call upon the Great Physician. This is really why Paul has introduced the diagnosis of man's sinful condition which takes up the first major division of his Epistle. And this is the reason we must preach the law. "Those who are well have no need of a physician, but those who are sick. . . . [Christ] came not to call the righteous, but sinners" (Matt. 9:12-13, RSV).

Paul is about to make the grand announcement of the gospel: that Great Physician *has* come! With rapture I now sing,

My Great Physician heals the sick;
The lost He came to save.
For me His precious blood He shed;
For me His life He gave.

I need no other argument;
I need no other plea.
It is enough that Jesus died,
And that He died for me.
—L. H. Edmonds

The Gospel of Justification

Romans 3:21-26

21 But now the righteousness of God without the law is manifested, being witnessed by the law and the prophets;
22 Even the righteousness of God which is by faith of Jesus Christ unto all and upon all them that believe: for there is no difference:
23 For all have sinned, and come short of the glory of God;
24 Being justified freely by his grace through the redemption that is in Christ Jesus:
25 Whom God hath set forth to be a propitiation through faith in his blood, to declare his righteousness for the remission of sins that are past, through the forbearance of God;
26 To declare, I say, at this time his righteousness: that he might be just, and the justifier of him which believeth in Jesus.

In his book, *Our Eternal Contemporary,* Walter Marshall Horton relates a conversation he had with a man he met aboard an Atlantic cruiser. "I have sinned," the man told Dr. Horton, "and I am making a trip to Rome to make it up to God." This psychological need to make things right with God is not only the basis of pagan sacrifices designed to appease offended deity but also explains *our* mechanisms of self-punishment. We must atone for our misdeeds, in the hope that we may remove the burden of guilt lying upon our consciences.

The history of religion is the story of man's attempt to span the gulf his sin has created between himself and God. The Pharisaism in which Paul had been reared must be understood as such an attempt. It was based on the Old Testament, but it had perverted God's covenant with Israel into a scheme of works-religion in which everything hinged upon perfect adherence to the all-embracing law of God.

Under this rigorous legalism Paul's food, his clothes, the way he cut his hair and washed his hands, and every detail of his life were planned. Yet he came eventually to discover the impotence of this religion of self-salvation. It produced no rightness with God, no assurance of pardon or release from sin. Instead it created in him an intense arrogance and an inward conflict which meant the end of all peace and satisfaction. From bitter experience he concluded "that no one can ever get into a right relationship with God through doing the things that any legal system provides" (3:20, Barclay).

So with a great sigh of relief Paul announces a new day in which God offers us a righteousness which we could never have won by ourselves. He proclaims—

1. *The New Gospel:* "But now the righteousness of God has been manifested apart from law" (21, RSV)—it has been shown in the cross of Jesus, His Son. In Christ a new era has begun. In Him, *God* has spanned the gulf of sin and death and provided a way of righteousness not based on law-works but offered as a free gift of grace to all who believe. This is the good "new news" of the Christian gospel.

> The Christian message—the Gospel—is that God has thus acted and by His action has altered man's whole status in life. Something has been done for man without his own contrivance, help or knowledge. After "D" Day in 1944, a battle was fought in Caen in Normandy which resulted in the liberation of all France. It was some time after the moment of victory before every Frenchman heard the news or shared in the fruits of victory, but the victory for all France was won in that battle. So the Cross is the victory of God which contains new life and freedom for all men.[8]

The gospel of Christ, which is *apart from law,* is indeed new. Yet it is not new. Its content (Christ crucified and raised from the dead as the world's Sin Offering) is new, but its method (salvation by grace through faith) is as old as God's dealings with His people. This is what Paul means when he reminds us that this divine righteousness is *witnessed by the Law and the Prophets* (NASB)—

by the Law, as his illustration of Abraham's justification (in chapter 4; cf. Gen. 15:5-6) will show; *by . . . the Prophets,* as his quotation from Hab. 2:4 has already indicated ("He who through faith is righteous shall live," 1:17, RSV).

Let us rejoice that "a new and living way" has been opened to us by the cross of Jesus Christ (Heb. 10:19-22).

2. *The New Redemption:* "This righteousness from God comes through faith in Jesus Christ to all who believe. There is no difference, for all have sinned and fall short of the glory of God, and are justified freely by his grace through the redemption that came by Christ Jesus" (22-24, NIV).

a. Consider, in the first place, how the Cross reveals the radical sinfulness of the human heart. The law pronounces all men guilty before God, but in the profoundest way the gospel exposes the ultimate meaning of sin—the crucifixion of Christ.

Human goodness joined with human wickedness to crucify Jesus. The Jewish ecclesiastics were trying to preserve Judaism and the Temple and believed they were doing God service in ridding themselves of One who openly said His teachings would burst the old wineskins of Jewish religion. The crowd who cried, "Crucify him," could claim they were right in calling for the death of One they were told was a blasphemer and impostor. The Roman soldiers were only carrying out their orders. Pilate condemned Jesus in the interests of preserving the peace of a troubled province. Even Judas was probably trying to force Jesus into an immediate action to bring in His kingdom. "The crucifixion of Jesus has demonstrated in actual history that the goodness and wisdom of men are corrupt because they do not recognize God; they crucify Him."[9]

Jeremiah said, "The heart is deceitful above all things, and desperately sick" (17:9, English Revised Version, hereafter ERV). Sin is a disease at the heart of man's goodness—a "goodness" which is so blind it cannot see God's holiness and truth and love in Jesus, and so self-assured it must crucify Jesus to maintain itself. The quintessence of sin is not wickedness but spiritual pride, and the logical consequence of such self-righteousness is the crucifixion of God.

b. But a second look discloses more than the depths of human depravity; the Cross also reveals the strength of God's love. For the Cross is not simply the act of sinful man; it is the deed of the God who was determined that His love would overcome the sin of the world. "God demonstrates his own love for us in this: While we were still sinners, Christ died for us" (5:8, NIV). If that is so, nothing can separate us from God's love. This is not a theory to be argued or even discussed; it is a truth which must be believed or disbelieved.

Faith cries out, 'Tis He! 'Tis He!
My God that suffers there.

Our sin is chronic, our plight is critical, even our religion fails us. But "I am persuaded that neither death, nor life, nor angels, nor principalities, nor powers, nor things present, nor things to come, nor height, nor depth, nor any other creature, shall be able to separate us from the love of God, which is in Christ Jesus our Lord" (8:38-39). For God himself, in His Son, has taken a Roman cross on His shoulders, climbed Golgotha's hill, and there has died in our stead.

"Do not fear even brother sin," St. Francis is reported to have said. "He is a leper. But when thou hast washed his sores thou wilt find them to be none other than the wounds of Jesus."

Would Jesus have the sinner die?
Why hangs He then on yonder tree?
What means that strange expiring cry?
(Sinners, He prays for you and me.)

"Forgive them, Father, oh, forgive!
They know not that by Me they live."
—Charles Wesley

c. Finally, the Cross reveals the meaning of God's redemption. In the Cross, "God presented him [Jesus] as a sacrifice of atonement, through faith in his blood. He did this to demonstrate his justice, because in his forbearance he had left the sins committed beforehand unpunished—he did it to demonstrate his justice at the present time, so as to be just and the one who justifies the man who has faith in Jesus" (25-26, NIV).

The phrase *sacrifice of atonement* translates the significant word *hilasterion,* which may be rendered either "propitiation" or "expiation." It literally means "mercy seat," the golden cover or lid on the ark of the covenant, which was behind the veil in the holy of holies. Beneath the mercy seat, within the ark, the oracles of God were deposited (Exod. 25:17-21). Above it God himself dwelt and manifested His presence in the midst of Israel (1 Sam. 4:4; 2 Sam. 6:2). Preeminently, it was the place where, on the great Day of Atonement, the people were reconciled to God by the sprinkling of blood (Lev. 16:14-15).

T. W. Manson has shown the arresting and beautiful meaning of this term by emphasizing the words *whom God hath set forth.* He says, "Paul's application of Day of Atonement ideas to the Gospel has, as its first fruits, the new and startling notion of the display of the *hilasterion.* It is no longer hidden behind the veil: it is brought out into the open for all to see."

> The culminating moment of the Day of Atonement liturgy is the entry of the High Priest alone into the Holy of Holies. No one except the High Priest was ever permitted to see the Holy of Holies or the *hilasterion;* he went in on behalf of the people. The whole transaction was wrapped in mystery, and carried out in great secrecy. The startling thing is that Paul here speaks of the public display of the *hilasterion;* it is no longer simply a piece of Temple furniture hidden behind the

> Veil to which only the High Priest had access. This divinely appointed *hilasterion;* Christ, in his Death (or through his blood) has been brought out into the open, and all men can go, by faith, directly into this Holy of Holies.[10]

But Burton Throckmorton writes, "It may well be that Paul's intention was, at least in part, to allude to the mercy seat . . . but it is also probably true that Paul did not intend to limit his meaning to 'mercy seat,' for most Gentiles would probably not have known what the mercy seat was." Since the majority of the Roman Christians were Gentiles when Paul wrote this Epistle, we must inquire further into the meaning of *hilasterion.* All scholars agree that the general meaning is either *a propitiation* or *an expiation* (RSV). The death of Christ was thus "a propitiatory sacrifice" or "an expiatory sacrifice." In reality both ideas are inherent in *hilasterion* and are necessary to a biblical doctrine of atonement. *Propitiation* has a *Godward* reference; through the death of Christ, God's wrath is overcome and His justice is demonstrated. *Expiation* has a *manward* reference; Christ's sacrifice removes the guilt of man's sin.

When we speak of Christ's sacrifice as a propitiation, we do so against the background of "the wrath of God" in 1:18. Of course this does not mean God needs to be appeased like an angry man. Such a perversion of the biblical doctrine of propitiation misses the fundamental point made everywhere in the Bible, that it is God himself who makes the sacrifice for man's sin. "For the life of the flesh is in the blood," we read in Leviticus; "and *I have given it to you* upon the altar to make an atonement for your souls" (Lev. 17:11, ERV, italics mine). And Paul writes of Jesus, "Whom God hath set forth to be a propitiation." The offering is God's own sacrifice.

God has dealt with sin in judgment, thereby vindicating His holiness and justice. As the Cross reveals the sin of man, it also reveals the judgment of God upon that sin in the person of Christ, whom He has provided as our

Sacrifice of atonement. "Christ died for our sin" (1 Cor. 15:3), that *God* may be "just, AND the justifier of him which believeth in Jesus."

O Love divine! what hast Thou done?
The immortal God hath died for me!
The Father's coeternal Son
Bore all my sins upon the tree.
The immortal God for me hath died;
My Lord, my Love, is crucified.

—CHARLES WESLEY

3. *The New Salvation.* Christ himself is the glorious new fact of our salvation, "who was delivered for our offences, and was raised again for our justification" (4:25). The Cross is central in the Christian gospel, but not divorced from the Resurrection. "If Christ has not been raised, then our preaching is in vain and your faith is in vain" (1 Cor. 15:14, RSV). Apart from the Resurrection, Jesus' death would have been only that of a martyr; by raising Him from the dead God has validated Christ as the Sin Offering for the world. Now in the presence of God the Saviour presents His blood and pleads in my behalf. The work of atonement is done!

Arise, my soul, arise.
Shake off thy guilty fears.
The bleeding Sacrifice
In my behalf appears.
Before the throne my Surety stands;
My name is written on His hands.

He ever lives above
For me to intercede,
His all-redeeming love,
His precious blood to plead.
His blood atoned for all our race,
And sprinkles now the throne of grace.

My God is reconciled;
His pard'ning voice I hear.
He owns me for His child;
I can no longer fear.
With confidence I now draw nigh,
And, "Father, Abba, Father," cry.
—Charles Wesley

Light from the Cross

Romans 3:27-31

27 Where is boasting then? It is excluded. By what law? of works? Nay: but by the law of faith.

28 Therefore we conclude that a man is justified by faith without the deeds of the law.

29 Is he the God of the Jews only? is he not also of the Gentiles? Yes, of the Gentiles also:

30 Seeing it is one God, which shall justify the circumcision by faith, and uncircumcision through faith.

31 Do we then make void the law through faith? God forbid: yea, we establish the law.

Dr. E. Stanley Jones explains that the Cross on which Jesus died was itself a symbol of His atonement. The upright beam represents God's justice, which has its foundation in the divine holiness. That justice is indifferent to persons; it will veer to neither the right nor the left. The upright beam thus announces *God's law:* "The soul that sinneth, it shall die." The horizontal beam, on the other hand, pictures *God's love:* His outstretched arms of mercy, which would embrace the whole world.

Christ's death, therefore, both upholds God's law and reveals God's love. In the cross of the Son of God, "Mercy and truth are met together; righteousness and peace have kissed each other" (Ps. 85:10).

Light on God's nature and the salvation He offers us through Jesus shines from the Cross.

In the Cross of Christ I glory,
Towering o'er the wrecks of time;

All the light of sacred story
Gathers round its head sublime.
—JOHN BOWRING

This is the mood of Paul in this passage. At the risk of seeming anticlimactic, he feels he must sum up the meaning of Christ's death as the divinely appointed means of our justification. He is now looking back at what he has just said about Christ's propitiatory sacrifice. As the apostle of God he cannot stop with the proclamation but must go on to an explanation of the Cross, in an endeavor to make clear the implications for us of the death of Christ.

Three conclusions follow: (1) The death of Christ provides a way of salvation that excludes all boasting (27-28); (2) it is a way of salvation that abolishes all human distinctions (29-30); (3) it is a way of salvation that establishes God's law (31).

1. First, *in Christ's death we find a salvation which excludes all boasting.* "Where, then, is boasting? It is excluded. On what principle? On that of observing the law? No, but on that of faith. For we maintain that a man is justified by faith apart from observing the law" (27-28, NIV).

a. The One in whom we boast tells all. The essence of sin is to boast in self; the essence of righteousness is to boast in Christ. To be a New Testament Christian is to say with Paul, "God forbid that I should glory, save in the cross of our Lord Jesus Christ" (Gal. 6:14; cf. 1 Cor. 1:30-31).

b. Boasting in Christ *apart from observing the law?* Yes. But we must be sure of what Paul is saying. He does not mean that God's laws must not be kept, but that salvation is not a matter of *our* works—or even our faith considered as a work! We are saved only by God's mercy proffered to us in the Cross—and there can be no pride or credit or merit in suing for mercy!

Martin Luther underlines *apart from works of the law* by adding the adverb "alone": "Man becomes righteous without works of the law, through faith *alone*." For this he was severely criticized. Luther, however, was right. Although the word is not here, this is surely the apostle's meaning: "It is by faith alone, and not by legal works, or by any other fancied means of justification, that men receive the righteous status which God by His grace bestows" (F. F. Bruce). Yet faith has no merit either, and no power apart from its Object. Faith is but "the hand of the heart" which gratefully receives God's gift of salvation. Our salvation is not *because of* our faith; it is only *by* or *through* faith. Christ alone saves.

When this is understood, we have no basis for self-congratulation as we contemplate our salvation. It is *sola gratia, sola fide, soli Deo gloria* ("by grace alone, through faith alone; to God alone be the glory").

c. Of course, this faith "worketh by love" (Gal. 5:5-6), and Paul will soon spell out this complementary truth. But at this point he is emphasizing that it is by faith, not by what a man does, that he receives God's justifying grace. That faith prompted John Wesley to confess, as he lay desperately ill in Bristol in 1783:

> I have been reflecting on my past life. I have been wandering up and down between fifty and sixty years, endeavoring in my poor way, to do a little good to my fellow creatures; and, now it is probable that here is but a few steps between me and death, and what have I to trust to for salvation? I see nothing which I have done or suffered, that will bear looking at. I have no other plea than this:
>
> *I the chief of sinners am,*
> *But Jesus died for me.*[11]

As he was dying in London eight years later, the modern apostle of holiness repeated those words, and then added, "The way into the holiest is by the blood of Jesus." The gospel excludes all boasting.

2. Furthermore, *in Christ's death we find a salvation which is suited to all men.*

First, the Cross means the obliteration of all *religious* distinctions between Jew and Gentile (28-30). Paul beautifully explains this in Eph. 2:11-22. The ancient Temple in Jerusalem with its "middle wall of partition" has been displaced by that temple of which Jesus Christ is the Chief Cornerstone. In the body of His death Christ has accomplished this unification of Jew and Gentile as well as their common reconciliation to the Father. In Colossians, Paul tells us what this means so far as the ceremonial law of Moses is concerned. The taboos of the Old Testament have ceased—Jewish circumcision, dietary and dress regulations, the seventh-day sabbath and all other Jewish feasts and sabbaths, the entire system of Moses (Col. 2:11-17). Christ has become the Substance of which all these were shadows and types. The gospel is our Magna Carta of freedom from Old Testament ceremonialism in every shape and form. "*We* are the circumcision," says Paul, "which worship God in the spirit . . . and have no confidence in the flesh" (Phil. 3:3).

Moreover, there are not two Gods (one for Jews, one for Gentiles). It is therefore unthinkable that the one God should have two methods of saving mankind. This puts to rest the popular notion of dispensationalism that Jesus came preaching "the Gospel of the Kingdom," but when He was rejected by Israel He began to proclaim "the Gospel of Grace"—along with the companion notion that after Jesus' second coming He will once again preach "the Gospel of the Kingdom" to Israel. No, all men *have been* and *are* and *will be* saved on the same terms—the grace of God which has been finally and fully revealed in the death of Christ. God is one, and He is unchanging. No one can be saved in any other way than by His mercy which has been manifested to all men through Christ's atoning sacrifice.

3. Finally, *in Christ's death we find a salvation which*

establishes the law. "Do we, then, nullify the law by this faith? Not at all! Rather, we uphold the law" (31, NIV).

Interpreters find Paul saying several different things here. Some believe he means that the law itself teaches justification by faith, as he will show in the next chapter, by the example of Abraham (from Gen. 15:5-6). Pharisaism had made a legalistic system of the old covenant, which was in reality a covenant of grace. From this perspective the gospel establishes the law by bringing out its true meaning: *Gospel and law are one.*

Others believe Paul is showing the relationship of justification to sanctification. He would then mean that when God justifies us through Christ's blood He also imparts to us the sanctifying Spirit, who enables *us* to fulfill the law in obedient love (8:1-4): *Gospel fulfills law.*

Both of these positions are Paul's teaching. But if he is still on his main subject of justification through Christ's death, he means that in His sacrifice *Christ* satisfies God's just demands and so makes it possible for God to remain just while He justifies the guilty sinner who believes in Jesus: *Christ fulfills the law.* Now God is free to pardon every penitent sinner who comes to Jesus in simple faith.

'Tis finished! the Messiah dies;
Cut off for sins, but not His own.
Accomplished is the sacrifice;
The great redeeming work is done.

'Tis finished! all the debt is paid;
Justice divine is satisfied;
The grand and full atonement,
God for a guilty world hath died.

Saved from the legal curse I am;
My Saviour hangs on yonder tree.
See there the meek, expiring Lamb!
'Tis finished! He expires for me.

—Charles Wesley

ROMANS 4

The Example of Abraham's Faith

Romans 4:1-12

1 What shall we say then that Abraham our father, as pertaining to the flesh, hath found?
2 For if Abraham were justified by works, he hath whereof to glory; but not before God.
3 For what saith the scripture? Abraham believed God, and it was counted unto him for righteousness.
4 Now to him that worketh is the reward not reckoned of grace, but of debt.
5 But to him that worketh not, but believeth on him that justifieth the ungodly, his faith is counted for righteousness.
6 Even as David also describeth the blessedness of the man, unto whom God imputeth righteousness without works,
7 Saying, Blessed are they whose iniquities are forgiven, and whose sins are covered.
8 Blessed is the man to whom the Lord will not impute sin.
9 Cometh this blessedness then upon the circumcision only, or upon the uncircumcision also? for we say that faith was reckoned to Abraham for righteousness.
10 How was it then reckoned? when he was in circumcision, or in uncircumcision? Not in circumcision, but in uncircumcision.
11 And he received the sign of circumcision, a seal of the righteousness of the faith which he had yet being uncircumcised: that he might be the father of all them that believe, though they be not circumcised; that righteousness might be imputed unto them also:
12 And the father of circumcision to them who are not of the circumcision only, but who also walk in the steps of that faith of our father Abraham, which he had being yet uncircumcised.

You may feel Paul is here dealing with a Jewish issue which should have been buried long ago in theological oblivion. Not so. In reality he is raising one of the most urgent questions of Christian faith: the relation of the New Testament to the Old, and the position of the Jew in relation to Christ.

A common misunderstanding which dies hard is the idea that the Old Testament teaches salvation by works. Paul shows this to be a fallacy. He makes it clear in this passage that there has always been only one covenant of grace, and that men and women in both dispensations have every one been saved on exactly the same terms, by grace through faith.

Paul demonstrates this by showing in the Old Testament itself that the two men most highly esteemed by Jews themselves—Abraham, their father; and David, the progenitor of the Messiah—were both justified by faith alone and not by works (cf. Matt. 1:1). The grace of God which culminated in the death of Christ on the Cross has always been the sole basis of God's accepting men and women into His favor.

Three truths are clearly seen in this passage: (1) In God's justification of Abraham we see His *method* of saving men (1-3); (2) we are shown also the *meaning* of justification (4-8); and (3) in Abraham's faith we see the *model* of Christian justification (9-12).

1. *Abraham and the METHOD of Justification.* Paul asks: "What then shall we say that Abraham, our forefather, discovered in this matter?" He answers: "If, in fact, Abraham was justified by works, he had something to boast about—but not before God" (1-2, NIV).

Notice the deference with which Paul treats the case of Abraham. He does not apply the logic of his preceding argument, which would have insisted that, "since all have sinned" (3:23), Abraham had sinned; and further, that, since "by the deeds of the law there shall no flesh be justified in his sight" (3:20), Abraham was no exception.

Abraham rightly deserves the rich honor accorded him by the Jews, but receiving honor from men is a different matter altogether from having "something to boast about—before God." Even Father Abraham, says Paul, cannot claim merit in God's presence. Before Him no human being can glory, not even Abraham.

"What does the Scripture say?" (NIV) Paul continues. He then quotes Gen. 15:6 from the Septuagint: *"Abraham believed God, and it was counted unto him for righteousness"* (3). He believed God's promise, "Look now toward heaven, and tell the stars, if thou be able to number them. . . . So shall thy seed be" (Gen. 15:5). Justifying faith is always based upon God's promise (cf. 10:17). Abraham's trust in that promise was counted to him for righteousness (5). He was justified because he put his trust in God's word.

Abraham's faith was *counted* (KJV), *reckoned* (RSV), or *credited* (NIV) *for* righteousness. We must not think of his faith as being itself a refined kind of righteousness. "Faith" and "righteousness" are in two separate categories. Faith is not a virtue. It is not a work. It derives its power solely from its Object. We are not justified by virtue of our faith but solely by God's grace. Otherwise *we* would have "whereof to glory; but not before God" (2). Justification by grace through faith is wholly apart from any trace of human merit—to the glory of God alone.

2. *Abraham and the MEANING of Justification.* "Now when a man works," Paul explains, "his wages are not credited to him as a gift, but as an obligation. However, to the man who does not work but trusts God who justifies the wicked, his faith is credited as righteousness" (4-5, NIV).

a. God "justifieth the ungodly" (5). He does not make us godly and then justify us. He justifies us just as we are, without works, while we are still ungodly. There is nothing beyond this in the Scriptures.

> The sinner stands trembling before the awful tribunal of divine justice; and has nothing to plead, but his own guilt, and the merits of the Mediator. Christ here interposes; justice is satisfied; the sin is remitted, and pardon is applied to the soul, by a divine faith wrought by the Holy Ghost, who then begins the great work of inward sanctification. Thus God justifies the ungodly, and remains just, and true to all His attributes. . . . If a man could possibly be made holy before he was justified, it would entirely set his justification aside; seeing he could not, in the very nature of the thing, be justified if he were not, at the very time, ungodly.[12]

This is what Martin Luther calls an "alien righteousness." "Everything," he says in his *Lectures on Romans,* "is outside us and in Christ." It is "an extraneous righteousness which does not originate in ourselves but comes to us from beyond ourselves . . . from heaven." Before we can receive this righteousness from God "our own personal righteousness must be uprooted," lest we trust in ourselves rather than in God alone.

b. Justification means divine pardon and acceptance. On the basis of God's grace in Christ we stand before Him as if we had never sinned. We exclaim with David, who also knew this blessedness of justification,

> *"Blessed are they whose offenses have been forgiven*
> *and whose sins have been covered.*
> *Blessed is the man whose sin the Lord will*
> *never count against him"* (7-8, NIV).

Abraham and David could know this happiness of pardon because the Cross that was raised on Calvary was eternal in the heart of God (Eph. 1:4-7). The death of Christ did not change God; it revealed His heart.

3. *Abraham as the MODEL of Justification.* Paul's last paragraph (vv. 9-12) underscores his point that justification is by faith alone, "apart from works of the law." At the same time, it shows the proper, if subordinate, place of rites and sacraments. The apostle reminds us that Abraham was justified by faith at least 14 years before he was circumcised (as recorded in Gen. 17:11). Circumcision was given "as a sign and seal of the righteousness that he had by faith while he was still uncircumcised" (11, NIV).

This puts all external rites in perspective. The Jews insisted on circumcision with fanatical zeal; Paul puts it in a place subordinate to faith. But though it is subordinate, we need signs and seals to prevent our faith from evaporating into abstract unreality. They keep the things of greatest importance firmly rooted in our common life and intimately related to the elements of everyday experience. *Signs* show us the essential relationship which exists between visible and invisible reality. They remind us we are living in a sacramental universe which points beyond itself to God. *Seals* serve as a visible confirmation of God's faithfulness—in terms people can see and understand—to perform what He has promised.

"The Christian analogue to circumcision is, of course, baptism as a rite symbolizing purification and admission to the redeemed community," C. Anderson Scott writes. "And there can be no doubt that all Paul had to say about circumcision he would say equally about baptism. Like circumcision, baptism 'had its value' (2:25), but, like circumcision, it had no value apart from a new creature."[13]

The faith that saves, signed and sealed by Christian baptism, is faith in *Christ alone.*

To God be the glory—great things He hath done.
So loved He the world that He gave us His Son,
Who yielded His life an atonement for sin,
And opened the Life-gate that all may go in.

Praise the Lord, praise the Lord,
Let the earth hear His voice!
Praise the Lord, praise the Lord,
Let the people rejoice!
O come to the Father, thro' Jesus, the Son,
And give Him the glory—great things He hath done.

—Fanny J. Crosby

Justification by Faith Alone

Romans 4:13-15

13 For the promise, that he should be the heir of the world, was not to Abraham, or to his seed, through the law, but through the righteousness of faith.
14 For if they which are of the law be heirs, faith is made void, and the promise made of none effect:
15 Because the law worketh wrath: for where no law is, there is no transgression.

Justification by faith alone is "the article upon which the Church stands or falls" (Luther). It means that our only hope of salvation is not, as Luther says,

our own but an extraneous righteousness which does not

originate in ourselves but comes to us from beyond ourselves, which does not arise on our earth but comes from heaven. . . . That is why our own personal righteousness must be uprooted. . . .

Christ wants all our feeling to be so bare that, on the one hand, we are not afraid to be cast into confusion on account of our faults, nor delight in praise and vain joy on account of our virtue.[14]

John Wesley was one with Luther on justification. It was while Wesley was listening to someone reading from Luther's *Preface to the Epistle to the Romans* that he found justifying faith:

About a quarter before nine, while he was describing the change which God works in the heart through faith in Christ, I felt my heart strangely warmed. I felt I did trust in Christ, Christ alone for salvation; and an assurance was given me that he had taken away *my* sins, even *mine,* and saved *me* from the law of sin and death.[15]

Thirty years later Wesley wrote: "I believe in justification by faith alone as much as I believe there is a God." A year before his death he said: "About fifty years ago I had a clearer view than before of justification by faith; and in this, from that very hour, I have never varied, no, not a hair's breadth. I am now on the border of the grave; but, by the grace of God, I still witness the same confession."

And on his deathbed he confessed, "I the chief of sinners am but Jesus died for me. . . . The way into the holiest is by the blood of Jesus."[16]

Here in Romans 4, Paul gives a three-point summary of the doctrine of justification: (1) It is by faith alone, and not by works (1-8); (2) It is by faith alone, and not by rites (9-12); (3) It is by faith alone, and not by law (13-15).

1. *Justification is by faith alone, and not by works.* Justification is an act of God by which, on the basis of Christ's atonement, He pardons and receives us into His favor. It is an act of sheer grace: God *justifieth the ungodly* (5). All we bring to God is our guilt and sin; on the merits of

Christ's blood He forgives our sins and accepts us "in the beloved" (Eph. 1:6). This is what Paul is talking about in 1-8.

a. To be justified by faith is to have "no confidence in the flesh." It is to count "as loss for the sake of Christ" all of those attributes, qualities, and works which a legalistic religion prizes. It is to say with Paul: "Indeed I count everything as loss because of the surpassing worth of knowing Christ Jesus my Lord. For his sake I have suffered the loss of all things, and count them as refuse, in order that I may gain Christ and be found in him, not having a righteousness of my own, based on law, but that which is through faith in Christ, the righteousness from God that depends on faith" (Phil. 3:4-9, RSV).

In the James Kennedy method of presenting the gospel to unbelievers, the second question brings into focus the crucial significance of justification by faith alone: "Suppose you were to die today and stand before God and He were to say to you, 'Why should I let you into My heaven?' what would you say?" Would you say with Edward Mote, "My hope is built on nothing less / Than Jesus' blood and righteousness"? If so, you know what it means to be justified by faith alone.

b. But is not repentance commanded? In his sermon "The Scripture Way of Salvation," Wesley says: "God does undoubtedly command us both to repent, and to bring forth fruits meet for repentance; which, if we willingly neglect, we cannot reasonably expect to be justified at all; therefore both . . . are, in some sense, necessary to salvation.

"But they are not necessary in the *same sense* with faith, nor in the *same degree.*" Repentance for Wesley means conviction of sin by the Spirit, along with a true self-knowledge that we are lost apart from Christ. In this sense repentance is "a low species of faith, i.e., a supernatural sense of an offended God." "Fruits meet for repentance" are works we perform which evidence that we are truly turning from sin to God. These should be done, Wesley says, "If there be time and opportunity for them. Otherwise a man may be justified without them, as was the thief on the cross; but he cannot be justified without faith. . . . Repentance and its fruits are only *remotely* necessary in order to faith; whereas faith is *immediately* and *directly* necessary."[17]

Repentance, therefore, is not a meritorious work we perform in order to win God's favor; it is rather faith itself in its beginnings, which prepares the way for saving trust in Christ.

c. Neither must faith be trusted in as a work we perform. We confess with Calvin: "We say that faith justifies, not that it is accounted as righteousness to us for its own worth, but because it is an instrument by which we freely obtain the righteousness of Christ."[18] Our faith is "counted for righteousness" (5). As previously stated, faith derives its strength, not from itself, but from its Object, Christ. In Christ alone are all merits of our salvation.

d. Finally, the works which faith produces have no merits of their own; the good works the justified man performs are acceptable to God because the man himself is "accepted in the beloved." Here Luther, Calvin, and Wesley also agree. I can never stand before God and plead my works; I can plead only the blood of Jesus. In 1771, Wesley and his preachers drew up the following declaration:

> We abhor the doctrine of Justification by Works as a most perilous and abominable doctrine; and pressed, we hereby solemnly declare, in the sight of God, that we have no trust or confidence but in the alone merits of our Lord and Saviour Jesus Christ, for Justification or Salvation either in life, death, or the day of judgment; and although no one is a real Christian believer (and consequently cannot be saved) who doth not good works, where there is time and opportunity, yet our works have no part in meriting, or purchasing our salvation from first to last, either in whole or in part.[19]

2. *Justification is by faith alone, and not by rites.* We have already seen that what circumcision was for Abraham baptism is for Christian believers: a sign and seal of the righteousness we have by faith alone.

This is a point easily lost if we take Paul's doctrine of baptism too literally. In 6:3 he says that we are "baptized into Jesus Christ . . . into his death." In 6:4 he writes that "we are buried with him by baptism into death: that like as Christ was raised up from the dead by the glory of the Father, even so we also should walk in newness of life" (cf. Col. 2:12). In Gal. 3:27 he writes, "For as many of you as have been baptized into Christ have put on Christ." Many commentators connect these passages with 1 Cor. 12:13 ("For by one Spirit are we all baptized into one body") and construct from them a doctrine of baptismal regeneration.

Baptismal regeneration, however, violates Paul's fundamental gospel of justification by faith alone. Abraham was justified long before he was circumcised. His righteousness was given to him *by faith* (11), 14 years before his circumcision.

Why then was circumcision given to Abraham? Let Paul answer: "as a sign or seal of the righteousness which he had by faith while he was still uncircumcised" (11, RSV). To *seal* means to authenticate. Of Christ it is written, "For him hath God the Father sealed" (John 6:27). This refers to Jesus' baptism, where He was publicly sealed as the Son of God by the descent of the Holy Spirit in the form of a dove upon Him. Jesus was visibly authenticated as God's Son by His baptism and the descent of the dove.

As Abraham believed God and on the ground of his faith alone was justified before God, so by faith alone are we justified. And as Abraham was circumcised as a sign and seal of the righteousness he had by faith, being uncircumcised, so we are baptized as a sign and seal of our justifying faith. Furthermore, circumcision pictured "putting off the body of flesh" (Col. 2:11, RSV), just as baptism graphically portrays our death and resurrection with Christ by which we "put off the old man with his deeds" and "put on the new man" (Col. 3:8-9), or Christ (Gal. 3:27).

Christian baptism dramatizes our death and resurrection with Christ, bringing this out of the purely "spiritual" realm into the area of public fact. In this way it is a sign that we have received God's righteousness. It also seals us as the children of God, being the outward token of the inward grace of the Spirit which accompanies our salvation.

To make baptism more than this is to violate "the truth of the gospel" (Gal. 2:14-21) and reintroduce salvation by works. Our trust for salvation is not in our baptism; it is in Christ alone, who gives our baptism validity. "For in Christ Jesus neither circumcision nor uncircumcision [baptism nor unbaptism] is of any avail, but faith working through love" (Gal. 5:6, RSV) and "a new creation" (Gal. 6:15, RSV).

3. *Justification is by faith alone, and not by law.* The point Paul makes in 13-14 is amplified in Galatians (3:15-22). The promise of God was made to Abraham 430 years before He gave the law at Sinai. Moreover, God's promise reached beyond the law, to Christ. The law was thus inserted as a kind of parenthesis in God's dealings with His people, and it can in no way invalidate the promise. "Why then the law? It was added because of transgressions, till the offspring should come to whom the promise had been made" (Gal. 3:19, RSV). "The law entered, that the offence might abound. But where sin abounded, grace did much more abound" (5:20). The law of Moses prepared the way for God's act of grace in Christ.

Promise and law are thus in two separate categories. *The law brings wrath,* not salvation, and turns sin into *transgression* (15, RSV). The law exposes our guilt (3:19-20) and sinfulness (7:8-9, 13), but it cannot save. Nevertheless, it is eternally valid as the mind and expression of the holy God (7:12; cf. Matt. 5:17).

What then? Here is Paul's answer in a nutshell: To try

to do "works of the law" to please God is to compound our guilt ("by the deeds of the law there shall no flesh be justified in his sight," 3:20); but to come to Christ is to "fulfil the law" (3:31; 8:3-4). Let us listen to part of Luther's *Preface to the Epistle to the Romans* which John Wesley heard that night in the society on Aldersgate Street:

> Doing the works of the law and fulfilling the law are two very different things. The work of the law is everything that one does or can do, towards keeping the law of his own free will or by his own powers. But since under all these works and along with them there remains in the heart dislike for the law, and the compulsion to keep it, these works are all wasted and of no value. That is what St. Paul means when he says: "By the works of the law no man becomes righteous before God." To fulfil the law, however, is to do its works with pleasure and love, and to live a godly life of one's own accord, without the compulsion of the law.
>
> This pleasure and love for the law is put into the heart by the Holy Ghost. But the Holy Ghost is not given except in, with and by faith in Jesus Christ. And faith does not come save only through God's word or gospel, which preaches Christ, that he is God's Son and a man, and has died and risen again for our sakes.
>
> Hence it comes that faith alone makes righteous and fulfils the law; for out of Christ's merit it brings the Spirit, and the Spirit makes the heart glad and free as the law requires that it shall be. . . . And thus it is impossible to separate works from faith, as impossible as to separate heat and light from fire.[20]

This was God's word to John Wesley which "strangely warmed" his heart and enabled him to "trust in Christ, Christ alone for salvation." Indeed, these words constitute the very core of the gospel.

Yet, in order to guard the gospel against a pietistic perfectionism, one final word must be added. Even those who, having been justified by faith alone, go on to be perfected in love by the Spirit can never be justified by their own righteousness or holiness. Listen to John Wesley:

> The holiest of men still need Christ . . . as their Priest, to make atonement for their holy things. Even perfect holiness is acceptable to God only through Jesus Christ. . . .
>
> The best of men need Christ as their Priest, their Atonement, their Advocate with the Father . . . on account of their coming short of the law of love. For every man living does so. . . . The perfect transgress the very law they are under. . . .
>
> As there is not a full conformity to the perfect law, so the most perfect do, on this very account, need the blood of atonement, and may properly for themselves, as well as for their brethren, say, "Forgive us our trespasses."[21]

This means, simply, that the truly sanctified are also justified by faith alone. They can never present their own works or righteousness or holiness to God as a basis of their acceptance. They will be as dependent on the blood of Jesus on the day of final judgment as when they first came to Christ for pardon.

From first to last, our salvation is "to the praise of the glory of his grace, wherein he hath made us accepted in the beloved" (Eph. 1:6).

Rock of Ages, cleft for me,
Let me hide myself in Thee.
Let the water and the blood,
From Thy wounded side which flowed,
Be of sin the double cure,
Save from wrath and make me pure.

Could my tears forever flow,
Could my zeal no respite know,
These for sin could not atone;
Thou must save, and Thou alone.
In my hand no price I bring;
Simply to Thy cross I cling.

—August M. Toplady

The Nature of Faith

Romans 4:16-25

16 Therefore it is of faith, that it might be by grace; to the end the promise might be sure to all the seed; not to that only which is of the law, but to that also which is of the faith of Abraham; who is the father of us all,
17 (As it is written, I have made thee a father of many nations,) before him whom he believed, even God, who quickeneth the dead, and calleth those things which be not as though they were.
18 Who against hope believed in hope, that he might become the father of many nations, according to that which was spoken, So shall thy seed be.
19 And being not weak in faith, he considered not his own body now dead, when he was about an hundred years old, neither yet the deadness of Sarah's womb:
20 He staggered not at the promise of God through unbelief; but was strong in faith, giving glory to God;
21 And being fully persuaded that, what he had promised, he was able also to perform.
22 And therefore it was imputed to him for righteousness.
23 Now it was not written for his sake alone, that it was imputed to him;
24 But for us also, to whom it shall be imputed, if we believe on him that raised up Jesus our Lord from the dead;
25 Who was delivered for our offences, and was raised again for our justification.

It would seem that Paul has exhausted his subject of justification by faith alone. He has—almost. His argument is coming to its conclusion, but the case of Abraham looms so large and is so important that it provides a perfect illustration of the whole matter.

Paul seems to be saying here: "I am trying to show you the meaning of justifying faith. If you are having trouble as to what faith means, or how justification comes to us through faith, we have a perfect example of it in the case of Abraham. We have used Abraham as an argument; now let us look at Abraham as an illustration."

Genesis tells us that Abraham believed God, and it was counted to him as righteousness. Let's take a close look at that faith, keeping in mind that the Genesis account is for us. The principle which Abraham's faith enshrines holds good for all believers in God, and especially those who believe in God as He is revealed in the gospel—

the God who delivered up Jesus to death because of our sins, but also raised Him up to procure our justification.

1. First, let us consider *the nature of God's promise.* With respect to this, we must see that God's promise was an expression of sheer grace. Abraham's personal righteousness had nothing to do with it. Law-keeping was out of the question, since the law was not given until more than 400 years later. God himself acted out of pure love and took the initiative. As Paul refers to God's promise to the patriarch, he seems to have in mind several scriptures.

In the immediate background is the promise referred to in 3 and quoted in 18*b*: "Look now toward heaven, and tell the stars, if thou be able to number them: and he said to him, So shall thy seed be" (Gen. 15:5). In 17 the apostle cites Gen. 17:5, "A father of many nations have I made thee." Finally, Paul doubtless has in mind Gen. 22: 17-18, to which he alludes in 13: "I will multiply thy seed as the stars of the heaven, and as the sand which is upon the sea shore; and thy seed shall possess the gate of his enemies; and in thy seed shall all the nations of the earth be blessed."

a. In the first place, God's promise was unconditional. Barclay tells us that the Greek language has two words for *promise.* One is *huposchesis,* which means a promise with conditions: "I promise to do this, if you promise to do that." But Paul uses the word *epaggelia,* which connotes a promise made unconditionally out of the goodness of one's heart. It is as if Paul is saying, "God's promise was not dependent on Abraham's keeping the law; it was not a matter of merit in any way; it was only a matter of God's own *agape* love" (see Deut. 7:6-8). God's promise was an expression of His redemptive purpose, which was not to be defeated by man (cf. c. 9, where Paul elaborates this).

b. Secondly, it was a promise that Abraham "should be the heir of the world" (13). This is not a formal quotation of a single recorded promise to Abraham, but an inference Paul draws from all the references in Genesis.

Delimited in geographical terms, Abraham's inheritance lies between Egypt and the Euphrates (Gen. 15:8; cf. 13: 14-17), but in the spiritual and permanent sense in which the promise is interpreted in the New Testament, his inheritance cannot be confined within such earthly boundaries: "For he looked for a city which hath foundations, whose builder and maker is God" (Heb. 11:10).

c. Finally, it was a promise of Christ and believers in Him. F. F. Bruce points out that the promise of Gen. 12:3 ("In thee shall all families of the earth be blessed") is repeated in Gen. 22:18 in the form "*In thy seed* shall all the nations of the earth be blessed" (italics added). He explains that in Galatians 3 "Paul takes up both forms of the promise and shows how the word 'seed' in the second form, being a collective singular, can and does refer primarily to Christ (verse 16) and consequently to the people of Christ (verse 29)."[22]

This promise of Christ and of a people made up of believing Jews *and* Gentiles is a promise whose validity has nothing whatever to do with the law or with the righteousness which depends on keeping the law. It was a promise of *grace,* calling only for *faith.* It was this promise which Abraham embraced with obedient trust.

This also is God's promise to us—Christ and salvation through Him alone. And it is true whether we embrace it or not. The gospel is not put in jeopardy by human sin or unbelief. But it does demand faith if we are to enjoy its blessings. It calls, not for our slavish attempts to placate God or please Him by our own works, but for simple trust, "that if thou shalt confess with thy mouth the Lord Jesus, and shalt believe in thine heart that God hath raised him from the dead, thou shalt be saved" (10:9).

2. Let us now consider *the nature of Abraham's faith.* As it was necessary to consider several passages in Genesis to grasp the full significance of God's promise, we must also consider all these scriptures to understand Abraham's faith.

a. First, his faith was an obedient response. Immediately after God's call and promise, "Abram departed, as the Lord had spoken unto him" (Gen. 12:1-4). "By faith Abraham, when he was called . . . obeyed" (Heb. 11:8). This is what Wesley calls "repentance faith." When God calls, faith obeys. For this reason Paul speaks of "the obedience of faith" (1:5; 16:26; cf. 15:18). If the essence of sin is the elevation of self as god, the beginning of faith is submission of self to God. We must turn from our own way before we can follow God. Such repentance is of the very essence of faith. It has no merit in itself, but we cannot trust Christ when our backs are to Him. Faith turns around to embrace the promise of God.

b. Repentance faith becomes saving faith the moment we trust God's word and put our whole weight upon it. Faith reckons God's word to be true, regardless of all apparently contrary evidence. Such absolute resting in the naked word of God is the link between repentance and justification. Let us see how Abraham illustrates this.

"I have made you the father of many nations," God says to Abraham (17, RSV). In the eyes of God, the patriarch *is* already what he shall become. Abraham regards himself as being in fact what God declares he shall become. *Before him whom he believed,* the aged patriarch was by faith already *a father of nations.* The "multitudes" who should be his inheritance were already present before God and before Abraham. Faith reckons absolutely on the promise of God, who quickeneth the dead and "summons things that are not yet in existence as if they already were" (NEB).

c. Abraham's faith was a resurrection faith. In the patriarch's own person, already a centenarian, and his wife almost as old as he, a resurrection would take place, in order to make the promise of God come true. It was this resurrection faith with later prompted Abraham to offer up Isaac, the promised heir through whom God's word would come to fulfillment, "accounting that God was able to raise him up, even from the dead" (Heb. 11:19).

> *Against all hope, Abraham in hope believed and so became the father of many nations, just as it had been said to him, "So shall your offspring be." Without weakening in his faith, he faced the fact that his body was as good as dead —since he was about a hundred years old—and that Sarah's womb was also dead. Yet he did not waver through unbelief regarding the promise of God, but was strengthened in his faith and gave glory to God, being fully persuaded that God had power to do what he had promised. This is why "it was credited to him as [eis,* for*] righteousness"* (18-22, NIV).

Without finding in the world of sense or reason the least ground for hoping, he nevertheless believed. His hope proceeded from a fact that the eye of reason could not perceive. *Against all hope, Abraham in hope believed.* Here Paul defines faith in harmony with Heb. 11:1: "Now faith is the substance of things hoped for, the evidence of things not seen." It bursts forth in the form of hope, "as seeing him who is invisible" (Heb. 11:27). Such hope is not mere wishful thinking; it is confident expectation in God's unbreakable word of promise.

Faith gives glory to God. It glorifies God's perfections: His holiness, His love, His grace, His faithfulness to His word, and His power to fulfill it, "being fully persuaded that what he . . . [has] promised, he . . . [is] able also to perform." "Being fully persuaded" translates a Greek word which means "to fill a vessel to the brim." "This word used in the passive applies to a man filled with a conviction which leaves no place in his heart for the least doubt" (Godet).

By such confidence we lay hold of God's promise, or better, God's promise lays hold of us, and we are justified. "Therefore it was imputed to him for righteousness" (22).

3. Finally, let us consider *the nature of Christian faith.* This narrative, Paul reminds us, "was not written for his [Abraham's] sake alone . . . but for us also . . . if we believe on him that raised up Jesus our Lord from the dead" (23-24). Our justification is identical to Abraham's, for it is rooted in the free and gracious will of God, who imputes faith for righteousness. Our faith is also identical to Abraham's, because it is in the same God, the God who brings life out of death. But for us the power of the living God can no longer be described in terms of Isaac's birth from aged parents. That which the Old Testament prefigured has become manifest in the death and resurrection of Jesus, in which God raised up His own Son, not from a dead womb, but from a grave.

In the deepest sense, our faith is not in Christ but in God, *who raised Jesus our Lord from the dead* (NIV). We trust in Christ as God's Sin Offering made in our behalf. The ultimate efficacy of that sacrifice lies in the power of God, who delivered Jesus "over to death for our sins" and raised Him "to life for our justification" (25, NIV). By His death Jesus satisfied sin's debt against us. His resurrection is proof that the debt is cancelled and sin is dead. By simple trust we receive this comforting word to the salvation of our souls.

Father, whose everlasting love
Thy only Son for sinners gave,
Whose grace to all did freely move
And sent Him down a world to save;

Help us Thy mercy to extol,
Immense, unfathom'd, unconfined;
To praise the Lamb who died for all,
The general Saviour of mankind.

Thy undistinguishing regard
Was cast on Adam's fallen race;
For all Thou hast in Christ prepared
Sufficient, sovereign, saving grace.

—Charles Wesley

ROMANS 5

New Life in Christ

Romans 5:1-11

1 Therefore being justified by faith, we have peace with God through our Lord Jesus Christ:
2 By whom also we have access by faith into this grace wherein we stand, and rejoice in hope of the glory of God.
3 And not only so, but we glory in tribulations also: knowing that tribulation worketh patience;
4 And patience, experience; and experience, hope:
5 And hope maketh not ashamed; because the love of God is shed abroad in our hearts by the Holy Ghost which is given unto us.
6 For when we were yet without strength, in due time Christ died for the ungodly.
7 For scarcely for a righteous man will one die: yet peradventure for a good man some would even dare to die.
8 But God commendeth his love toward us, in that, while we were yet sinners, Christ died for us.
9 Much more then, being now justified by his blood, we shall be saved from wrath through him.
10 For if, when we were enemies, we were reconciled to God by the death of his Son, much more, being reconciled, we shall be saved by his life.
11 And not only so, but we also joy in God through our Lord Jesus Christ, by whom we have now received the atonement.

In one of his books H. G. Wells tells of a prominent man who was living under such stress he was in serious danger of a complete nervous and mental breakdown. His doctor told him the only thing that could save him would be to find the peace that fellowship with God can give. "What!" he said, "to think of that, up there, having fellowship with me! I would as soon think of cooling my throat with the Milky Way or shaking hands with the stars!"

The despair of this distraught soul is typical of countless persons who do not or will not believe the gospel. What a different note Paul sounds here! He bursts into lyrical praise as he sings of the peace, joy, hope, and love he has found through trusting Christ. "He who through faith is righteous *shall live*" (1:17, RSV). Paul's accent from this point on is upon the *new life* of holiness and hope and love which opens to one who puts his trust in the crucified Christ.

This compact passage is difficult to outline. It is actually a summary and preview of chapters 6 through 8, but Paul's heart is so full of exultation as he writes that he does not fall into theological argumentation. He sings his way through the Christian heights.

What are the salient features of the new life we receive from Christ?

1. First, it is *a life of peace.* "Therefore, since we have been justified through faith, we have peace with God" (1, NIV). If this is an exhortation, as some of the best ancient manuscripts indicate, it could be translated, "Let us *continue* to enjoy peace with God through our Lord Jesus Christ."

The peace we enjoy, however, is entirely a gift of God through Christ. We do not "make our peace with God"; Christ has made our peace with the Father through His death on the tree. We receive this peace as a boon when we come in penitent trust to the Cross. And we continue in peace as we live out a life of "faithing obedience" in Christ. "He is our peace" (Eph. 2:14).

But how can we describe this peace? We perhaps may paraphrase Bernard of Clairvaux and say,

The peace of Jesus, what it is,
None but the pardoned know!

The peace of God is in Hebrew *shalom*—the soul's health, happiness, and well-being in God. As former rebels, we have not been merely pardoned; we have been introduced into the very presence of God. Such is the meaning of the Greek word rendered *access.* Through Christ we have entered into a state of grace in which we "rejoice in hope of the glory of God" (2).

Peace thus merges into joy. Peace and joy are twin blessings of the gospel. F. F. Bruce quotes the old Scots preacher who put it, "Peace is joy resting; joy is peace dancing."

2. So our new life in Christ is *a life of joy.* Three objects of rejoicing are here mentioned.

a. First of all, *we rejoice in [our] hope of the glory of God.* This is the end for which He created us: the glory of uninterrupted communion, the glory of perfect love, the glory of His presence with nothing between.

We have an anticipation of this glory now in the indwelling Spirit, who is the "foretaste" of the glory that shall be revealed when Christ returns. When in the Spirit we spontaneously utter, "Glory!" we are experiencing an advance installment of heaven. But our little 100-watt bulbs cannot now receive the high-voltage of God's unveiled presence. Nevertheless, *hope maketh not ashamed; because the love of God is shed abroad in our hearts by the Holy Ghost* (5). This indwelling of God's Spirit, flooding our hearts with His love, gives us a "sure hope" of heaven. We rejoice, therefore, *in hope of the glory of God.*

b. We also rejoice in sufferings. If this seems strange, we need to remind ourselves that afflictions are viewed as normal experiences for Christians. The apostles warned their converts that "we must through much tribulation enter into the kingdom of God" (Acts 14:22); when tribulations came their way, they were not to consider it "strange."

Affliction, tribulation, and persecution are not only regarded in the New Testament as the inevitable lot of Christians, but are also a sign that God counts those who endure them as worthy of His kingdom (2 Thess. 1:5). Besides, they have a positive effect on those who suffer them, for they help them to cultivate *perseverance* and *character* (3-4, NIV); when such endurance and steadfastness are the outcome of true Christian faith, our *hope* is all the more stimulated (5).

c. Preeminently, *the Christian life is a life of rejoicing in God himself.* Paul concludes, "We also rejoice in God through our Lord Jesus Christ, through whom we have now received reconciliation" (11, NIV). The hope of glory was a rejoicing hope, and those who knew why they were suffering trials and persecutions could rejoice even amidst their tribulations, and even because of them. But no joy is to be compared with the joy that is found in God himself, when we have been reconciled to Him through Christ's blood.

3. Supremely, our new life in Christ is *a life of love.* Reconciled to God through Christ's death, "we love because he first loved us" (1 John 4:19, NIV). Ours is an answering love.

As a husband and wife know each other in the intimacy of personal communion, so we know and love God in Christ.

The love of Jesus, what it is,
None but His loved ones know.
—Bernard

a. It was love which caused Christ to lay down His life for us when we were helpless. In prevenient grace the Spirit awakens us when we are asleep, enables us to respond to God, gives us the strength to repent and believe. Without this gracious assistance of the loving Spirit we could never be saved. But thank God, "while we were powerless to help ourselves" (6, Phillips) "in due time Christ died for the ungodly." We would have remained forever ungodly except for God's awakening and enabling love.

b. Again, "while we were yet sinners" and "when we were enemies," Christ died for us (8, 10). Human love will go to death itself for those who are its objects, but not for the unlovely and hostile. Yet this is where the character of God shines brightest; God proves His love to us in the fact that Christ died for us while we were in a state of wickedness and rebellion. Everywhere in the New Testament the death of Christ is the supreme manifestation of the love of God: "Herein is love," says John, "not that we loved God, but that he loved us, and sent his Son to be the propitiation for our sins" (1 John 4:10). Behind the atonement is the self-giving, self-sacrificing love of God. The Cross does not change God from a wrathful Deity to a loving Father; it reveals Him as love.

c. Finally, through the risen Christ we experience the fullness of divine love. "For if, when we were God's enemies, we were reconciled to him through the death of his Son, how much more, having been reconciled, shall we be saved through his life!" (10, NIV). This is Paul's version of Christ's exaltation, making possible the Pentecostal gift of the Spirit (cf. John 7:39; Acts 2:32-33). In Acts 2, Peter speaks of the outpouring of the Spirit, made possible through the risen Christ. Here in Romans 5, Paul gives this an ethical interpretation. "God has poured out his love into our hearts by the Holy Spirit, whom he has given us" (5, NIV). By the infilling and indwelling of the Spirit our very beings are suffused and possessed by God's *agape* love.

God's love flooding our hearts completely cancels the fear of His outpoured wrath. For those who know that love through the Spirit, there is only the confident expectation of the unveiling of divine glory. This love "shed abroad in our hearts" is the foretaste and guarantee of the glory which shall be ours when Christ returns to consummate our salvation.

Once heaven seemed a far-off place,
Till Jesus showed His smiling face.
Now it's begun within my soul;
'Twill last while endless ages roll.

—C. F. Butler

Peace, joy, hope, and love, then—the true fruit of the Spirit—fill the hearts of those who have been justified by faith. The guilty past has been cancelled; the glory of the future is assured; here and now the presence and power of the Holy Spirit secure to us all the grace we need to endure trial, to resist evil, and to live as those who wear the beautiful name of Christ.

God's Eternal Purpose in Christ
(Rom. 5:12—11:36)

Christ and Adam

Romans 5:12-21

12 Wherefore, as by one man sin entered into the world, and death by sin; and so death passed upon all men, for that all have sinned:
13 (For until the law sin was in the world: but sin is not imputed when there is no law.
14 Nevertheless death reigned from Adam to Moses, even over them that had not sinned after the similitude of Adam's transgression, who is the figure of him that was to come.
15 But not as the offence, so also is the free gift. For if through the offence of one many be dead, much more the grace of God, and the gift by grace, which is by one man, Jesus Christ, hath abounded unto many.
16 And not as it was by one that sinned, so is the gift: for the judgment was by one to condemnation, but the free gift is of many offences unto justification.
17 For if by one man's offence death reigned by one; much more they which receive abundance of grace and of the gift of righteousness shall reign in life by one, Jesus Christ.)
18 Therefore as by the offence of one judgment came upon all men to condemnation; even so by the righteousness of one the free gift came upon all men unto justification of life.
19 For as by one man's disobedience many were made sinners, so by the obedience of one shall many be made righteous.
20 Moreover the law entered, that the offence might abound. But where sin abounded, grace did much more abound:
21 That as sin hath reigned unto death, even so might grace reign through righteousness unto eternal life by Jesus Christ our Lord.

Dr. James B. Chapman used to advise preachers, "Grapple with a difficult biblical theme occasionally, even if it throws you!" This, indeed, is wise counsel. It is only as we struggle with the great themes of the gospel that our understanding of the faith grows and deepens. And when one of these divine truths is illuminated by the Spirit, we are sometimes transported to the heights of prophetic inspiration.

Paul himself has reached such a high point of revelation and ecstasy. Through the preceding chapters he has been mountain climbing. Suddenly he reaches a vista point, a veritable Everest of biblical revelation, from which he is able to view in retrospect all he has thus far said and just as clearly to see what lies ahead. As he surveys the panorama of redemption, the apostle is "lost in wonder, love, and praise." His thoughts leap forth like a torrential mountain stream, and rush forward with such force that they do not always come to carefully formed expression.

Let us try to stand with Paul on this peak of Christian truth and look through his eyes. To do so, we must lay aside the presuppositions of our decidedly individualistic way of thinking and adopt the biblical concept of "social solidarity." For Paul, as for the Old Testament, Adam was actually the first man. But he was more than a historical individual; he was what his name means in Hebrew—"mankind" (cf. Gen. 5:1-2).

As such, Adam was *the figure* (*tupos,* or "type") *of him that was to come* (v. 14), i.e., Christ. Christ is "the last Adam" (1 Cor. 15:45). He is more than the Jesus of history we meet in the Gospels; having been raised from the dead by the Father, He is the risen Christ, into whose body the Holy Spirit incorporates all believers (1 Cor. 12: 12-13).

Paul's thought can readily oscillate between Adam and sinful humanity, on the one hand, and between Christ and His Church on the other. This is not myth; it is reality. This solidarity with our fellows is a fact we tend to overlook in the assertion of our individuality.

> No man is an island, entire of itself; every man is a piece of the continent, a part of the main. If a clod is washed away, Europe is the less as well as if a promontory were or a manor of thy friends. Every man's death diminishes *me,* because I am involved in mankind. And

> therefore never send to know for whom the bell tolls; it tolls for thee.

This famous quotation from John Donne expresses something of what Paul meant when he penned, "In Adam all die" (1 Cor. 15:22). Each of us is a personal manifestation of a humanity which began to die in Adam.

But, thank God,

> *A second Adam to the fight*
> *And to the rescue came!*

"'As in Adam all die, *even so in Christ all shall be made alive.*' A new creation has come to birth: the old 'Adam-solidarity' of sin and death has been broken up to be replaced by the new 'Christ-solidarity' of grace and life."[1] "In God's sight," the seventeenth-century Thomas Goodwin said quaintly, "there are two men—Adam and Christ—and these two men have all other men hanging at their girdle strings." That is, before God every individual is "in Adam" or "in Christ." In Adam we have ruin; in Christ, rescue (Barclay).

1. *Sin and Death Through Adam.* Mankind's ruin, Paul says, can be traced back to the Fall. "By one man sin entered into the world, and death by sin" (12). There is both revelation and mystery here.

a. One key to understanding this disputed passage is to note the distinction Paul makes between Adam's *sin* (16, RSV) and "the" *sin* (or Sin) which entered into the world by his disobedience.

(1) Adam *sinned* (16); i.e., he missed the mark. But not because he was a bad marksman! He chose the wrong target: self instead of God. His was an act of *disobedience* (19) or *transgression* (14) of the revealed will of God (cf. Gen. 2:15-17; 3:6). Paul also calls this an *offence* (15, 18) (against the divine sovereignty and love). "Man was created looking directly to God, as his last end; but falling into sin, he fell off from God, and turned into himself" (Wesley). This was man's fall.

(2) Thereby *sin entered into the world.* The word

for "sin" here is *he hamartia,* literally, "the sin." *Hamartia* with the definite article occurs at least 28 times between 5:12 and 8:10, and it always means Sin, "the sin principle" or "the principle of revolt issuing in many transgressions."

In 7:20 it is described as "sin that dwelleth in me." Adam's disobedience opened our human existence to "indwelling sin," an irrational, tyrannical force of evil—a slumbering power which is aroused when God's commandment comes (cf. 7:8-11). I am the bondslave of this sin (7:14). It has captured my "body" (or personality), so that it is now "the body of sin" (6:6) or "Sin's body." My flesh is "sinful flesh" (8:3) or "Sin's flesh." Because of the Fall my body, my flesh, my very person *belongs to* Sin. Sin "reigns" in me like a false king. It causes me to cry out in anguish,

> *I do not understand my own actions. For I do not do what I want, but I do the very thing I hate. . . . I can will what is right, but I cannot do it. For I do not do the good I want, but the evil I do not want is what I do. . . . Wretched man that I am!* (7:15, 18-19, 24, RSV).

b. Furthermore, by Adam's sin *death* also entered and *passed upon all men.* In Adam the dike broke, and the whole race was engulfed in death. Although Paul must certainly mean that physical death is fallen man's lot, he intends far more. What makes death so tragic is Sin: "The sting of death is sin" (1 Cor. 15:56). Dying in guilt and alienation from God is the supreme penalty of Sin, and it is this which gives death its horror and its tragic quality.

We cannot know what man's existence would have been had he not sinned. Would he have continued to live as an immortal creature on earth? Would he have been translated like Enoch and Elijah? Would he have fallen into a serene sleep, to awake in God's presence? We do not know.

But we all know what spiritual death means. Paul said, "When the commandment came, sin revived, and I died" (7:9). Because *all have sinned* as a consequence of Sin which entered by the Fall, spiritual death reigns (cf. 3:23).

c. This *death reigned from Adam to Moses,* even over those who had not, like Adam, disobeyed God's specific commandment (13). Indwelling Sin produced death in them, despite the fact that they revealed "the work of the law written in their hearts" (2:15). Some, like Enoch, Noah, and Abraham, responded to God's grace and were saved; but the situation was no different than it now is in paganism: because of original sin men become actual sinners when they come to the age of "conscience." With the Latin poet Ovid such persons must confess,

I see the right, and approve it too;
I hate the wrong, and yet the wrong pursue!

Standing on this high peak and viewing the human situation and Paul's analysis of it in Romans, we see that it is this *spiritual death* which reigns because of Adam's sin. We are not damned for Adam's sin, but for personal transgression. One does not die because of his fathers' sins, or because of Adam's sin. Guilt is a matter of personal and conscious responsibility. "The soul that sinneth, it shall die" (cf. Ezek. 18:1-4). We must be wary, therefore, of attaching "guilt" to Adam's sin; the Old Testament itself opposes such an idea. Paul plainly says in this passage that "sin is not imputed when there is no law" (13).

Let us recapitulate. Because of the solidarity of the race, in Adam *all men sinned* (12, RSV). In this primal sin the human race cut itself off from God. This alienation resulted in the corruption of indwelling Sin. This Sin now rules our lives and, taking advantage of God's commandment, deceives us into disobeying God and so kills us spiritually (7:11).

Thus, Sin reigned in death, not only *from Adam to Moses,* but in a more pronounced way since Sinai. "The law entered, that the offence might abound" (20). The law cannot dislodge Sin; it only intensifies its activity. The old lady had a point who objected to the recitation of the Ten Commandments in church "because they put so many ideas into people's minds"!

Such is our human predicament. "Explain original sin any way you wish," Dr. Edward Ramsdell once said in a university lecture, "you cannot explain it away. It is an empirical fact." As members of a humanity which has fallen from the divine intention for the race, we are bound up together in a solidarity of sin, guilt, and death. And no human power can extricate us, not even God's holy law. "Wretched man that I am! Who will deliver me from this body of death? Thanks be to God through Jesus Christ our Lord!" (7:24-25, RSV).

2. *Grace and Life Through Christ.* We have now arrived at the point where Paul began: in his grateful awareness that his existence had been re-created through Christ (cf. 2 Cor. 5:17). This scripture is not a piece of speculative theory for Paul; it is bedrock spiritual reality. As he views the human situation from the perspective of his new creation in Christ, Paul sees the entire human family caught in the inextricable situation in which he struggled and suffered before he met the risen Lord on the Damascus Road. All men, Gentiles without God's law and Jews with that law, are fighting a losing battle against Sin. The only hope of deliverance, he knew, was "through Jesus Christ our Lord."

The first Adam had failed; but now God has created a "second Adam." F. F. Bruce has said it perfectly:

> The idea of God's man as the fulfiller of God's purpose is a recurring one in the Old Testament; he is "the man of thy right hand . . . the son of man whom thou madest strong for thyself" (Psalm lxxx. 17).
>
> When one man fails in the accomplishment of God's purpose (as, in measure, all did), God raises up another to take his place—Joshua to replace Moses, David to replace Saul, Elisha to replace Elijah. But who could take the place of *Adam*? Only one who was competent to undo the effects of Adam's sin and become the

inaugurator of a new humanity. The Bible—and, indeed, the history of the world—knows of one man only who has the necessary qualifications. Christ stands alone (in Carlyle's translation of Luther's hymn) as

"the Proper Man
Whom God Himself hath bidden."[2]

In developing this theme Paul first draws a comparison between Adam and Christ, then a contrast.

a. By comparison, the action of both Adam and Christ had racial effects. In both cases, "one died for all." Adam's death brought Sin and death to the race; Christ's death brought resurrection and life. Let us listen to what Paul says to the Corinthians: "The love of Christ controls us, because we are convinced that one has died for all; therefore all have died. And he died for all, that those who live might live no longer for themselves but for him who for their sake died and was raised" (2 Cor. 5:14-15, RSV).

"One has died for all; therefore all have died." The entire race of sinners (provisionally) died in and with Christ on the Cross. The old humanity in Adam has been put to death with Christ on Calvary. The death of Christ was the death of the first Adam.

"And he died for all, that those who live might live no longer for themselves [that is, in sin] but for him who for their sake died and was raised." The new race (provisionally) arose with Christ in His resurrection. In union with Christ and in the power of His risen life we may now live "in righteousness and true holiness" (Eph. 4:24). The resurrection of Christ was the creation of "the new man" *(ibid.)*, the body of Christ, or the new humanity.

b. By contrast, Adam died because he disobeyed God (his sin was an act of human perfidy); Christ died because He obeyed God (His righteousness was an act of divine grace). "But the gift is not like the trespass. For if the many died by the trespass of one man, how much more did God's grace and the gift that came by the grace of the one man, Jesus Christ, overflow to the many!" (15, NIV).

Paul would probably be displeased with us for giving so much attention to Adam. Adam was "old hat" to Paul, merely a "type" or pattern of what we are here shown in Christ. The fact that Sin and death came into the world through this one man, bringing the world under divine condemnation, is simply a reminder to us that through Christ—the one unique Man—grace and righteousness and life have come into the world (16).

This unique Christ has brought us salvation, by His obedience. What does it matter if Adam was disobedient? Christ "became obedient unto death—even death on a cross!" (Phil. 2:8, NIV). What does it matter if Adam undermined the dike? Christ has opened the floodgates of heaven, so that peace has poured in upon the lower-lying world—"peace . . . as a river, and . . . righteousness as the waves of the sea" (Isa. 48:18). What does it matter if Sin began to reign in Adam? Through Christ it has been cast down off its throne, that "grace [might] reign through righteousness unto eternal life by Jesus Christ our Lord" (21).

In Christ, death has died! "O death, where is thy sting? O grave, where is thy victory? The sting of death is sin; and the strength of sin is the law. But thanks be to God, which giveth us the victory through our Lord Jesus Christ" (1 Cor. 15:55-57).

In Christ, condemnation is lifted and justification is given. "Therefore as by the offence of one judgment came upon men to condemnation; even so by the righteousness of one the free gift came upon all men unto justification of life" (18).

In Christ, a race of righteous men has been created. "For just as through the disobedience of one man the many were made sinners, so also through the obedience of the one man the many will be made righteous" (19, NIV).

In Christ, true sanctification has been made available. "Moreover the law entered, that the offence might abound. But where sin abounded, grace did much more abound:

that as sin hath reigned unto death, even so might grace reign through righteousness unto eternal life by Jesus Christ our Lord" (20-21). In Christ, abounding Sin has been displaced by abounding grace.

To rejoice in this great salvation one must know for himself the power of Christ's blood and Spirit. But those who have tasted this wondrous deliverance join with Charles Wesley in testifying:

That Blood applied by faith I feel,
And come its healing power to tell,
Through which I know my sins forgiven;
A witness I, that all may find
The peace deserved for all mankind,
And walk with God, my God, to heaven.

I come to testify the grace
My Lord obtain'd for all our race,
Enough ten thousand worlds to save.
Salvation is in Jesus' name,
Which every soul of man may claim.
And all that seek the grace shall have.

Salvation from the power of sin,
Salvation from the root within,
Salvation into perfect love
(Thy grace to all hath brought it near)—
An uttermost salvation here,
Salvation up to heaven above.

ROMANS 6

The New You

Romans 6:1-14

1 What shall we say then? Shall we continue in sin, that grace may abound?
2 God forbid. How shall we, that are dead to sin, live any longer therein?
3 Know ye not, that so many of us as were baptized into Jesus Christ were baptized into his death?

4 Therefore we are buried with him by baptism into death: that like as Christ was raised up from the dead by the glory of the Father, even so we also should walk in newness of life.
5 For if we have been planted together in the likeness of his death, we shall be also in the likeness of his resurrection:
6 Knowing this, that our old man is crucified with him, that the body of sin might be destroyed, that henceforth we should not serve sin.
7 For he that is dead is freed from sin.
8 Now if we be dead with Christ, we believe that we shall also live with him:
9 Knowing that Christ being raised from the dead dieth no more; death hath no more dominion over him.
10 For in that he died, he died unto sin once: but in that he liveth, he liveth unto God.
11 Likewise reckon ye also yourselves to be dead indeed unto sin, but alive unto God through Jesus Christ our Lord.
12 Let not sin therefore reign in your mortal body, that ye should obey it in the lusts thereof.
13 Neither yield ye your members as instruments of unrighteousness unto sin: but yield yourselves unto God, as those that are alive from the dead, and your members as instruments of righteousness unto God.
14 For sin shall not have dominion over you: for ye are not under the law, but under grace.

Man has been trying to understand himself since the time of Socrates, when philosophy began to address the mystery of the human psyche and thus initiated what we now call psychology. With the advent of modern psychology, especially since depth psychology, the quest for self-understanding has become a popular exercise. Many today are familiar with Freud's analysis of the psyche which distinguishes the id (instinctual drives), ego (reason), and superego (conscience). Keith Miller writes about the "warfare" between these "brothers" in the "inner family" of personality.[3] In somewhat the same way, transactional analysis helps us understand the struggle which goes on within all of us between the "parent," the "child," and the "adult" who make up each self.[4]

Christians can profit by these psychological studies. They help us to understand ourselves, perhaps Paul would say, as we are by nature—"in Adam." The gospel, however, gives us a new picture of ourselves; it shows us who we are as re-created persons in Christ. It is important that we know ourselves as we are by nature, but it is essential that we understand ourselves as we are by grace.

Here in Romans 6, Paul is expressly summoning us to look at ourselves as the gospel depicts us. *Reckon ye also yourselves to be dead indeed unto sin, but alive unto God through Jesus Christ* (11). That is: Take into account who you really are as Christian believers. You have undergone with Christ a death to sin and have been raised with Him to new life in the Spirit. "So you also must consider yourselves" (RSV).

Have you taken into account who you really are? What Paul writes here is the picture of "the new you," if indeed you are in Christ.

1. In the first place, "the new you" is *dead to Sin.* You have been crucified with Christ, you have truly entered into the Saviour's death at Calvary. Let this *fact* take full possession of your understanding. This is how Paul begins his doctrine of Christian sanctification in Romans 6.

a. The suggestion that we as Christians should "go on sinning so that grace may increase" (1, NIV) is not only *ghastly* (Phillips); it is also illogical. Nothing Paul has said about Christ and Adam in the previous chapter points in this direction. Rather, reigning grace through Christ now displaces Sin, which has reigned since Adam's fall. "Grace reign[ing] through righteousness unto eternal life by Jesus Christ our Lord" has brought to an end Sin's reign unto death—for all who are in Christ and under His lordship. This is Paul's argument in 5:12-21.

But the apostle is willing to hear his objector out. So he comes back with a question of his own for the objector: *How CAN we who died to sin still live in it?* (2, RSV). It is as contradictory for a Christian to go on sinning as for a dead man to continue living. "The new life involves a decisive break with the old—that is why it is fantastic to suggest that we *continue in sin,*" writes Gerald Cragg. "Death itself is not more final than the Christian's severance from the past."[5] For the person in Christ "the old has passed away, behold, the new has come" (2 Cor. 5:17, RSV).

b. Behind this declaration, as we have said, is Romans 5, which announces that Christ's death was the death of the old Adam-humanity, the end of Sin's rule over humankind. *By faith we enter into Christ's death to sin, and His death becomes our death!* By thus being "co-crucified" with Christ we are set free from Sin. Our body (or self) ceases to be "Sin's body." "The body given over to Sin" is "cancelled out." Sin having lost its grip upon me, I am now free to put my body (my person) with all its powers at God's disposal. Such is the meaning of Rom. 6:6: "We know that the man we once were has been crucified with Christ, for the destruction of the sinful self, so that we may no longer be the slaves of sin" (NEB).

Our baptism has taken place in view of this very death (3-4). Only the dead are buried. The creed declares that Christ was "crucified, dead, and buried." Paul says the same thing about us, and he cites our baptism as proof. Our baptism means that we have become incorporated into Christ and His death. We have been "grafted into" Christ (the meaning of 5). Everything Christ procured for us by His atonement is now ours in Him (cf. 1 Cor. 1:30-31). In Christ and His body I find spiritual completion (cf. Col. 2:9-17).

c. The new man in Christ is therefore actually living a holy life in Christ and in the power of the Spirit. The old man he once was in Adam has ceased to be. An incident in Augustine's early Christian life illustrates this. Before his conversion he had a mistress named Claudia. Shortly after he found Christ, Claudia saw him on the street in the city. "Augustine! Augustine!" she cried after her old paramour. Augustine paid no heed. "Augustine! Augustine!" she cried out again; "it is Claudia!" "But it is no longer Augustine," he replied, as he continued on his way.

So you must consider yourself—*dead indeed unto sin . . . through Jesus Christ.*

2. In the second place, "the new you" is *alive to God in Christ Jesus* (RSV). You have not only died with Christ to

Sin; you have been raised with Him to *newness of life* (4).

Of course, death and resurrection cannot be separated —either for Christ or for those of us who are in Him. The separation is possible only in thought. In experience, dying with Christ and being raised with Him to "new life of the Spirit" (7:6, RSV) are two parts of one experience. "I have been crucified with Christ; it is no longer I who live, but Christ who lives in me; and the life I now live in the flesh I live by faith in [or, 'by the faith of,' KJV] the Son of God, who loved me and gave himself for me" (Gal. 2:20, RSV).

Christ dying *for* me is my justification; Christ living *in* me is my sanctification. This sanctification *begins* in the new birth, as I begin to appropriate the merits of both His death and His resurrection. John Wesley has said it well:

> Christian faith is not only an assent to the whole gospel of Christ, but also a full reliance . . . upon Him as our atonement and our life, as *given for us* and *living in us;* and in consequence hereof, a closing with Him, and cleaving to Him, as our "wisdom, righteousness, sanctification, and redemption," or, in one word, our salvation.[6]

Our sanctification through Christ becomes *entire* when we permit His risen life to possess us completely, as we yield ourselves utterly to His sovereign lordship over us. Bishop H. C. G. Moule speaks of "Christ *for* us on the Cross, as our peace with God. . . . Christ *in* us for our emancipation from the tyranny of self, for the conquest of temptation, for the power to 'walk and to please God.' . . . Christ *over* us, the Master, by every claim of lordship, sovereignty, and possession."

Bill Bright shares with us his life in Christ:

> I usually awaken with a psalm of praise on my lips, with an attitude of thanksgiving: "Oh, Lord, I thank You that I belong to You. I thank You that You live within me, and I thank You that You have forgiven my sins. I thank You that I am a child of God. Now as I begin this day, as I continue throughout the day, I thank You that You walk around in my body, love with my

heart, speak with my lips and think with my mind. I thank You that, during the course of the day, You promised to do greater things through me than You did when You were here on the earth. By faith I acknowledge Your greatness, Your power, Your authority in my life, and I invite You to do anything You wish in and through me."

Then I slip out of bed on my knees, as a formal act of acknowledging His lordship.[7]

3. Finally, the "new man" must be *yielded to God.* If we are to experience the divinely intended scope of sanctification and life, we must put ourselves utterly at His disposal. This has both negative and positive implications.

a. Negatively, *Let not sin therefore reign in your mortal bodies, to make you obey their passions. Do not yield your members to sin as instruments of wickedness* (12-13, RSV). By our yielding to our bodily passions or "desires" *(epithumiais),* Sin may once again be "conceived" in us (cf. Jas. 1:14-15) and *reign* once more "unto death" (cf. 6:16).

The desires of the body are morally neutral, but they become the occasion of certain temptations. As those *who have been brought from death to life* (13, RSV) we must "by the Spirit . . . put to death the deeds of the body" if we are to maintain spiritual life (8:13, RSV). Our natural desires must be sacrificed for the higher spiritual ends for which Christ sacrificed His very life (cf. 1 Cor. 9:27).

b. Positively, we must *yield . . . [ourselves] to God, as men who have been brought from death to life, and . . . [our] members to God as instruments of righteousness* (13, RSV). The word translated *yield* is *parastesate.* "The aorist certainly implies a critical resolve, a *decision* to surrender" (Moule). It means to *offer* (NIV) ourselves to God, to put ourselves into His hands for His holy purposes. "The 'self-presentation' of the Gospel . . . is done in the fulness of personal decision and consciousness. . . . It is the placing of the surrendered self into Hands which will both foster its true development as only its Maker can, as He fills it with His presence, and will use it in the bliss of an eternal serviceableness for His beloved will."[8]

It is this act of Christian consecration, accompanied by appropriating faith, which makes possible the full possession and sanctification of our beings by the Holy Spirit. In chapter 8 (verses 2-4), Paul shares with us His personal experience of the Spirit-filled life. It is preeminently a love-filled life which delights in God's holy will and service. To be "filled" with the Spirit does not mean to receive more of God, but to give Him *all of ourselves*.

c. Dr. E. Stanley Jones has given classic testimony to this deeper commitment to which Christ calls us all:

> I was a Christian for a year or more when one day I looked at a library shelf and was struck with the title of a book, *The Christian's Secret of a Happy Life.*
>
> As I read it my heart was set on fire to find this life of freedom and fullness. I reached page forty-two when the Inner Voice said very distinctly, "Now is the time to find." I pleaded that I did not know what I wanted, that when I finished it, I would seek. But the Inner Voice was imperious, "Now is the time to seek." I tried to read on, but the words seemed blurred. I was up against a divine insistence, so closed the book, dropped on my knees and asked, "What shall I do?" The Voice replied, "Will you give me your all—your very all?" After a moment's hesitation I replied, "I will." "Then take my all, you are cleansed," the Voice said with a strange, inviting firmness. "I believe it," I said and arose from my knees. I walked around the room affirming it over and over, and pushing my hands away from me as if to push away my doubt. This I did for ten minutes, when suddenly I was filled with a strange refining fire that seemed to course through every portion of my being in cleansing waves. It was all very quiet and I had hold of myself—and yet the divine waves could be felt from the inmost center of my being to my fingertips. My whole being was being fused into one, and through the whole there was a sense of sacredness and awe—and the most exquisite joy.
>
> Very emotional? So be it! But I knew then, and I

know now, that I was not being merely emotionally stirred, but the very sources of my life were being cleansed and taken possession of by Life itself. My will just as much involved as my emotion. The fact is the whole of life was permanently on a higher level.[9]

The Holy Life

Romans 6:15-23

15 What then? shall we sin, because we are not under the law, but under grace? God forbid.
16 Know ye not, that to whom ye yield yourselves servants to obey, his servants ye are to whom ye obey; whether of sin unto death, or of obedience unto righteousness?
17 But God be thanked, that ye were the servants of sin, but ye have obeyed from the heart that form of doctrine which was delivered you.
18 Being then made free from sin, ye became the servants of righteousness.
19 I speak after the manner of men because of the infirmity of your flesh: for as ye have yielded your members servants to uncleanness and to iniquity unto iniquity; even so now yield your members servants to righteousness unto holiness.
20 For when ye were the servants of sin, ye were free from righteousness.
21 What fruit had ye then in those things whereof ye are now ashamed? for the end of those things is death.
22 But now being made free from sin, and become servants to God, ye have your fruit unto holiness, and the end everlasting life.
23 For the wages of sin is death; but the gift of God is eternal life through Jesus Christ our Lord.

Paul's gospel of grace is at the same time a gospel of sanctification. Justification decisively breaks the claim of sin upon us as guilt. At the Cross, that enfeebling and exhausting burden rolls from our backs and disappears in our Lord's grave! Freed from sin's guilt, we are also released from its power. Justification by faith thus provides the creative power for a life of *righteousness unto holiness* (19).

"Thou shalt call his name JESUS:" the angel announced, "for he shall save his people from their sins" (Matt. 1:21)—from their *sins,* not merely from judgment and hell. God justifies us in order to sanctify us. Nothing short of a life of "true righteousness and holiness" (Eph. 4:24, RSV) is consistent with "the form of teaching to which you were committed" (17, NIV). Justification and holiness are so interrelated that we can say, "No justification, no holiness; no holiness, no justification."

1. The holy life *begins in justification.* Pardoning love initiates the process of sanctification. With joyous assurance Paul writes, "But thanks be to God that, though you used to be slaves to sin, you wholeheartedly obeyed the form of teaching to which you were committed. You have been set free from sin and have become slaves to righteousness" (17-18, NIV).

This is clearly a word of thanksgiving for the Romans' conversion to Christ and the gospel. "You obeyed from the heart the mould of teaching to which you were handed over" (H. C. G. Moule). "The apostolic Doctrine . . . of the acceptance of the guilty for the sake of Him who was their Sacrifice . . . has, as it were, grasped them as its vassals, to form them, to mould them, for its issues."[10]

To be *committed* to, or "handed over" to, the apostolic doctrine of justification by faith, with an obedience "from the heart," is a life-changing experience. One who has striven *under law* (15, RSV) to gain God's acceptance, and then has heard and wholeheartedly received the comforting truth of pardon and acceptance through the crucified Saviour, is thereafter a captive of the gospel. For through Christ's blood sin's guilt has been dissolved and sin's power broken. He can then only say with Paul, "I am not ashamed of the gospel of Christ: for it is the power of God unto salvation" (1:16).

"Sin shall not be your master, because you are not under law, but under grace" (14, NIV). To be justified is to be free, for the first time, to obey God. I found this freedom in my teens, and in that glorious moment I was "handed over" to the gospel I now preach. Not fully understanding what had happened to me, I testified the next night after my conversion, "God has sanctified me!" He had—initially and outwardly (cf. 1 Cor. 6:9-11). My life had been recreated in Christ. Sanctification actually *begins* in justification. To deny this is to deny Paul's gospel: "When you were slaves to sin, you were free in regard to righteousness. . . . But now that you have been set free from sin and have become slaves of God, the return you get is sanctification and its end, eternal life" (20, 22, RSV).

The Greek word rendered *return* is *karpon,* which is literally "fruit." Sanctification is not something for which the justified Christian strives or works; it is the natural fruit of his new relationship to God. He has been sin's slave; he is now God's slave. He has been "washed . . . sanctified . . . justified, in the name of the Lord Jesus, and by the Spirit of our God" (1 Cor. 6:11)—cleansed from his old sinful practices, renewed in his inner nature by the Holy Spirit, loosed from the power of sin. "Pardoning love is the root of it all," Wesley says. The joy and freedom of pardon are the basis of Christian holiness.

2. The holy life *calls for total consecration to God.* "Having been set free from sin . . . now yield your members to righteousness for sanctification" (18-19, RSV)—the "through and through" sanctification of 1 Thess. 5:23.

Paul is issuing this call to complete consecration and inward sanctification, but it is not the urging of mere man; it is the call of the Holy Spirit himself. The Spirit who comes to live in the Christian's heart relentlessly urges him on to true and full sanctification. "For God hath not called us unto uncleanness, but unto holiness. He therefore that rejecteth, rejecteth not man, but God, who hath also given us his *holy* Spirit" (1 Thess. 4:7-8, mg.).

a. Initial sanctification is deliverance from *reigning* sin; entire sanctification, from *remaining* sin.

What is the sin that remains in the heart of the justified? Paul's exhortation in 19 implies clearly that it is a remaining self-sovereignty. "I am speaking in human terms," he writes the Romans, "because of your natural limitations. For just as you once yielded your members to impurity and to greater and greater iniquity, so now yield your members to righteousness for sanctification" (RSV). That is, "As you once abandoned yourselves to sin and its servitude, so now you must abandon yourself to God and His service."

Why are some of us who were once such lusty sinners now such timid saints? Why is our former zeal for sinning not matched by our Christian zeal for holiness? Why are some Christians who were once such faithful servants of the devil such halfhearted servants of God? Is not the root of the problem what Oswald Chambers calls "my claim to my right to myself"? He adds:

> The imperative need of spirituality is to sign the death warrant of the disposition of sin, viz., my claim to my right to myself. . . . When I come to a moral decision [to surrender this claim] and act upon it, then all that Christ wrought *for* me on the Cross is wrought *in* me. The free committal of myself to God gives the Holy Spirit the chance to impart to me the holiness of Christ.[11]

b. The imagery in Paul's mind here is undoubtedly that of Exod. 21:2-6, where a Hebrew slave, freed in the year of jubilee, chooses to become a love slave of his benevolent master. In this vein Bishop Moule paraphrases Paul:

> You are, with infinite rightfulness, the bondmen of your God. You see your deed of purchase; it is the other side of your warrant of emancipation. Take it, and write your own unworthy names with joy upon it, consenting and assenting to your Owner's perfect rights. And then live your life, keeping the autograph before your eyes. Live, suffer, conquer, labour, serve, as men who have themselves walked to their Master's door, and presented the ear to the awl which pins it to the doorway, saying, "I will not go out free."
>
> To such an act of the soul the apostle calls these saints, whether they had done the like before or not. They were to sum up the perpetual fact, then and there, into a definite and critical act (*parastasate,* aorist) of thankful will.
>
> And he calls us to do the same today. By the grace of God, it shall be done. With the eyes open, and fixed on the Master who claims us, and with hands placed

> helpless and willing within His hands, we will, we do, present ourselves bondservants to Him; for discipline, for servitude, for all His will.[12]

3. Finally, the holy life *is a life of perpetual obedience to God.* Let us turn to the opening question in verse 15: *Shall we sin, because we are not under law, but under grace?* Are the Lord's freedmen free to sin? The aorist tense means "Shall we make provision *for one act* of disobedience and infidelity to our new Master?" "By no means! Don't you know that when you offer yourselves to someone to obey him as slaves, you are slaves to the one whom you obey—whether you are slaves to sin, which leads to death, or to obedience, which leads to righteousness?" (15-16, NIV).

A. M. Hunter comments: "The very suggestion that freedom from law means freedom to sin is absurd, he [Paul] says. Let them regard their conversion *as a change of masters.* It is a law governing all service that the slave must yield his master exclusive obedience; no man may be a slave to two at the same time."[13]

The liberty of the gospel is not the license to sin. Sin is a power which, once yielded to, takes possession of us. "Once yield for a second to lust, whether it be the lust of the flesh or the lust of the mind," Oswald Chambers warns —"once yield and, though you may hate yourself for having yielded, you are bondslave to that thing." If this happens, only the redemptive power of Christ's blood can free you again (cf. 1 John 2:1-3).

But we need not sin. The freedom of the gospel is the freedom not to sin. "Sin is not meant to be your master —you are no longer living under the Law, but under grace" (14, Phillips). The freedom of Christ is the freedom to obey God, constantly and perpetually. Having been liberated from sin and consecrated to God, we are now "servants of liberty." The service of God is perfect freedom.

Yet this freedom must be guarded. "For freedom Christ has set us free; stand fast therefore, and do not submit again to a yoke of slavery" (Gal. 5:1, RSV)—either the yoke of legalism or the yoke of disobedience. Stand fast in the grace of Christ!

Make me a captive, Lord,
And then I shall be free;
Force me to render up my sword,
And I shall conqueror be.
I sink in life's alarm
When by myself I stand;
Imprison me within Thine arms,
And strong shall be my hands.

My heart is weak and poor
Until its Master find;
It has no spring of action sure—
It varies with the wind.
It cannot freely move,
Till Thou hast wrought its chain;
Enslave it with Thy matchless love,
And deathless it shall reign.

My will is not my own
Till Thou hast made it Thine;
If it would reach a monarch's throne
It must its crown resign.
It only stands unbent,
Amid the clashing strife,
When on Thy bosom it has leant
And found in Thee its life.

—George Matheson

ROMANS 7

The Freedom of the Gospel

Romans 7:1-25

1 Know ye not, brethren, (for I speak to them that know the law,) how that the law hath dominion over a man as long as he liveth?
2 For the woman which hath an husband is bound by the law to her husband so long as he liveth; but if the husband be dead, she is loosed from the law of her husband.

3 So then if, while her husband liveth, she be married to another
man, she shall be called an adulteress: but if her husband be dead, she
is free from that law; so that she is no adulteress, though she be
married to another man.
4 Wherefore, my brethren, ye also are become dead to the law by the
body of Christ; that ye should be married to another, even to him who
is raised from the dead, that we should bring forth fruit unto God.
5 For when we were in the flesh, the motions of sins, which were by
the law, did work in our members to bring forth fruit unto death.
6 But now we are delivered from the law, that being dead wherein we
were held; that we should serve in newness of spirit, and not in the
oldness of the letter.
7 What shall we say then? Is the law sin? God forbid. Nay, I had not
known sin, but by the law: for I had not known lust, except the law
had said, Thou shalt not covet.
8 But sin, taking occasion by the commandment, wrought in me all
manner of concupiscence. For without the law sin was dead.
9 For I was alive without the law once: but when the commandment
came, sin revived, and I died.
10 And the commandment, which was ordained to life, I found to be
unto death.
11 For sin, taking occasion by the commandment, deceived me, and
by it slew me.
12 Wherefore the law is holy, and the commandment holy, and just,
and good.
13 Was then that which is good made death unto me? God forbid.
But sin, that it might appear sin, working death in me by that which is
good; that sin by the commandment might become exceeding sinful.
14 For we know that the law is spiritual: but I am carnal, sold under
sin.
15 For that which I do I allow not: for what I would, that do I not; but
what I hate, that do I.
16 If then I do that which I would not, I consent unto the law that it is
good.
17 Now then it is no more I that do it, but sin that dwelleth in me.
18 For I know that in me (that is, in my flesh,) dwelleth no good
thing: for to will is present with me; but how to perform that which is
good I find not.
19 For the good that I would I do not: but the evil which I would not,
that I do.
20 Now if I do that I would not, it is no more I that do it, but sin that
dwelleth in me.
21 I find then a law, that, when I would do good, evil is present with
me.
22 For I delight in the law of God after the inward man:
23 But I see another law in my members, warring against the law of
my mind, and bringing me into captivity to the law of sin which is in my
members.
24 O wretched man that I am! who shall deliver me from the body of
this death?
25 I thank God through Jesus Christ our Lord. So then with the mind
I myself serve the law of God; but with the flesh the law of sin.

This chapter should be good news for anyone whose religion is a straightjacket. Many good people are all bound up—by their idea of the law, by rules and regulations. They know no freedom of Spirit. They "take pains" and give them to everybody else! Paul's gospel of freedom is just the opposite of this. It came in part out of his own personal deliverance from the law's tyranny. This emancipation has been beautifully captured by Earl B. Marlatt in a poem entitled "Paul":

He found life a pattern
Woven by the Law
And men, colorless threads in the fabric;
Save one,
Whose face shone
While jagged rocks carved the last darkness,
And Another,
Whose light and voice
Illumined a desert road.
Thereafter,
Frail but unafraid,
He journeyed into the dawn—
Tearing the pattern to shreds
To free souls
From the tyranny of the dark.

"Do you not know, brethren," Paul asks, "that the law is binding on a person only during his life?" (1, RSV). His question means, "Surely you know this—that the reign of law has been superseded by that of grace. Or do you need to be told that death brings an end to the claims of law, and therefore the dispensation of the law ceased with the death of Christ?"[14]

Many good church people seem *not* to know this. They have not learned that the love of Christ provides both adequate motivation and proper safeguards for the fulfillment of God's requirements. So in their very sincerity they have fallen into bondage, and they are anything but a good advertisement for the gospel. These "good" people need the help Paul can give them here in Romans 7. This chapter is *really* good news!

1. *Freedom from the Law.* A woman who has a husband, Paul says, is bound by the law to the husband only as long as he lives; when he dies, she is free to marry another. "Wherefore, my brethren, ye also are become dead to the law by the body of Christ [crucified on the Cross and raised by the Father]; that ye should be married to another, even to him who is raised from the dead, that we should bring forth fruit unto God" (4).

The clue to Paul's illustration is found in 6:6, which means that "our old man" died in and with Christ—provisionally at Calvary and experientially in our conversion. The "old man" (Adam—and the old Adamic humanity) is dead. Therefore the law that bound us to him is dissolved. We are now free to be married to Christ and *bring forth fruit unto God.*

Paul's analogy is consistent. *(a)* The woman is the true "self" capable of passing through different states or stages. We may live either under law (bound to Adam) or under grace (united to Christ). *(b)* The law is basically the Mosaic law, but since Paul omits the definite article in verse 1 he means also religion conceived of as a legalistic relationship to God. *(c)* The first husband is the old Adam, to whom we are bound under the law. *(d)* The new husband is the risen Christ, to whom we are united by faith (cf. Eph. 5:31-32).

Under law we are married to the old Adam, and this is life in the flesh: "For when we were in the flesh, the motions of sins, which were by the law, did work in our members to bring forth fruit unto death" (5). The *fruit unto death* is "the works of the flesh . . . immorality, impurity, licentiousness, idolatry, sorcery, enmity, strife, jealousy, anger, selfishness, dissension, party spirit, envy, drunkenness, carousing, and the like" (Gal. 5:19-21, RSV).

Under grace we are married to Christ, and this is *new life of the Spirit* (6, RSV). "But now we are delivered from the law, that being dead wherein we were held; that we should serve in newness of spirit, and not in the oldness of the letter" (6). Deliverance from the law does not mean license; it means just the opposite: the power through the Spirit to serve God in love and thus fulfill the law's true requirement. "The fruit of the Spirit is love, joy, peace, patience, kindness, goodness, faithfulness, gentleness, self-control; against such there is no law" (Gal. 5:22-23, RSV). Since those who are Spirit-filled do God's will spontaneously in love, the law has no claims against them.

2. *The Function of the Law.* Paul's analogy seems to raise a serious question about the law. If the law causes me to bring forth *fruit unto death,* is the law itself sin? "It now begins to look as if sin and the Law were very much the same thing. Can this be a fact?" (7, Phillips).

Paul rejoins, *God forbid.* The *law* is not sinful; *I* am.

Earlier (3:19-20) Paul has explained the function of the law with reference to *justification;* it pronounces us guilty before God, but it has no power to put us right with Him. A mirror cannot cleanse us. Here Paul shows us the function of the law with reference to *sanctification:* (a) It reveals to us the depravity of our hearts (7-13) and *(b)* thereby reduces us to self-despair, so that we spontaneously cry out to Christ for deliverance (14-25).

a. God's law reveals to me the native depravity of my heart—the exceeding sinfulness of Sin (7-13). "If it had not been for the law, I should not have known sin. I should not have known what it is to covet if the law had not said, 'You shall not covet.' But sin, finding opportunity in the commandment, wrought in me all kinds of covetousness. Apart from the law sin lies dead" (7-8, RSV). "The law is not simply a reagent by which the presence of sin may be detected," C. K. Barrett observes; "it is a catalyst which aids and even initiates the action of sin upon man." The law activates self-will.

The law thus "worketh wrath" by turning Sin into "transgression" (4:15; 5:13). It "slipped in" to make Sin reign and abound (5:20-21). Irenaeus characterized the law as God's poultice He applies to bring Sin to a head. The law is always preliminary to grace. Chronologically, the dispensation of law preceded that of grace. Personally, the same order is followed. God shows me my sin through the law, that I might see my deep need of His grace. "They that be whole need not a physician, but they that are sick."

Paul's confession in 9 is probably a reference to his *Bar Mitzvah,* when as a Jewish boy of 13 he became a "Son of the Commandment." In that experience he heard within the depths of his consciousness God's "Thou shalt not!" Whereupon something within him rejoined, "I will!" "When the commandment came, sin revived and I died; the very commandment which promised life proved to be death for me. For sin, finding opportunity in the commandment, deceived me and by it killed me" (9-11, RSV). Sin is the culprit. And as Paul has already said in 5:14, it is there whether we have God's written commandment or not. So this is more than Paul's confession; it is Mr. Everyman's autobiography. It is every person's experience as he passes the threshold of moral accountability (3:23).

Sin is not the fault of the law. The law is *spiritual* (14) and *holy* (12). It is the gift and revelation of the Holy One. "And the commandment is holy and just and good" (12, RSV). The commandment is *just* because it describes right relations: between man and God, and between man and man. It is *good* in the way the Psalmist means when he exclaims, "The statutes of the Lord are right, rejoicing the heart" (Ps. 19:8). When we are right with God and our neighbor, we experience a deep sense of peace and well-being. But indwelling Sin turns this holy law into "the law of sin and death" (8:2). It turns peace into condemnation, the light of God's love into the darkness of His wrath. And this, by divine intention—to show us that we are deep-dyed sinners in need of redemption.

b. God's purpose in giving the law, therefore, is to reduce us to total despair in our own efforts to find freedom from Sin. Like an unwanted in-law, Sin has moved in and created domestic discord. The more we struggle against it, the greater the conflict in the house of Mansoul.

"I do not understand my own actions," Paul complains (15, RSV). The NEB renders this, "I do not even acknowledge my own actions as mine." (This translation uses *ginosko* in accord with the biblical sense that to "know" is to "choose." "I do not determine my own actions," is perhaps his meaning.) "For I do not do what I want, but I do the very thing I hate. Now if I do what I do not want, I agree that the law is good. So then it is no longer I that do it, but sin which dwells within me. . . . I can will what is right, but I cannot do it" (16-18, RSV). Possessed by Sin, Paul still understood God's will and yearned to do it, but he was powerless to turn his good resolve into righteous action. This is Luther's "bondage of the will."

As creatures of flesh, our wills *are* bound. We are the slaves of Sin. But God has left one door open. While we cannot free ourselves from Sin, *we can choose a new Master*. We *can* turn to Christ. "O wretched man that I am!" Paul cries, "who shall deliver me from the body of this death? *I thank God through Jesus Christ our Lord*" (24-25, italics added).

The law has done its proper work in me when I come to see that *I left to myself* (25, Moffatt—*autos ego,* "I of myself") can never save or sanctify myself. The latter half of 25 is the key to this chapter. It means that, relying on my own resources, I am morally bankrupt. I cannot save or deliver myself; or, for that matter, remain holy in heart and life *except as I rely on Christ*.

Here in these agonizing verses Paul is essentially describing his preconversion struggle. C. H. Dodd observes, "It would stultify his whole argument if he now confessed that, at the moment of writing, he was a 'miserable wretch, a prisoner of sin's law.'" A concession, however, must be granted. Paul's thesis throughout chapter 7 is clear: *The law cannot sanctify*. To the extent a Christian believer is depending upon his own self-effort for sanctification, *to that extent* he is under the law. Having begun in the Spirit he is seeking to be made perfect by the flesh (Gal. 3:3). Not until he ceases "from his own works" does he enter the rest of heart holiness (Heb. 4:9-10). Something of this struggle therefore continues until by the full possession of the sanctifying Spirit his obedience is made perfect in love.[16]

To turn back from Christ-reliance to self-reliance at any time is to turn back to the *flesh*—and to reopen the door to the struggle of these verses. So God's law *drives me to Christ* and *keeps me close to Him* as my only Salvation, my only Holiness.

3. *The Fulfillment of the Law.* Although not in this chapter, we must look for a moment to Paul's conclusion in 8:1-4. Here we find Paul's present testimony. This is the joyous witness of everyone who has turned completely to Christ, trusted Him solely, and yielded fully to His lordship.

What we could never do for ourselves, God in Christ has done for us: by His obedience "unto death, even the death of the cross" (Phil. 2:8), the incarnate Son of God has defeated and destroyed *sin in the flesh,* potentially sanctifying our human existence. Now exalted at the Father's right hand, He imparts to us *the Spirit of life,* which sets us *free from the law of sin and death.* The Holy Spirit reproduces in us the very holiness of Christ, flooding our hearts with the love which fulfills *the just requirement of the law* (RSV).

In closing, let us reframe Paul's opening illustration. A woman was married to a stern, exacting man—"a male chauvinist pig," to use today's parlance. He laid out each day's duties he expected her to perform. She was to arise at a certain time, prepare his breakfast, and help him get off to work. As soon as he left the house she was to wash the dishes, clean up the kitchen, then sweep and dust the house. When he returned in the evening, he made it a point to check to see if she had carried out all his orders. Finally, to simplify his requirements he drew up 10 rules, which he placed on the kitchen wall in plain view.

In the course of time the wife's love was turned to bitterness. She felt herself reduced to abject slavery. She was frozen in fear, as her life became a barren round of duty.

Then her husband died. Some time later she met a fine man who knew the meaning of love and marriage. They became man and wife. This marriage was altogether different from the former. Her husband was generous, kind, and thoughtful. He did not have to command her to get up and prepare the breakfast. She enjoyed awakening him each morning with the aroma of coffee and frying bacon, and when he left for work she washed the dishes and did her chores with genuine delight.

One day as she was rummaging through a drawer she came on the 10 old rules her former husband had drawn up. To her amazement she was observing them all! "Love does nothing the law forbids—and more than the law requires."

That blessed law of Thine,
Jesus, to me impart.
Thy Spirit's law of love divine,
Oh, write it in my heart!

Implant it deep within,
Whence it may ne'er remove,
The law of liberty from sin,
The perfect law of love.

Thy nature be my law,
Thy spotless sanctity,
And sweetly every moment draw
My happy soul to Thee.

Soul of my soul remain;
Who didst for all fulfill,
In me, O Lord, fulfill again
Thy Heavenly Father's will!

—Charles Wesley

ROMANS 8

Life in the Spirit

Romans 8:1-11

1 There is therefore now no condemnation to them which are in Christ Jesus, who walk not after the flesh, but after the Spirit.
2 For the law of the Spirit of life in Christ Jesus hath made me free from the law of sin and death.
3 For what the law could not do, in that it was weak through the flesh, God sending his own Son in the likeness of sinful flesh, and for sin, condemned sin in the flesh:
4 That the righteousness of the law might be fulfilled in us, who walk not after the flesh, but after the Spirit.
5 For they that are after the flesh do mind the things of the flesh; but they that are after the Spirit the things of the Spirit.
6 For to be carnally minded is death; but to be spiritually minded is life and peace.
7 Because the carnal mind is enmity against God: for it is not subject to the law of God, neither indeed can be.
8 So then they that are in the flesh cannot please God.
9 But ye are not in the flesh, but in the Spirit, if so be that the Spirit of God dwell in you. Now if any man have not the Spirit of Christ, he is none of his.
10 And if Christ be in you, the body is dead because of sin; but the Spirit is life because of righteousness.
11 But if the Spirit of him that raised up Jesus from the dead dwell in you, he that raised up Christ from the dead shall also quicken your mortal bodies by his Spirit that dwelleth in you.

Flesh and *Spirit* are the words that dominate this passage. These are Bible words for two diametrically opposing ways of life. They are *not* psychological terms for "passion" and "reason," as the Greeks would say, or for the "lower" and "higher" natures of man.

Flesh in Scripture basically means "mere man." Life *after the flesh* is life "according to oneself" as a mere creature of time and sense. The fleshly (carnal) life is an existence in, by, and for oneself as a creature who has separated himself from God. The *flesh* is self-centered in itself, living for itself, relying on itself as a part of created existence—living as if God did not exist or care. This is the very essence of sin: living for self and the world rather than for God and the Kingdom.

By contrast, *Spirit* means God's indwelling Presence.

We *are* flesh; we *receive* the Spirit. Theologically, *the Spirit of God* (9*a*) is the Third Person of the Triune Godhead, who now *dwells in you* (9*b*, RSV) if you are *in Christ Jesus* (1). The Spirit is also *the Spirit of Christ* (9*c*), for by the Spirit *Christ is dwelling within you* (10, NEB).

An existence centered in self and set on this world—this is life *in the flesh* (9). An existence centered in Christ and oriented toward God is life *in the Spirit* (9). So, not to the saints in heaven, but to the saints in Rome, Paul writes, "You are not in the flesh, you are in the Spirit, if the Spirit of God really dwells in you" (RSV).

1. *Life in the Flesh.*

a. "Flesh" sometimes means the flesh-substance man has in common with beasts. It generally stands, in both Testaments, for "man." Man *is* flesh. "I conferred not with flesh and blood" (Gal. 1:16) means "with no other human beings." "No flesh" means simply "nobody" (Rom. 3:20; Gal. 2:16). "The Word was made *flesh*" (John 1:14) means He became *human*. Flesh is something man *is*.

Flesh is also something man *has*; it is the sphere of his existence in the world. In this neutral sense Paul says in Gal. 2:20, "The life that I now live *in the flesh* I live by . . . faith." The morally neutral flesh possesses "desires" *(epithumia)*, "passions" *(pathemata)*, and "wishes" *(thelemata)* (cf. Rom. 13:14; Gal. 5:16, 24; Eph. 2:3). In this sense "flesh" and "body" are used almost interchangeably.

Man as a creature who is and *has* flesh is not sinful, but by contrast to God he is finite, weak, and mortal (cf. Isa. 31:3). "Flesh represents mere man, man in contrast with God—hence man in his weakness and mortality."[17]

b. Paul, however, introduces a difference of meaning when he says that fallen man is *carnal*. Fallen man not only *is* and *has* flesh; he *uses* his flesh as the basis of his life.[18] He lives *for* the flesh and *by* the flesh, as a creature bound up in the flesh with a world subject to sin and death.

"Those who live according to the flesh set their minds

on the things of the flesh" (5, RSV). Fallen men have a "mind-set" or "disposition" (Greek, *phronema*) of the flesh; they are *carnally minded,* which means *death* (6). "The carnal mind is enmity against God: for it is not subject to the law of God, neither indeed can be. So then they that are in the flesh cannot please God" (7-8).

The "carnal" is not sinful. When Paul says, "The flesh lusteth against the Spirit, and the Spirit against the flesh" (in Gal. 5:17), he is not referring to the conflict between man's reason and his passions. This should be obvious from the fact that his list of 15 "works of the flesh" which follows contains 10 which have nothing to do with the sensual nature (Gal. 5:19-21). As Wesley says, the majority are sins which a being without a body could commit. By the flesh Paul means the *entire human person under the power of sin*—his mind and spirit as well as his body.

(1) To live *after the flesh* is sinful, therefore, not because the flesh is sinful *per se,* but because man is living, not in creaturely obedience to God, but *for himself.* To be carnal is to make the "belly" one's god (cf. 16:18; Phil. 3:19), to love "this present world" (cf. 12:2; 2 Tim. 4:10; 1 John 2:15-17), to set one's mind on things that are upon the earth (Col. 3:2), which is essentially idolatry (Col. 3:5). To live *after the flesh,* then, is to live "according to oneself"—for one's own pleasure, indulging his own desires, passions, and wishes (cf. Eph. 2:3).

(2) But the flesh also stands for reliance upon one's own efforts or resources in the endeavor to do God's will. Paul's last word for carnal-mindedness is putting "confidence in the flesh" by depending on one's own character and works for salvation (Phil. 3:2-3). The "wretched man" of Romans 7 is the person who, relying on himself to keep God's law, finds he cannot please God. "Left to myself" (*autos ego,* 7:25), says Paul, I am powerless (cf. 8:3, "weak through the flesh"). "For I know that nothing good dwells within *me,* that is, in *my flesh.* I can will what is right, but I cannot do it" (7:18, RSV).

Paul puts a question to the Galatians that you and I

also should face: "Having begun in the Spirit, are ye now made perfect by the flesh?" (3:3). The NIV translates this, "Are you now trying to attain perfection by human effort?"

The "last-ditch stand" of the flesh is not rebellion against God (which ceases at conversion); it is false self-reliance. "Those who belong to Christ Jesus have crucified the flesh with its passions and desires" (Gal. 5:24, RSV). They have also renounced all "confidence in the flesh" (Phil. 3:3). They have died to both self-indulgence and self-effort.

So Paul's final word on the flesh simply summarizes the message of the Old Testament: "Cursed be the man that trusteth in *man,* and maketh *flesh* his arm, whose heart departeth from the Lord" (Jer. 17:5, italics added).

2. *Life in the Spirit.* We cannot say too quickly, or too emphatically, that life in the Spirit is possible only *in Christ Jesus* (1). The Spirit is given only to those who trust Christ and receive Him as their Life. "The law of the Spirit of life *in Christ Jesus* has set me free from the law of sin and death" (2, RSV, italics added). Life in Christ—and only in Christ—is life in the Spirit.

a. It is Christ who brought an end to life *according to the flesh* (4, RSV). It is He who has introduced life *according to the Spirit* (RSV). He has accomplished this deliverance and made possible this life by His incarnation and His cross: "What the law could not do, in that it was weak through the flesh, God sending his own Son in the likeness of sinful flesh, and for sin, condemned sin in the flesh: that the righteousness of the law might be fulfilled in us, who walk not after the flesh, but after the Spirit" (3-4). He became flesh, that we might receive the Spirit!

Christ came in the *likeness* of "sin-controlled flesh" (the meaning of the phrase *sinful flesh*). *Our* flesh is "Sin's flesh"—it belongs to Sin, as a consequence of the Fall. Christ had a physical form like every man; He was completely human—sin excepted. His existence, from the moment of His miraculous conception by the Spirit to His death, was an existence in the Spirit. He therefore sanctified every stage of human life from the womb to the tomb.

Christ's flesh was "holy flesh." He was mistaken by men as a sinner, but this was because "man looketh on the outward appearance." "He was numbered with the transgressors." Yet in His inner life the Son of God was holy —in perfect self-control because He was fully under the control of the Spirit. At the last, "through the eternal Spirit" (Heb. 9:14), He offered up His life *for sin* (3). By His obedience "unto death, even the death of the cross" (Phil. 2:8), He executed Sin in the flesh. "Sin was thenceforth deposed from its autocratic power."[19] "By His life of perfect obedience and His victorious death and resurrection, the reign of sin over human nature has been broken."[20] He has "killed its claim and power for all who are in Him, making man's earthly conditions the scene of sin's defeat."[21] Christ has sanctified our human situation.

b. Holiness, then, is our Christian inheritance. Christ has been made for us Sanctification as well as Justification and Redemption (1 Cor. 1:30). He died not only to make possible our pardon and acceptance, but also our purification and restoration to the divine image. He has made propitiation for our *sins,* and He has pronounced the doom of *Sin itself.*

The holiness Christ procured for us by His life, death, and resurrection may be reproduced in us by the Spirit. The whole work of Christ for us had as its grand aim making us holy, "in order that the just requirement of the law might be fulfilled in us, who walk not according to the flesh but according to the Spirit" (4, RSV). Christ fulfilled the law *for* us in order that it might be fulfilled *in* us. The love which moved Him to obey the Father and give himself for others now motivates us for that devotion which fulfills the divine requirement for man (cf. 13:8-10; Matt. 22: 36-40).

c. Christ has made possible our life *in the Spirit,* which means a life indwelt by the *Spirit of Christ,* having

Christ dwelling within (9-10). When the Spirit really indwells us—possesses, controls, and pervades our beings —*Christ* indwells us, lives His life in and through us. This is New Testament holiness.

> *"Called unto holiness," praise His dear name!*
> *This blessed secret to faith now made plain:*
> *Not our own righteousness, but Christ within,*
> *Living and reigning and saving from sin.*
>
> —Mrs. C. H. Morris

Of course there are degrees of divine indwelling and therefore stages of holiness. Every Christian *has* the Spirit (9*b*), but not every Christian is *filled* with the Spirit. These degrees of indwelling are indicated in Paul's letter to the Ephesians. It was precisely because they were "a dwelling place of God in the Spirit" (Eph. 2:22, RSV) that the apostle prays for them, "that . . . he may grant you to be strengthened with might through his Spirit in the inner man, and that Christ may dwell in your hearts through faith . . . that you may be filled with all the fulness of God" (Eph. 3:16-17, 19, RSV). Clearly, Paul is praying that these Christians who had received the Spirit should enjoy His inward strengthening as the promised Comforter and the fullness of His indwelling. At the heart of the prayer is the petition: "that Christ will *make his home* in your hearts" (TEV).

Bishop Moule points out that the indwelling of Christ for which Paul here prays is "so deep and great, as to constitute a practically new arrival, and remaining where He so arrives not as a Guest, precariously detained, but as a Master resident in His proper home."[22]

"I have just given Christ the key ring to every room in my heart, and He has filled me with His Spirit!" In these words a seminarian shared with me his entrance into the Spirit-filled life. He had heard one of his professors tell of F. B. Meyer's quest for the Spirit's fullness. Dr. Meyer had offered Christ the entire key ring to his heart—except for one small key. The Lord was turning sadly away when

Meyer reached into his pocket and restored the little key. Immediately He was filled with the Spirit. And so it had been with the seminary student.

d. After explaining several kinds of Spirit-filling taught in the Scriptures, Daniel Steele describes the "ethical fullness" which means New Testament holiness. In an important paragraph in his *Defense of Christian Perfection,* Steele writes:

> But there is another kind of fullness of the Spirit which must imply entire sanctification—the permanent gracious presence in the soul of the Holy Spirit, in his fullness, not as an extraordinary gift but as a person having the right of way through soul and body, having the keys to the inmost rooms, illuminating every closet and pervading every crevice of the nature, filling the entire being with holy love.

This full possession of the heart by the Holy Spirit is the norm of New Testament Christianity. It is the end for which Christ came, and the life of which Paul speaks when he writes to the Romans: "You are not in the flesh, you are in the Spirit, if the Spirit of God really dwells in you" (9*a,* RSV). The fullness of the Spirit means the end of life *in the flesh.*

e. Even so, our *mortal bodies* remain. "But if the Spirit of him that raised up Jesus from the dead dwell in you, he that raised up Christ from the dead shall also quicken your mortal bodies by his Spirit that dwelleth in you" (11).

The *flesh* is destroyed, but the *body* is assured a glorious future, organically one with this living present. The body, once so defiled, is now precious to the Father because it is the habitation of the Spirit, the very temple of the triune God. H. C. G. Moule comments:

> Not only so; that same Spirit, who, by uniting us to Christ, made actual our redemption, shall surely, in ways to us unknown, carry the process to its glorious crown, and be somehow the Efficient Cause of "the redemption of our body." . . .

Wonderful is this . . . Gospel for the body. In Christ, the body is seen to be something far different from the mere clog, or prison, or chrysalis, of the soul. It is its destined implement . . . for the life of glory. As invaded by sin, it must needs pass through either death or, at the Lord's Return, an equivalent transfiguration. . . . No mere material sequences will bring this about. It will be "because of the Spirit"; and "because of the Spirit *dwelling in you,*" as your power for holiness in Christ.[23]

Father of everlasting grace,
Thou hast in honour of Thy Son
The GIFT unspeakable sent down,
The Spirit of life, and power, and love:
The purchased Comforter is given,
For Jesus is return'd to heaven,
To claim, and then THE GRACE impart.
Our day of Pentecost is come,
And God vouchsafes to fix His home
In every poor expecting heart.

—Charles Wesley

Holiness by the Spirit

Romans 8:12-17

12 Therefore, brethren, we are debtors, not to the flesh, to live after the flesh.
13 For if ye live after the flesh, ye shall die: but if ye through the Spirit do mortify the deeds of the body, ye shall live.
14 For as many as are led by the Spirit of God, they are the sons of God.
15 For ye have not received the spirit of bondage again to fear; but ye have received the Spirit of adoption, whereby we cry, Abba, Father.
16 The Spirit itself beareth witness with our spirit, that we are the children of God:
17 And if children, then heirs; heirs of God, and joint-heirs with Christ; if so be that we suffer with him, that we may be also glorified together.

There have always been those in the Church who think that holiness is simply a matter of rules and regulations, such as "Touch not; taste not; handle not," which Paul calls "commandments and doctrines of men" (Col. 2:21-22). "These have indeed an appearance of wisdom," the apostle admits, "in promoting rigor of devotion and self-abasement and severity to the body, but they are of no value in checking the indulgence of the flesh" (Col. 2:23, RSV).

Nevertheless, the holy life is both a duty and a discipline. This passage opens with the reminder *We are debtors.* For a moment Paul tells us what we are *not* indebted to: *the flesh,* or the self-life (12). It is clear, however, that his main purpose is not negative but positive; he wants us to understand we are indebted to *the Spirit.* That is, holiness is our duty *in the Spirit.* This obligation works out in a life of discipline; to be Christian is to be empowered by the Spirit to "put to death the deeds of the body" (13, RSV) and to be *led by the Spirit* into a life of Christlike obedience to the Father (14).

Talking about duty and discipline is absolutely essential, but unless we see clearly that this is an altogether different matter from "rigor of devotion and self-abasement and severity to the body," we may be imperceptibly brought back under the "spirit of bondage again to fear" (15). Christian holiness does *not* reintroduce a spirit of slavish fear. It is living daily in the joyous realization, given to us by the witnessing Spirit, that we are the children of God alongside our Elder Brother, Christ (16-17). At its deepest, holiness is not simply duty and discipline, it is our delight as God's sons and daughters.

1. Holiness is our *debt* in the Spirit. Too often in Christian history, holiness has been considered the special interest of the few who have chosen to heed "the counsel of perfection" or who perhaps have had special instincts for piety. But whatever holiness is, it is not for a minority of would-be "saints" or a special concern of merely "the holiness movement." In scripture, holiness is a sacred and binding debt owed by *all* who are the children of God. Holiness is not an option; it is a debt we owe as those who have received the *Holy* Spirit. We are bound, every one of us who names the name of Christ, to be separate from sin and to be holy as He is holy.

How miserable to be in debt and unable to pay! Whether one guiltily ignores his obligations or finds his means insufficient to meet them, he is—unless his conscience is dead—a haunted man. But when he has the means to pay and does so, such punctuality becomes one of life's pleasures.

As Christians, we owe a debt, but we are able to pay. Once we owed and had no means; we were morally bankrupt. Now we owe and have Christ in us by the Spirit; in Him we are sufficient. *We are debtors.* But He who makes His claims upon us has first immeasurably given. Christ is our Life; His very Spirit dwells within us. In the Spirit we have "the riches of grace" from which to pay.

"Holiness is beauty," Bishop Moule says. "But it is first duty, practical and present, in Jesus Christ our Lord."[24]

2. Holiness is a *discipline* in the Spirit. "If you live according to the flesh," Paul warns, "you will die, but if by the Spirit you put to death the deeds of the body you will live" (13, RSV).

It is death either to gratify the flesh or to live by the resources of the flesh. Fleshly living may take the form of either self-gratification or self-reliance. Of course, the wages of sinful indulgence are death (6:23). But also to turn back from Spirit-dependence to one's own wits and resources is to invite Satan to attack and destroy us. "For we wrestle not against flesh and blood, but against principalities, against powers, against the rulers of the darkness of this world, against spiritual wickedness in high places," and only the Christian who has on "the whole armour of God" is "able to withstand" (Eph. 6:12-13). "The arm of flesh will fail you!" There is no stage in the Christian life when we can dispense with the power of the Holy Spirit as our victory and deliverance from temptation.

Even though we are "not in the flesh, but in the Spirit" (9), we are still in the body. By the term Paul means the physical organism, of course; but he means more. The body is what man *is*. "Indeed, *soma* (body) is the nearest equivalent to our word 'personality.' . . . The *soma* is the whole person: 'Your body is the temple of the Holy Ghost. . . . Glorify God therefore in your body.'"[25]

The deeds of the body, which we are commanded to *put to death,* are the psychological as well as the physical impulses—all the mechanistic tendencies of the psyche (to rationalize, to overcompensate, etc.) along with the instinctual urges and drives of our common humanity. The Spirit-filled believer remains a human ego with natural tendencies, and he still possesses the Freudian id with its pressures and proddings. Since these impulses reside beneath the level of consciousness, they are morally neutral; but they may easily lead to sin and must therefore be controlled and subjugated by the power of the Holy Spirit. If we "repress" them by denying their existence, we not only deceive ourselves; we may make ourselves sick. By the Spirit we must "suppress" them by acknowledging and surrendering them to God and permitting Him to give us victory over them.

W. E. Sangster has a helpful passage in his book *The Pure in Heart,* where he insists that "life, as it bubbles out of the subconscious, is amoral, and should be regarded merely as instinct or 'reaction' until the conscious self identifies itself with the end desired." He continues:

> When I feel a sudden stab of jealousy, is it I?—I, in the very instant that I feel it? Is it I, when some surge of pride stiffens my spirit? Is it I, in the moment when some carnal appetite stirs in my flesh?
>
> Certainly, in that split second, it feels like me. Is this effort to disown the shabby desires of my nature no more respectable than an incontinent man denying the paternity of his illegitimate children? Is that carnality, pride, jealousy, self-pity or any other member of the dirty litter—is it mine?—mine in the second that I feel it: mine whether I disown it or not?
>
> I cannot feel that it is. As a conscious moral being, it is not mine till my will makes it mine. I have an

> amoral nature, with race and family memories and tendencies. But, as a person, and with the help of the Holy Ghost, the animal nature can be curbed, chained, subdued, mastered. No more of it need be admitted to my moral life than fellowship with God allows. In the moment it stirs in me, trying to wrest my moral life to what I judge to be evil, it is still only temptation. It is true that I need not solidify it in a deed for it to become a sin. If I finger it awhile and glut my imagination in it, it becomes sin, even though it has not issued in a deed, because I have taken it as my own.
>
> I will not take it as my own. I will learn from the saints how to assess it swiftly in the light of God and, seeing it to be evil, blast it with a prayer.
>
> It was never mine. It was amoral instinct. It was only impulse bidding for moral stature. It was recognized in the white light of God in its evil tendency, and never passed the moral guard.[26]

By the power of the indwelling Spirit we *may* subjugate, master, control, all our impulses to the glory of God! This is suppression, but not of sin; it is the control of amoral human nature, by the Spirit. The Spirit-indwelt Christian is not exempt from temptations to the flesh, but he has within him the divine and all-effectual "Counteragent" to the subtlest of all his foes. Filled with the Spirit, he is able to *defeat* temptation.

3. Finally, holiness is our *delight* in the Spirit. The fact that holiness is our duty and discipline in the Spirit must not be permitted to obscure the fact that it is also our genuine delight as children of God who enjoy the witness of the Spirit.

A life of holiness is really assured only to those who by simple trust and filial obedience live daily in the warmth of God's love in Christ. As the children of God, "we have received the Spirit of adoption" ("sonship," RSV). "When we cry, 'Abba! Father!' it is the Spirit himself bearing witness with our spirit that we are children of God, and if children, then heirs, heirs of God and fellow heirs with Christ" (16-17, RSV).

In a parallel passage Paul says, "Because you are sons, God has sent the Spirit of his Son into our hearts, crying, 'Abba! Father!'" (Gal. 4:6, RSV). Jesus is God's Son *by nature;* we are children of God *by adoption.* But by the Spirit we are introduced into the same intimate relationship with the Father which the Son has known from eternity. When we thus pray, we use the very word the disciples heard the Son of God use when He prayed—"Abba." The Spirit of the Son in our hearts cries, "Father! Dear Father!" This inward awareness that we are beloved of God as His very children is the root of all holiness. In his second discourse on "The Witness of the Spirit," Wesley explains how this is true:

> We must be holy in heart before we can be conscious that we are so. But we must love God before we can be holy at all, this being the root of all holiness. Now we cannot love God, till we know he loves us: "We love him, because he first loved us." And we cannot know his love to us, till his Spirit witnesses it to our spirit. Till then we cannot believe it; we cannot say, "The life which I now live, I live by faith in the Son of God, who loved me, and gave himself for me."[27]

Then, only then we feel
Our interest in his blood,
And cry, with joy unspeakable,
Thou art my Lord, my God!

Most deeply, holiness is the natural outflow of this filial relationship to God, the simple expression of the love of God shed abroad in our hearts by the Holy Spirit, who has been given to us (5:5). Living the life of holiness, then, is not a matter of flinty determination or the rigor of self-abasement; its source is the strength and joy of divine sonship. "The joy of the Lord is your strength." The secret of holiness is a daily walk with Christ in the school of prayer and discipleship. It is living so naturally and consistently in *the Spirit of the Son* that we cry joyously with Him, "I delight to do thy will, O my God."

Joys are flowing like a river
Since the Comforter has come.
He abides with us forever,
Makes the trusting heart His home.

Springing into life and gladness
All around this glorious Guest,
Banished unbelief and sadness,
And we just obey and rest.

—MANIE PAYNE FERGUSON

The Hope of Glory

Romans 8:18-27

18 For I reckon that the sufferings of this present time are not worthy to be compared with the glory which shall be revealed in us.
19 For the earnest expectation of the creature waiteth for the manifestation of the sons of God.
20 For the creature was made subject to vanity, not willingly, but by reason of him who hath subjected the same in hope,
21 Because the creature itself also shall be delivered from the bondage of corruption into the glorious liberty of the children of God.
22 For we know that the whole creation groaneth and travaileth ir pain together until now.
23 And not only they, but ourselves also, which have the firstfruits of the Spirit, even we ourselves groan within ourselves, waiting for the adoption, to wit, the redemption of our body.
24 For we are saved by hope: but hope that is seen is not hope: for what a man seeth, why doth ye yet hope for?
25 But if we hope for that we see not, then do we with patience wait for it.
26 Likewise the Spirit also helpeth our infirmities: for we know not what we should pray for as we ought: but the Spirit itself maketh intercession for us with groanings which cannot be uttered.
27 And he that searcheth the hearts knoweth what is the mind of the Spirit, because he maketh intercession for the saints according to the will of God.

"Glory" is a divine word. It means the brightness or radiance which shines from the presence of God. It appeared in the pillar of cloud (Exod. 16:10), on Mount Sinai (Exod. 24:16), in the Tabernacle (Exod. 40:34) and Temple (1 Kings 8:11).

God's glory originally shone on the countenance of

Adam, but it was lost, along with the moral image, when he fell (cf. 3:23). In Christ, this lost glory has been restored (John 1:14). It was veiled, however, during the days of His humiliation, except for the brief interlude of His transfiguration (Matt. 17:1-5). But after His passion and death He was glorified, by the Resurrection.

Through Christ we experience God's glory. "By the *glory* of the Father" we are "raised" to "newness of life" (6:4). This is an eschatological phrase which means God has "transferred us to the kingdom of his beloved Son" (Col. 1:13, RSV). By the Spirit we have "tasted the powers of the age to come" (Heb. 6:5, RSV), but in a sense we are already living in it (cf. John 5:25). The Spirit who indwells us and witnesses to us is himself the Guarantee and Foretaste of *the glory which shall be revealed* when Christ returns (18). Like Christ's earthly glory, ours is a veiled glory. Although "God . . . hath shined in our hearts, to give [us] the light of the knowledge of the glory of God in the face of Jesus Christ. . . . We have this treasure in earthen vessels" (2 Cor. 4:6-7).

By the same token, just as Christ is now glorified after His passion and death, so too we shall share in His inheritance of glory, as we do now actually share in "the fellowship of his sufferings" (cf. Phil. 3:10-11). "In this hope we were saved" (25, RSV), the hope of sharing *His* glory.

1. *Glory Anticipated.* Our Christian existence has three tenses: past, present, and future. It is based upon the Foundation which has been laid—Christ (1 Cor. 3:11); it lives in the present by the power of the Spirit; it presses toward the full redemption of the future. Paul now turns to the third tense: the hope for the future that we have in Christ. Even here, the Spirit is still central, as the Foretaste of this future glory which shall be ours when Christ returns.

Paul sees the entire natural order, cursed because of man's sin (Gen. 3:17), groaning in birth pangs for the final deliverance which shall come when Christ is revealed. His vision in 19-22 is of "the new heavens and the new earth" promised in Isa. 66:22. God's ultimate purpose is the creation of a new cosmos, now being preceded by birth pains (cf. Isa. 66:7-9). But nature's redemption is linked up with *the manifestation of the sons of God* (19). Phillips phrases it: "The whole creation is on tiptoe to see the wonderful sight of the sons of God coming into their own." This is what the late Professor G. T. Thomas of Edinburgh calls "a scientific fact viewed theologically."

But Paul's concern is not with creation for its own sake but with the certainty of the future salvation of God's children. *The whole creation* groans and travails in the labor of childbirth *until now.* "And not only they, but ourselves also, which have the firstfruits of the Spirit, even we ourselves groan within ourselves, waiting for the adoption, to wit, the redemption of our body" (22-23). "Not only so" (NIV) indicates that he is carrying his argument one step forward. We believers, who enjoy *the firstfruits of the Spirit,* have an inward anticipation of God's glory which will burst upon creation when Christ appears.

The Spirit who dwells in our hearts, flooding them with the love of God (5:5), is an actual Foretaste of our heavenly glory. "The *firstfruits* are a specimen crop of the glory which shall be ours when Christ returns. As the grapes of Eshcol, brought back by Caleb and Joshua from the land of Canaan, were meant to whet the appetite of the Hebrews for the Promised Land, so the Holy Spirit introduces us to the taste of heaven."[28]

Heaven is not gates of pearl and streets of gold; these are but external trappings. Heaven is the presence of God; and in the Spirit, God's immediate presence is given to us.

Once heaven seemed a far-off place,
Till Jesus showed His smiling face.
Now it's begun within my soul;
'Twill last while endless ages roll.

—C. F. Butler

2. *Glory Veiled.* The immediate link between the present scripture and the preceding is "the Spirit of adoption"

(15). Our adoption is realized, but it is incomplete. It is assured to us by the witnessing Spirit, but it is not yet apparent to the world. It is a concealed sonship, obscured by the body of our humiliation. But at the end of the age, when our Lord returns with His own and for His own (cf. 1 Thess. 4:13-17), our sonship will be revealed. All will then see our adoption is a fact. "The Spirit of adoption" is the guarantee of that coming disclosure. "Beloved, we are God's children now; it does not yet appear what we shall be, but we know that when he appears we shall be like him, for we shall see him as he is" (1 John 3:2, RSV).

a. "This present time" (18) of our Christian existence is an *interim period,* a "time between the times." It is life in the Kingdom which has been inaugurated but not consummated. The Kingdom *has come* in Christ—in His incarnate life, death, resurrection, and ascension; it came "with power" at Pentecost, when the exalted Christ poured out the Holy Spirit upon His Church. But, it has *not yet come* in its *final* manifestation and glory; the Church awaits "the blessed hope" of its Lord's appearing. For this reason, we speak of the Church as "the end-time community." It exists between Pentecost and the Parousia.

b. "This present time" is a time of "sufferings" for the Christian (18). It corresponds in many ways with the period of Jesus' earthly humiliation. As our Lord was subject to temptation, sufferings, and death during the days of His flesh, so are we. "The disciple is not above his master." Our present existence is in "the body of our humiliation" (Phil. 3:21, ASV). Even though our body is dead to sin (6:6-7), if we are completely yielded to God (6:13) and indwelt by the Spirit (8:3-4, 9), and therefore truly sanctified (6:19), it is still mortal (8:10) and must be constantly sacrificed to God by the power of the Spirit (8:13). As such it is "the temple of the Holy Ghost," in which we may "glorify God" (1 Cor. 6:19-20); but it has not yet been redeemed from its infirmities and weaknesses which cause us to "groan within ourselves" as we await our "adoption as sons, the redemption of our bodies" (23, RSV).

These groanings come from the awareness of our human frailties: the racial effects of sin in our bodies and minds, the scars from our past sins, our prejudices and warped attitudes, our neuroses which bring emotional depressions and make us at times "act out of character," our temperamental idiosyncrasies, our human weariness and fretfulness, and a thousand faults to which our mortal flesh is heir. As the old southern spiritual goes,

Sometimes I feel discouraged
And think my work's in vain,
But then the Holy Spirit
Revives my soul again.

Thank God, "the Spirit also helpeth our infirmities" (26). Yet they remain. An honest doctrine of Christian perfection must be formulated within the framework of *this present time* which is characterized by *infirmities*. When we are indwelt by the Holy Spirit, we are no longer "in the flesh." The *sinfulness* of the flesh is destroyed by the Spirit (8:8-9), but not its *weakness*. At every stage in my Christian pilgrimage I must confess with Paul, "I know that in me (that is, in my flesh [myself apart from Christ]) dwelleth no good thing" (7:18). Without Him I can do nothing (John 15:5).

c. Because I am not yet resurrected with Christ, "I am not yet perfected" (Phil. 3:12, literal translation). Although God's glory fills my heart, it is a veiled glory. This "earthen vessel" often obscures Christ, and at times even hides Him from my own consciousness. As Paul writes in another letter, "Here indeed we groan, and long to put on our heavenly dwelling. . . . For while we are still in this tent, we sigh with anxiety; not that we would be unclothed, but that we would be further clothed, so that what is mortal may be swallowed up by life" (2 Cor. 5:2, 4, RSV).

3. *Glory Revealed.* Someone has penned my testimony:

I'm a person God is making,
Like a statue God is shaping;
God is changing me, correcting—
God's intent on my perfecting.

"I am not yet perfected," but thank God, *I am being perfected:* "And we all, with unveiled face, beholding the glory of the Lord, are being changed into his likeness from one degree of glory to another" (2 Cor. 3:18, RSV). By the Spirit of Christ, I am being transformed "in ever-increasing splendor into his own image" (Phillips); besides that, I have the hope that one day I shall stand perfected in His likeness. "We know that, when he shall appear, we shall be like him; for we shall see him as he is" (1 John 3:2).

a. "In this hope we were saved," says Paul (24, RSV)—in the confident expectation that Christ will return and "transform the body of our humble state into conformity with the body of His glory" (Phil. 3:21, NASB).

"If our Christianity be not altogether restless eschatology," Barth says with characteristic incisiveness, "there remains in it no relationship whatever to Christ." Only as we experience suffering mingled with hope do we live in true dependence upon Christ.

b. Christian hope sanctifies: "Every man that hath this hope in him purifieth himself, even as he is pure" (1 John 3:3).

c. It heartens and makes glad: "We . . . rejoice in hope of the glory of God. And not only so, but we glory in tribulations also: knowing that tribulation worketh patience; and patience, experience; and experience, hope; and hope maketh not ashamed; because the love of God is shed abroad in our hearts by the Holy Ghost which is given unto us" (5:2-5).

This hope is not wishful thinking; it is a sure confidence, "knowing that he who raised the Lord Jesus will raise us also with Jesus and bring us . . . into his presence" (2 Cor. 4:14, RSV).

Oh, what a blessed hope is ours!
While here on earth we stay,
We more than taste the heavenly powers,
And antedate that day.
We feel the resurrection near,
Our life in Christ concealed,
And with his glorious presence here
Our earthen vessels filled.

—CHARLES WESLEY

If God Be for Us!

(The following exposition is by Paul S. Rees)[29]

Romans 8:28-39

28 And we know that all things work together for good to them that love God, to them who are the called according to his purpose.
29 For whom he did foreknow, he also did predestinate to be conformed to the image of his Son, that he might be the firstborn among many brethren.
30 Moreover whom he did predestinate, them he also called: and whom he called, them he also justified: and whom he justified, them he also glorified.
31 What shall we then say to these things? If God be for us, who can be against us?
32 He that spared not his own Son, but delivered him up for us all, how shall he not with him also freely give us all things?
33 Who shall lay any thing to the charge of God's elect? It is God that justifieth.
34 Who is he that condemneth? It is Christ that died, yea rather, that is risen again, who is even at the right hand of God, who also maketh intercession for us.
35 Who shall separate us from the love of Christ? shall tribulation, or distress, or persecution, or famine, or nakedness, or peril, or sword?
36 As it is written, For thy sake we are killed all the day long; we are accounted as sheep for the slaughter.
37 Nay, in all these things we are more than conquerors through him that loved us.
38 For I am persuaded, that neither death, nor life, nor angels, nor principalities, nor powers, nor things present, nor things to come,
39 Nor height, nor depth, nor any other creature, shall be able to separate us from the love of God, which is in Christ Jesus our Lord.

This is the great challenge that St. Paul set on its sturdy feet and sent marching down the far-from-easy path of the Christian centuries. I wish, by Heaven's help, to set it ringing in our ears and in our hearts. . . .

If God be for us, who can be against us? With these terms does a bold Christian confidence gird itself. It rises, all rugged and splendid, out of the midst of a great marshalling of majestic truth; for the eighth chapter of Romans marks one of the highest levels of revelation in all this Book of God. As someone has pointed out, it begins with "No Condemnation" and ends with "No Separation"! The last 13 of its 39 verses constitute the immediate setting of the text; and, with them as a background, let us examine this thrillingly triumphant word.

Let us, however, remark in a general way on the contrast that is here declared. For and against! Explain it as we may, deny it we cannot; there is a dualism in life from which it is impossible to escape. A moral cleavage cuts its keen and uncoverable way straight through the universe. There are things that are for us and there are things that are against us. And these things, according to the inspired conception of the Apostle Paul, not only group themselves, not only exist in conflicting confederacy, but, traced up to their sources, are found to be centralized and personalized. Our text names the One, the High and Holy One, who gathers up unto himself and presides over the things that are leagued for goodness and for all who seriously purpose goodness for themselves. And while it does not name him, the text does, by the use of the personal pronoun, suggest the personalization of evil, whether the opposition be human or satanic.

But the point is that the contest is not an equal one. God is almighty; Satan is not. Wickedness may make more noise, but righteousness can muster greater strength. Life's insurrectionary and destructive forces are formidable, yes, devastating—let no one be so stupid as to deny their reality or their vitality—but they are no match for the redemptive and healing energies released from the broken heart of God on the mount called Calvary. Show me the man who aligns himself with God, takes bold stand there, makes unconditional surrender there, and I will show you a man who is so divinely environed, so linked with omnipotence, as to secure for himself the restful assurance of final and everlasting triumph. Swing him from the gibbet, burn him at the stake, grind him to powder, and before you are done with your thankless task the vaulted skies will ring with his victory-shout, flung full-throated from the battlements of glory: "Thanks be unto God, which always causeth us to triumph in Christ."

If God be for us, who can be against us?

Now, an attempt to interpret these words in the line of thought of which they are a part will lead us to consider that:

1. *God Is for Us ELECTIVELY in the Purposes of His Grace.*

That is the point of verse 29, which reads: *For whom he did foreknow, he also did predestinate to be conformed to the image of his Son, that he might be the firstborn among many brethren.*

Thus in a vast stretch of thought are we carried back to mystic beginnings, back of Calvary with its shadows and anguish, back of Bethlehem with its cradle song, back of Sinai with its thunder-toned pronouncements of law, back of the Garden of Eden with its sinless symphony of physical beauty and moral purity, back of creation's wonder chorus when the morning stars sang together and the sons of God shouted for joy—back, back, back, where in the counsels of the infinite Mind and Heart the story of man got its start. Even there and then we—you and I—were given a place in the eternal purpose of God.

Well aware am I that this is treading ground strewn with the weapons and scalps of many a theological gladiator. Not for a moment does one presume to offer any final word on the mystery of how the divine foreknowledge and foreordination are to be reconciled with human freedom and human responsibility. He who speaks too glibly or dogmatically here commits the folly of rushing in where angels fear to tread. But of one thing we may be very sure—it is an unshakable conviction born of an effort to hold a balanced view of the teachings of God's Word—and that is that if a man is saved it is by the grace of God, and if a man is lost it is by his own refusal of the offer of that grace. Any view of the doctrine of election that arbitrarily limits the atonement of our Lord Jesus Christ, or that arbitrarily elevates certain individuals to eternal life while it consigns certain others to eternal death, can be held only by eyes blind to the fact that "God willeth not the death of any" but rather that "all men should come to repentance."

When a candidate for the ministry told John McNeil that he was perturbed with the thought that he might sometime offer free grace to one who was not of the elect, the noted Edinburgh preacher is reported to have answered: "Oh, mon, don't let that bother ye. If ye should happen to get the wrong mon saved, God will forgive ye." Thus it is that betimes a bit of humor happily rescues us from the peril of extremes to which we seem driven by the rigor and vigor of our often too cold theologies.

In taking leave of this thought of God's eternal purpose of grace there are two suggestions that one would lift into prominence. First, you, my friend, and you, have a place in that purpose. You are dear to God. You mean something to Him. You are even now the subject of influences and the object of plannings the origin of which is older than proud Egypt's pyramids and finds its home in the heart of the Eternal Father. The second suggestion is that the blessedness to which you are elected in the filling of your place in His purpose is nothing short of holiness, or Christlikeness. I use the words synonymously because the Scriptures do. The same Holy Spirit who declares in the context, *Whom he did foreknow, he also did predestinate to be conformed to the image of his Son,* declares in Eph. 1:4 that "he hath chosen us in him before the foundation of the world, that we should be holy and without blame before him in love." There is a large sense in which Christlikeness must ever remain merely an approximation with us; but there is a proper sense in which it can be, by the grace of God, an actual, living realization. Christ was holy and without *fault*—there is your approximation. We can be holy and without *blame*—there is your realization. A heart cleansed from all sin by the precious blood of Christ is a heart whose moral texture of motive and purpose is inwoven with the mind of Christ.

And this suggests the second proposition to which our study brings us:

2. *God Is for Us EFFICACIOUSLY in the Cross of His Son.*

The question of the text is followed by another question. *If God be for us, who can be against us?* Then the apostle seems to say in effect, Do you doubt that He is for you? If you do, answer this further question: *He that spared not his own son, but delivered him up for us all, how shall he not with him also freely give us all things?*

What God has purposed in eternity He has provided for in time in the incarnation and atonement of the Lord Jesus Christ. Let us not be confused by the clamor of contradictory voices heard on every hand; the delivering up of Jesus, His vicarious sacrifice upon the Cross, is the central fact in the whole revelation and realization of God's redemptive purpose. To it all preceding ages point the way; from it all succeeding ages take their rise. The Cross effectively removes those barriers in the divine nature that would prevent a holy God from making cheap concessions to sin and it effectively produces the highest type of moral appeal to morally responsive beings, inciting them, as nothing else has ever done, to a hatred of sin and a love of righteousness.

Ah, yes, He was delivered up for us all! And since He was, says St. Paul, shall not the Father God give us all things? Such things, for example, as the luminous chapter unveils?

Shall He not forgive us our sins? Answer: *Whom he called, them he also justified.* "Therefore being justified by faith, we have peace with God through our Lord Jesus Christ" (Rom. 5:1).

Shall He not confer upon us, who are by nature aliens and by choice rebels, the title of sons, sons of God? Answer: "Ye have received the Spirit of adoption, whereby we cry, Abba, Father. The Spirit itself beareth witness with our spirit, that we are the children of God."

And, having forgiven us our transgressions, having put upon us the benediction of His pardoning peace, shall He not deliver us from our carnal-mindedness, from the subtle enmity of self-will and self-love? Answer: "For the law of the Spirit of life in Christ Jesus hath made me free from the law of sin and death." The *life of sinning* is one thing; the *law of sin* is another thing. The life of willful sinning ceases at conversion, but victory and freedom as touching the law of sin in our moral nature is the glorious privilege of God's children who will be filled with His sanctifying Spirit.

Shall He not, moreover, teach us the secret of that mysterious ministry which we call prayer, that something by which, as Tennyson put it, more things are wrought than this world dreams of? Answer: *Likewise the Spirit also helpeth our infirmities: for we know not what we should pray for as we ought: but the Spirit itself maketh intercession for us with groanings which cannot be uttered.*

And would not time fail us to tell of *all* those divine ministries and human benefits that flow down to us in an endless stream from that crimson fountainhead at Calvary? God went the limit at "The Old Rugged Cross." He gave us His best. And that best is the red banner we lift in confidence that "no good thing will he withhold from them that walk uprightly."

3. *God Is for Us ENCOURAGINGLY in the Mysteries of His Providence.*

Blessedly familiar are the pertinent words of the twenty-eighth verse: *And we know that all things work together for good to them that love God, to them who are the called according to his purpose.* Mark the certainty of it. *We know!* That is characteristically the language of Christian conviction. But do not fail to mark the limitation of it: *to them that love God, to them who are the called according to his purpose.* To *them* the immense pledge is given, concerning *them* the inclusive declaration is made, that *all things work together for good.*

I stood one day with a friend in a salon of Marshall Field's in Chicago where magnificent tapestries were on display. In front of us was one whose rare beauty of design and marvelous skill in execution made it particularly impressive. Curious about its cost, I stepped over and turned up the corner to see if I could find a price mark. I found it—$6,000. But I found something else. I made the discovery that this expensive tapestry had two sides, and that if Marshall Field's had hung it up wrong side out it would not have brought $6.00, to say nothing of $6,000. That back side was utterly without design. Threads ran crazily in this direction and that. It all looked like the work of a nitwit. Yet those were the very threads that, worked by the masterly hand of the artist, had produced the exquisite picture that appeared on the other side.

Have you put your life in the hands of the Infinite Artist? Have you really? Then have the faith and courage to believe that, however strangely the threads may seem to run, however cruelly the needle may stab out, it is His hand at work—and back of His hand His heart.

Then, changing the figure, let this be your steadfast stand:

I will not doubt, though all my ships at sea
Come drifting home with broken masts and sails;
I will believe the Hand that never fails,
From seeming evil worketh good for me.
And though I weep because those sails are tattered:
Still will I cry, while my best hopes lie shattered:
"I trust in Thee."

I will not doubt, though sorrows fall like rain,
And troubles swarm like bees about a hive;
I will believe the heights for which I strive
Are only reached by anguish and by pain;
And though I groan and writhe beneath my crosses
I shall see through my severest losses
The greater gain.

I will not doubt. Well anchored in this faith,
Like some staunch ship, my soul braves every gale;
So strong its courage that it will not quail
To breast the mighty unknown sea of death.
Oh, may I cry, though body parts with spirit,
"I do not doubt," so listening worlds may hear it,
With my last breath.

It can be done by those who abide in the faith that *all things work together for good to them that love God.*

But we have not yet reached the climax of the discourse out of which the text speaks so significantly. *If God be for us, who can be against us?* For us *electively* in the purposes of His grace, for us *efficaciously* in the cross of His Son, for us *encouragingly* in the mysteries of His providence, the apostle now reveals Him as the One who will be for us forever.

4. *God Is for Us ETERNALLY in the Fellowship of His Love.*

Who shall separate us from the love of Christ? Is the daring defiance that Paul lifts against all comers. He feels himself in the warm embrace of the love that will not let him go, a love that now whispers and now sings of the life of love that is to be, "unmeasured by the flight of years"; a love for which he counts all things but loss and holds life itself as a consecrated forfeit to that infinite affection.

This is no cheap faith we hold and preach, this Pauline, this Christian faith. No puppy love transferred to the realm religious. Here is a love-bond that nothing but sin can break—not tribulation, or distress, or persecution, or famine, or nakedness, or peril, or sword. "In all these things we are more than conquerors through him that loved us. For I am persuaded, that neither death, nor life, nor angels, nor principalities, nor powers, nor things present, nor things to come, nor height, nor depth, nor any other creature, shall be able to separate us from the love of God, which is in Christ Jesus our Lord."

The evidence is in. The argument is finished. God is for us—has been for us through the eternity that stretches back of us, wants to be for us throughout the eternity that rolls ahead of us. There is but one point unsettled. And what is that?

In a critical hour in the Civil War a somewhat fearful individual exlaimed to Mr. Lincoln: "O Mr. President, I am most anxious that the Lord shall be on our side!"

Back came the Lincoln reply, characteristically terse and penetrating: "Well, strangely enough, that gives me no anxiety at all. The thing that I worry about is to make sure that *I* am on the *Lord's* side!"

And therein lies the point! The divine position has been taken and announced. What shall ours be? Who is on the Lord's side? That is the supreme question of the hour. I appeal to you: Answer it aright. Take stand with Him, that you too may lift your confident challenge: *If God be for us, who can be against us?*

ROMANS 9

The Majesty of God's Ways

Romans 9:1-29

1 I say the truth in Christ, I lie not, my conscience also bearing me witness in the Holy Ghost,
2 That I have great heaviness and continual sorrow in my heart.
3 For I could wish that myself were accursed from Christ for my brethren, my kinsmen according to the flesh:
4 Who are Israelites; to whom pertaineth the adoption, and the glory, and the covenants, and the giving of the law, and the service of God, and the promises;
5 Whose are the fathers, and of whom as concerning the flesh Christ came, who is over all, God blessed for ever. Amen.

6 Not as though the word of God hath taken none effect. For they are
not all Israel, which are of Israel:
7 Neither, because they are the seed of Abraham, are they all chil-
dren: but, In Isaac shall thy seed be called.
8 That is, They which are the children of the flesh, these are not the
children of God: but the children of the promise are counted for the
seed.
9 For this is the word of promise, At this time will I come, and Sarah
shall have a son.
10 And not only this; but when Rebecca also had conceived by one,
even by our father Isaac;
11 (For the children being not yet born, neither having done any good
or evil, that the purpose of God according to election might stand, not
of works, but of him that calleth;)
12 It was said unto her, The elder shall serve the younger.
13 As it is written, Jacob have I loved, but Esau have I hated.
14 What shall we say then? Is there unrighteousness with God? God
forbid.
15 For he saith to Moses, I will have mercy on whom I will have mercy,
and I will have compassion on whom I will have compassion.
16 So then it is not of him that willeth, nor of him that runneth, but of
God that sheweth mercy.
17 For the scripture saith unto Pharaoh, Even for this same purpose
have I raised thee up, that I might shew my power in thee, and that my
name might be declared throughout all the earth.
18 Therefore hath he mercy on whom he will have mercy, and whom
he will he hardeneth.
19 Thou wilt say then unto me, Why doth he yet find fault? For who
hath resisted his will?
20 Nay but, O man, who art thou that repliest against God? Shall the
thing formed say to him that formed it, Why hast thou made me thus?
21 Hath not the potter power over the clay, of the same lump to make
one vessel unto honour, and another unto dishonour?
22 What if God, willing to shew his wrath, and to make his power
known, endured with much longsuffering the vessels of wrath fitted to
destruction:
23 And that he might make known the riches of his glory on the
vessels of mercy, which he had afore prepared unto glory,
24 Even us, whom he hath called, not of the Jews only, but also of the
Gentiles?
25 As he saith also in Osee, I will call them my people, which were
not my people; and her beloved, which was not beloved.
26 And it shall come to pass, that in the place where it was said unto
them, Ye are not my people; there shall they be called the children of
the living God.
27 Esaias also crieth concerning Israel, Though the number of the
children of Israel be as the sand of the sea, a remnant shall be saved:
28 For he will finish the work, and cut it short in righteousness: be-
cause a short work will the Lord make upon the earth.
29 And as Esaias said before, Except the Lord of Sabaoth had left us
a seed, we had been as Sodoma, and been made like unto Gomorrha.

Romans 9 has been called "The Hardest Chapter in the Bible." It may be, if we think Paul is here advocating the doctrines of absolute predestination and particular election. Or, on the other hand, if we don't understand the biblical doctrine of divine sovereignty.

Paul is not a systematic theologian; he is a preacher of the unsearchable riches of God's grace. To read back into him the stupendous, rigid, and logical system of John Calvin is to misconceive completely what he is doing here. As Chester Warren Quimby says, "If Paul had any such fully developed and integrated system of Sovereignty and Election as Calvin later worked out, he left little trace of it."[30]

No, Paul is agonizing here with the problem of why his fellow Jews have rejected the gospel. And you can plainly see that it was no theoretical matter with him. "I have great heaviness and continual sorrow in my heart," he sighs. "For I could wish that myself were accursed from Christ for my brethren, my kinsmen according to the flesh" (2-3). Although Christ was his very Life and his only Hope, he was willing to be personally damned and cut off from Him if only his brethren would thereby turn to Jesus! Paul's word can mean only this. What a far cry from "It's too bad, but you're a sinner, so you must go to hell." No, no! Rather, the truly godly say, "Save them, or do not save me!"

1. *God's Sovereign Purpose* (6-9). Paul is not only heartbroken over his unbelieving kinsmen; he is also absolutely convinced that God's sovereign purpose is moving majestically onward in history, despite Israel's present rejection of the Saviour. "It is not as though God's word had failed. For not all who are descended from Israel are Israel" (6, NIV). Israel has never been constituted by blood and soil, like Greece or Rome, but always by the promise of God. The true Israel has ever been the *ecclesia,* the Church which lives by God's word.

Since from the beginning God's purpose envisioned the coming of Christ, the Church is one, from Abraham's call to the very end of time. The Christian Church is the "Israel of God" (Gal. 6:16), the heir of God's promise to Abraham: "In Isaac shall thy seed be called" (7). In his Galatian letter, Paul makes clear the meaning of this promise (3:16, 29; cf. Gen. 12:3; 22:18). God's purpose in election centers in Christ and operates through Him.

It is in Ephesians, however, that we see the full sweep of God's sovereign purpose in Christ: "For he chose us in him before the creation of the world to be holy and blameless in his sight. In love he predestined us to be adopted as sons through Jesus Christ, in accordance with his pleasure and will—to the praise of his glorious grace, which he has freely given us in the One he loves" (Eph. 1:4-6, NIV).

God's predestination is His gracious purpose before all worlds to save mankind through Christ; all who believe in Christ are "elect" in Him (cf. John 3:16). "Predestination, instead of locking the door, opened it!"[31] The divine predestination is the election of Jesus Christ to be the world's Saviour. Before the creation of the world God elected Him, and in free obedience to the Father, the Son elected to become man and die for the sins of the world. All who receive Christ and put their trust in Him are God's children, chosen to be holy and blameless and "accepted in the beloved" (Eph. 1:6). In God's Elect Man you and I are elected. This, Paul declares, is God's eternal purpose. The fact that Israel refused Christ in no way thwarts God's sovereign purpose to have a holy people. "Our God is marching on!"

2. *God's Sovereign Freedom* (10-21)

a. This is indeed a difficult passage, unless we keep in mind two basic considerations:

(1) Paul is not talking about God's choice of individuals to eternal life or damnation but of the selection of a people to carry forward His redemptive purpose in history. By Jacob and Esau, Paul does not mean those individuals, but rather their descendants, the Israelites and the Edomites (see Mal. 1:2-4). God chose the former over the latter, in His sovereign purpose, to have a believing servant people through whom the Seed should eventually come.

(2) Paul's purpose in the instances he cites (His choice of Jacob over Esau and His raising up of Pharaoh) is but to illustrate his main point that God is free to proceed as *He* will and choose whom He will in the carrying out of His sovereign purpose to have a holy people to serve Him. Is it unjust for God to fix the conditions upon which He will constitute men and women as His children? To have mercy only on those who believe? Who are *we* to call God's hand?

b. Paul means that everything depends upon the divine sovereignty. God does as He wills, and none can call Him to account. As to justice and mercy, God chooses. He is His own Dispenser of grace and punishment. Everything rests in the hands of God. As the clay cannot challenge the potter, neither can we summon God to judgment.

All this tends to leave us cold today. But when we understand Paul properly, his meaning and intention are indispensable in understanding the ways of God. Paul is not dealing with secondary causes. Although what he says about Pharaoh's hardening in no way rules out the latter's freedom of choice, the apostle's perspective is that of God's sovereignty in history. God *is* accountable only to himself. His purpose *is* working out in history. Everything *does* rest on God's will. He will have mercy on whom He will have mercy, and whom He will He hardens. But all this is the outworking, not of arbitrary power, but of *love*. "In love he predestined us" (Eph. 1:4-5, NIV). God's sovereign freedom is always under the control of His holy love; its very center is the cross of Jesus Christ.

So what Paul is driving home is that God has fixed the terms of His mercy. We do not determine the operation of His mercy toward men. We cannot say, "We will accept it so, but we will not have it thus." We do not ask God to revise, extend, or rescind. He alone determines how His mercy shall be given. He offers it *on His own terms*. It is like becoming a naturalized citizen of another nation. We do not fix the terms of naturalization. We do not say, "I will do this. I will do that. Then I'll make them take me in." We know this cannot be. That nation fixes the conditions and we meet them.

> We did not invent the mercy of God. We do not set the terms of its conditions, nor say how we shall or shall not accept its blessings. God's mercy is revealed to us. God set its terms. We can but reject or accept. We can become Christians, be saved, only because God in his self-sacrifice has offered himself and his salvation to us in Christ. If he had not so offered his mercy, we could never obtain it. But he has, and we may, though only on his terms. What saves his offer from despotism is that his one condition for receiving his mercy everyone can meet. His mercy is unto everyone who will believe by faith.[32]

3. *God's Sovereign Mercy* (22-29). Many, in reading this chapter, have heard Paul saying that God has arbitrarily foreordained some to be saved, others to be damned. But Paul's gospel was universal: "[Christ] died for *all*. . . . God was in Christ, reconciling *the world* unto himself" (2 Cor. 5:14, 19, italics added).

Paul's purpose here is not to show that certain souls are lost, whether or no. He is not even discussing this question. He is setting forth the great patience of God, which has endured the blindness and obstinacy of Israel precisely because in His sovereign mercy He will have a people, "not only from the Jews but also from the Gentiles" (24, NIV). He quotes Hos. 2:23 and 1:10 as prophecies of God's calling and creating Gentiles as His people, making them "children of the living God" (25-26). He then cites Isa. 10:22-23 and 1:9 as prophesying the remnant of Israel through whom God works while the majority continue in unbelief (27-29). Paul's conclusion will come later, "And so all Israel shall be saved," and that God "might have mercy upon all" (11:26, 32). As he declared in the previous chapter when describing the benefits of salvation, "For whom he did foreknow, he also did predestinate to be conformed to the image of his Son" (8:29). This divine foreknowledge, this divine predestination, this divine sovereignty are moved by only one purpose and to one end, the salvation of both Jews and Gentiles through Christ and their conformity to the image of the Son. God's purpose is universal.

The majesty and mystery of God's ways! We dare not be glib in talking about God. Our minds ask many questions which He has chosen not to answer for us. Like: Why was I born into a Christian home with all the gracious influences pointing me to Christ from my tenderest years, while another was born "with one foot in hell"? Questions such as this can be multiplied. But the New Testament makes one thing crystal-clear: "The Lord is . . . not willing that any should perish, but that all should come to repentance" (2 Pet. 3:9). And, as Hebrews tells us, it was the gracious purpose of God that Christ "should taste death for every man" (Heb. 2:9).

God's thoughts are not our thoughts, neither are His ways our ways. "For as the heavens are higher than the earth," He reminds us, "so are my ways higher than your ways, and my thoughts than your thoughts" (Isa. 55:8-9). Thank God, the final judgment of each individual is in *His* hands. When that judgment has been dispensed, it will be seen by all that the Judge of the earth has done right. Meanwhile we can afford to leave our unanswered questions with Him, remembering always that "now we see through a glass, darkly; but then face to face" (1 Cor. 13: 12). And in the time of our honest questioning the scripture teaches us always to say, with Whittier,

To one fixed hope my spirit clings:
I know that God is good!

God's ways are majestic, but they are merciful. God's power is over all, but it is controlled by love. The sovereign God is sovereign Mercy, whose purposes embrace all mankind to the end of time.

The Sin of Unbelief

Romans 9:30—10:21

30 What shall we say then? That the Gentiles, which followed not after righteousness, have attained to righteousness, even the righteousness which is of faith.

31 But Israel, which followed after the law of righteousness, hath not attained to the law of righteousness.
32 Wherefore? Because they sought it not by faith, but as it were by the works of the law. For they stumbled at that stumblingstone;
33 As it is written, Behold, I lay in Sion a stumblingstone and rock of offence: and whosoever believeth on him shall not be ashamed.
10:1 Brethren, my heart's desire and prayer to God for Israel is, that they might be saved.
2 For I bear them record that they have a zeal of God, but not according to knowledge.
3 For they being ignorant of God's righteousness, and going about to establish their own righteousness, have not submitted themselves unto the righteousness of God.
4 For Christ is the end of the law for righteousness to every one that believeth.
5 For Moses describeth the righteousness which is of the law, That the man which doeth those things shall live by them.
6 But the righteousness which is of faith speaketh on this wise, Say not in thine heart, Who shall ascend into heaven? (that is, to bring Christ down from above:)
7 Or, Who shall descend into the deep? (that is, to bring up Christ again from the dead.)
8 But what saith it? The word is nigh thee, even in thy mouth, and in thy heart: that is, the word of faith, which we preach;
9 That if thou shalt confess with thy mouth the Lord Jesus, and shalt believe in thine heart that God hath raised him from the dead, thou shalt be saved.
10 For with the heart man believeth unto righteousness; and with the mouth confession is made unto salvation.
11 For the scripture saith, Whosoever believeth on him shall not be ashamed.
12 For there is no difference between the Jew and the Greek: for the same Lord over all is rich unto all that call upon him.
13 For whosoever shall call upon the name of the Lord shall be saved.
14 How then shall they call on him in whom they have not believed? and how shall they believe in him of whom they have not heard? and how shall they hear without a preacher?
15 And how shall they preach, except they be sent? as it is written, How beautiful are the feet of them that preach the gospel of peace, and bring glad tidings of good things!
16 But they have not all obeyed the gospel. For Esaias saith, Lord, who hath believed our report?
17 So then faith cometh by hearing, and hearing by the word of God.
18 But I say, Have they not heard? Yes verily, their sound went into all the earth, and their words unto the ends of the world.
19 But I say, Did not Israel know? First Moses saith, I will provoke you to jealousy by them that are no people, and by a foolish nation I will anger you.
20 But Esaias is very bold, and saith, I was found of them that sought me not; I was made manifest unto them that asked not after me.
21 But to Israel he saith, All day long I have stretched forth my hands unto a disobedient and gainsaying people.

Everyone who knows Christ and rejoices in the hope of the gospel knows that the glory of salvation belongs to God alone; through His grace we have been called, converted, and cleansed. "We love him, because he first loved us"—from eternity. And we first sought Him because He had already found us. Our salvation is solely by His free choice, "that the purpose of God according to election might stand" (9:11), "to the praise of the glory of his grace, wherein he hath made us accepted in the beloved" (Eph. 1:6). Such is the majestic truth of sovereign grace Paul has just affirmed.

God's sovereignty, however, does not stand alone; it is but one pole of divine revelation. The other is human freedom and responsibility: "Choose you this day whom ye will serve" (Josh. 24:15). The gospel is an ellipse which revolves around these two poles of revealed truth. If I am saved, it is by God's grace alone; if I am not, it is because of my willful perversity. Like ancient Israel, I may "resist the Holy Ghost" and be damned. It is this solemn truth of human accountability before God which the apostle now declares.

Paul's one aim in this scripture is to show that God's rejection of Israel was not an arbitrary expression of divine sovereignty. God has rejected Israel because Israel has rejected her Messiah (9:30-33). In the Israelites' very zeal for God and His law they refused their only Redeemer (10:1-13). Their guilt is inexcusable; God has called Israel, faithfully and repeatedly, but they have obstinately refused to heed His invitation (10:14-21). This was not merely the sin of ancient Israel; it is the sin of unbelief, which always and everywhere closes the doors of divine mercy. "To day if ye will hear his voice, harden not *your* hearts" (italics added).

1. *Unbelief is blind to God's love* (9:30-33). God's dealings with Israel have brought us face-to-face with the paradox of divine sovereignty and human freedom. The very data of divine revelation thrust this enigma upon us. What then shall we say? History itself gives us the answer: "That the Gentiles, who did not pursue righteousness, have obtained

it . . . but Israel, who pursued a law of righteousness . . . stumbled" (30-32, NIV). They altogether missed it.

a. There is, however, an answer to Paul's question; and it lifts the problem out of the realm of sheer mystery into a region where it gives moral significance to our quest for salvation. The key to this transformation is the word *righteousness,* which is central to Paul's gospel and the point at which he took issue most sharply with the Jews. As they used the word it meant a pattern of behavior demanded by God, a kind of life we can live if we simply follow the law. But for Paul *righteousness* means basically a right relationship to God made possible by Christ's death and resurrection. "The righteousness which is of faith" (30) consequently stands in sharpest contrast to "the righteousness which is of the law" (10:5).

Because Israel had misconceived the nature of righteousness, the Jews have pursued it in a way which inevitably leads to frustration and failure. Righteousness by the law is a dead-end street. To seek God and salvation by works is to take a path which can end only in futility. A legalistic religion can never bring an experience of salvation. This is where the real tragedy of the situation shows itself.

From his own past experience Paul knew the high purpose which inspired the Jewish quest for righteousness. There can be no question that they pursued "the righteousness which is based on the law" (10:5, RSV). But such seriousness of endeavor proves to be its own undoing. "For whosoever will save his life shall lose it," even in this highest of all quests. Religious earnestness is virtuous; its defect is that we take ourselves too seriously and overestimate what we ourselves can do.

b. The tragedy is that in the way of human righteousness the good becomes the enemy of the best. Religious self-reliance creates spiritual pride and arrogance. Self-righteousness not only makes us judgmental and unkind toward others but, most tragically, it blinds us to God's mercy, which alone can save us. Thus the Jews "stumbled at that stumblingstone" (32), while countless Gentiles believed and were not "ashamed" (33). People who do not strive for righteousness find it, while others who pursue it do not achieve it! Just as tax collectors and harlots entered the Kingdom during the ministry of Jesus, so believing Gentiles who had shown no previous interest in God were now turning to Christ and being saved. But Israel, which strove to be righteous, was being judged unrighteous. These were the facts of history Paul saw so vividly.

c. The greatest of all sins is to imagine that we need no divine mercy. Spiritual pride creates this delusion. This is the tragedy of human morality, "the badness of goodness." Our very earnestness and sincerity blind us to our need of Christ. "If righteousness could be gained through the law, Christ died for nothing!" (Gal. 2:21, NIV). The self-righteous do not see this, so they crucify the Son of God afresh by their unbelief. They stumble over the "stumblingstone." All the while the self-despairing, hearing the preaching of the gospel, discover faith and thereby stumble unexpectedly upon the hidden treasure of the Kingdom and go on their way rejoicing (Matt. 13:44).

ROMANS 10

2. *Unbelief is ignorant of God's righteousness* (10:1-13). Paul has made the point in the previous chapter that "it is not of him that willeth, nor of him that runneth, but of God that sheweth mercy" (9:16). That is here confirmed; had it depended on the will or exertion of man, Israel should surely have been saved. But being ignorant of God's way of righteousness, they found the doors of mercy closed.

a. "I bear them witness," says Paul, "that they have a zeal for God, but it is not enlightened" (2, RSV). Exemplary though their zeal for God and His law is, in *one* respect they are deeply disobedient to God. "Being ignorant of God's righteousness," they zealously go about establishing their own righteousness. Having given them the law, which is indeed "holy, and just, and good" (7:12), God has offered them something better than the law—Christ, the Redeemer. And in their very zeal for the law they fail to discern how the whole of it points to Christ with most urgent insistence. Christ is the Fulfillment of the law and consequently the *end of the law* (4).

> For sheer zealous persistence in the good Commandments of God they reject the even better offer of Christ. They simply will not admit that the sending of Christ is the "record achievement" of the love of God, which dwarfs all God's previous gifts. It is as if, having received the gift of "Moses and the prophets," they have refused to allow God to give them the Redeemer in Christ. At the point where God intends the very best for them, they turn down His offer. They will not "submit to God's righteousness" (3). . . . They have found pearls of God in the Law and the Prophets, but now that God wants to give them the one pearl of great value they draw back their hands.[33]

b. Is this the sin of only the Jews? Is not the tendency to cling to what *we* believe, what is so familiar and traditional to *us,* the selfsame thing? What began as gospel in the Reformation or the Wesleyan revival may easily become a law to us, something we think we possess and have a sort of monopoly upon. We begin to trust, not in God's saving word to us in Christ, but in our tradition or our "gospel." Behind this tendency is "the demon of the ego," which regards itself and what it believes and thinks as all-important and secretly wants itself to be the focal point of the world. The self which formerly garbed itself in the robes of the world now dons its gown of self-righteousness!

So the holiness which was first given to us as a radical gift of God's grace may become a legalism: "The man who practices the righteousness based on the law shall live by it" (5, RSV). Or, the person who "believes the doctrine" and "lives the life" shall be saved. No, no! It is personal, vital faith in Christ!

c. For Paul, the man who would like to be saved by the law, or by his own holiness, without Christ and complete dependence upon Him at every stage, wants to "ascend into heaven" or "descend into the abyss" (6-7, RSV). To quote Luthi again at this point:

> For that is what we should have to do if we wanted to be saved independently of Christ; we should have to do what Christ did and descend into hell and clean it out, and ascend into Heaven and open it up. The man who tries to be saved through his own righteousness is trying to substitute his own descent into hell and ascent into Heaven for Christ's![34]

d. Salvation is through Christ alone, including initial salvation, full salvation, and final salvation. It is by "the word of faith, which we preach; That if thou shalt confess with thy mouth the Lord Jesus, and shalt believe in thine heart that God hath raised him from the dead, thou shalt be saved" (8-9). Salvation is a heart matter! It derives solely from Christ, with whom we must die and be raised, and whom we trust absolutely for righteousness, holiness, and acceptance in the day of judgment. It yields to His lordship over life and time and eternity. Any other scheme of salvation, however pious or religiously correct it may appear, is blasphemous unbelief. Humiliating though it is to confess one's poverty and lack of means, yet where salvation is concerned, we are all poor—Jews and Gentiles alike, the reputable and the disreputable. God alone is rich and "bestows his riches upon all who call upon him" (12, RSV).

3. *Unbelief is deaf to God's invitation* (10:14-21). We perhaps should pause here to remind ourselves that Paul is not indulging any anti-Semitism in this passage. No, his "heart's desire and prayer to God for the Israelites is that they may be saved" (10:1, NIV). Israel is simply an illustration of the tragic sin of unbelief.

Paul's strong insistence in this present passage is that Israel's downfall is not due to ignorance, or to lack of opportunity to be saved, but to sheer disobedience.

The apostle's four questions in verses 14-15 take into account an objection someone might advance that, in fact, Israel had never had a fair chance to be saved. Paul raises these questions to rebut them. In effect he asks, What conditions must be present before anyone can call on Christ and be saved? The answer implied in the questions is: (1) a preacher sent from God, (2) a gospel to proclaim, and (3) someone to hear the gospel and believe it. In Israel's case these conditions *have* been fulfilled; still they have not believed. Why? Because they have not heard? This is absurd, Paul says: Gospel preachers have "gone out into all the earth, their words to the ends of the world" (18, NIV). Why then have they not been saved? *Because they will not believe the gospel.*

While the proclamation of the gospel is essential to saving faith, we may hear and still refuse the good news. Faith comes from "what is heard . . . through the preaching of Christ" (17, RSV), but the very message that saves the one who believes hardens the one who will not believe. The one message is "the savour of life unto life" *and* "the savour of death unto death" (2 Cor. 2:16). The difference is in the response of the hearer. "Whoever believes and is baptized will be saved, but whoever does not believe will be condemned" (Mark 16:16, NIV). By the grace of God everyone who hears the gospel has the "response-ability" to believe and be saved.

Some do not understand the gospel because they *will not* understand. Self will not yield to Christ. They hear the gospel proclaimed. It is clear and intelligible. The Spirit accompanies the word and applies it with conviction to their hearts; yet they resist the Holy Spirit. They *will not* come to Christ. "All day long," the Lord complains, "I have held out my hands to a disobedient and obstinate people" (21, NIV). Does this make sense if God had foreordained them to hell?

Beware of unbelief! Of the Holy Spirit's coming, Jesus said, "He . . . will convict the world . . . concerning sin, because they do not believe in Me" (John 16:8-9, NASB). I go to the physician and he finds that I have a small malignancy which can be removed by surgery. He is confident my life can be saved if I will believe him and submit to an operation. If I refuse the surgery and die, it will not be cancer that kills me; it will be my unbelief.

"To day if ye will hear his voice, harden not your hearts." Repent now! Ask God's forgiveness of your obstinacy and unbelief. Pray God to soften your heart by His Spirit. Call upon Him now! God is rich in mercy and He "bestows his riches upon all who call upon him" (12, RSV).

ROMANS 11

The Salvation of Israel

Romans 11:1-36

1 I say then, Hath God cast away his people? God forbid. For I also am an Israelite, of the seed of Abraham, of the tribe of Benjamin.
2 God hath not cast away his people which he foreknew. Wot ye not what the scripture saith of Elias? how he maketh intercession to God against Israel, saying,
3 Lord, they have killed thy prophets, and digged down thine altars; and I am left alone, and they seek my life.
4 But what saith the answer of God unto him? I have reserved to myself seven thousand men, who have not bowed the knee to the image of Baal.
5 Even so then at this present time also there is a remnant according to the election of grace.
6 And if by grace, then is it no more of works: otherwise grace is no more grace. But if it be of works, then is it no more grace: otherwise work is no more work.
7 What then? Israel had not obtained that which he seeketh for; but the election hath obtained it, and the rest were blinded
8 (According as it is written, God hath given them the spirit of slumber, eyes that they should not see, and ears that they should not hear;) unto this day.
9 And David saith, Let their table be made a snare, and a trap, and a stumblingblock, and a recompence unto them:
10 Let their eyes be darkened, that they may not see, and bow down their back alway.
11 I say then, Have they stumbled that they should fall? God forbid: but rather through their fall salvation is come unto the Gentiles, for to provoke them to jealousy.
12 Now if the fall of them be the riches of the world, and the diminishing of them the riches of the Gentiles; how much more their fulness?

13 For I speak to you Gentiles, inasmuch as I am the apostle of the
Gentiles, I magnify mine office:
14 If by any means I may provoke to emulation them which are my
flesh, and might save some of them.
15 For if the casting away of them be the reconciling of the world,
what shall the receiving of them be, but life from the dead?
16 For if the firstfruit be holy, the lump is also holy: and if the root be
holy, so are the branches.
17 And if some of the branches be broken off, and thou, being a wild
olive tree, wert graffed in among them, and with them partakest of the
root and fatness of the olive tree;
18 Boast not against the branches. But if thou boast, thou bearest
not the root, but the root thee.
19 Thou wilt say then, The branches were broken off, that I might be
graffed in.
20 Well; because of unbelief they were broken off, and thou standest
by faith. Be not highminded, but fear:
21 For if God spared not the natural branches, take heed lest he also
spare not thee.
22 Behold therefore the goodness and severity of God: on them
which fell, severity; but toward thee, goodness, if thou continue in his
goodness: otherwise thou also shalt be cut off.
23 And they also, if they abide not still in unbelief, shall be graffed in:
for God is able to graff them in again.
24 For if thou wert cut out of the olive tree which is wild by nature,
and wert graffed contrary to nature into a good olive tree: how much
more shall these, which be the natural branches, be graffed into their
own olive tree?
25 For I would not, brethren, that ye should be ignorant of this
mystery, lest ye should be wise in your own conceits; that blindness in
part is happened to Israel, until the fulness of the Gentiles be come
in.
26 And so all Israel shall be saved: as it is written, There shall come
out of Sion the Deliverer, and shall turn away ungodliness from Jacob:
27 For this is my covenant unto them, when I shall take away their
sins.
28 As concerning the gospel, they are enemies for your sakes: but as
touching the election, they are beloved for the fathers' sakes.

29 For the gifts and calling of God are without repentance.

30 For as ye in times past have not believed God, yet have now
obtained mercy through their unbelief:

31 Even so have these also now not believed, that through your mercy
they also may obtain mercy.

32 For God hath concluded them all in unbelief, that he might have
mercy upon all.

33 O the depth of the riches both of the wisdom and knowledge of
God! how unsearchable are his judgments, and his ways past finding
out!

34 For who hath known the mind of the Lord? or who hath been his
counsellor?

35 Or who hath first given to him, and it shall be recompensed unto
him again?

36 For of him, and through him, and to him, are all things: to whom
be glory for ever. Amen.

Paul now returns to his initial problem: *Has God rejected his people?* (1, RSV). Up to this point the apostle has handled this question from two points of view. In his first answer he has spoken of the sovereignty of God: God chooses whom He will, and whom He will He rejects; man can present no claims to Him. God's people are freely chosen by grace through faith (9:6-29). In his second answer he has shown that Israel's rejection is their own fault. God's promises depend upon faith; but Israel, seeking their righteousness by the law, have been rejected for their unbelief (9:30—10:21).

What would be the situation if Paul said no more? It would mean that Israel's rejection is final; that God intended it to be so, and Israel deserved it. But this is not the last word on the problem. In dealing with Israel's salvation the apostle becomes a prophet. In sharing with us the "mystery" God has revealed to him (25), Paul goes beyond anything he says elsewhere. Has God repudiated the people He chose to be His servant to the Gentiles? The answer is a resounding *God forbid.* God's judgment upon Israel is *not* final: for (1) even now there is a remnant of Israel within the Church (1-10); (2) the fall of Israel has become the salvation of the Gentiles, and therein we see an intimation of her final acceptance (11-24); and (3), in the last place, Israel as a whole is destined to receive Christ (25-32). "And so all Israel shall be saved" (26). It is such a breathtaking thought that Paul bursts out in an ecstatic doxology: "O the depth of the riches, the wisdom and the knowledge of God!" (33, NIV).

How helpless we feel when faced with this vision! What are people like us to say when the apostle is so overcome he can hardly find words to express himself? *O the depth of the riches!* Paul writes. He does not mean the kind of depth that ends in nothingness. He is not discussing the abyss of darkness. This abyss is filled with light. It is not the abyss of hell; it is the abyss of heaven, illuminated with the light of God's fatherly wisdom and mercy. O Spirit, who "searcheth the deep things of God," shed Thy light into our hearts and minds, that we may receive and proclaim Thy truth!

1. *The Remnant of Israel.* Paul has ample proof that Israel is not entirely rejected: he himself has been saved. "I am an Israelite myself, a descendant of Abraham, from the tribe of Benjamin" (1, NIV). As the original Saul of the tribe of Benjamin had persecuted David, the apple of God's eye, so Saul of Tarsus had persecuted the Descendant of David, Jesus, in His Church (cf. Acts 9:4-5). And what happened? God changed this arch-persecutor into the apostle to the Gentiles and the messenger of the grace of Christ! More than most of his fellow Jews, Saul was victim of that zeal which is blind to Christ. But God was able to open his eyes and transform him. How inscrutable the ways of God, who makes Saul into Paul! If God saved this man, then whom is He not capable of saving?

Admittedly, Paul's conversion is far from the salvation of all Israel. But we must not overlook the fact that often in God's kingdom we find almost imperceptible signs that point to greater things. To illustrate this point Paul goes back to the time of Elijah, in the days of Ahab, Jezebel, and the priests of Baal. At that time even the prophet Elijah could see no hope for Israel; everything seemed to be over for God's people. The prophet was convinced he was the only one left who had not bowed before Baal, so he decided to abandon the Promised Land.

Retracing the way God's people had entered the Holy Land, Elijah came to Mount Sinai. There he encountered the Lord. "'Lord, they have killed your prophets and torn down your altars,'" Elijah complained; "'I am the only one left, and they are trying to kill me.'" But God replied, "'I have reserved for myself seven thousand who have not bowed the knee to Baal.'" In the Lord's answer to the prophet the apostle finds a word for us: "So too, at the present time there is a remnant of grace" (3-5, NIV). In a way Paul is repeating what he has already said in chapter 9, that God has always had His remnant in Israel. Yet the tone is different here. "There the word was: only a remnant. Here it is: *already* a remnant!"[35] The remnant is the firstfruit of Israel's restoration.

Nevertheless, the condition of Israel seems hopeless. A terrible judgment lies upon them. God has hardened their hearts. He has given them "a spirit of stupor"—literally, "petrified" them. Their table, which God so richly set, has become "a snare and a trap" (8-9, NIV). Yet, as we shall see, this too is a part of the divine strategy in furthering the gospel.

2. *The Hardening of Israel.* In His dealing with men and nations on probation, God's judgment is always mingled with mercy. So with His hardening of Israel. As the discussion proceeds, it will be increasingly apparent that Paul understands God to be using the failure of Israel as a means of perfecting His plans. With a slightly different emphasis, he is restating his conviction that in everything God works for the good of those who are His called ones (cf. 8:28, RSV). But mercy cannot achieve its purpose in one step, and Paul here suggests the several stages by which God's sovereign love accomplishes its ends. The apparent rejection of Israel cannot be final; it is a necessary part of God's wider plan. "Because of their transgression, salvation has come to the Gentiles" (11, NIV).

Walter Luthi has translated Paul's thought in an unforgettable paragraph:

> The Jews crucified their Lord. What did they achieve by it? They buried the seed-corn in the earth, but the same seed-corn brought forth a rich profusion of fruit. Saul the Jew attacked the young community of Christ. With what success? The result was that he scattered the Christians of Jerusalem, and the fugitives became missionaries in lands far beyond the frontier of the Holy Land. And when Paul himself was cruelly persecuted by the Synagogue from his very first day as missionary to the Gentiles, and was hunted like a wolf or a wild boar, what was the outcome? Time and again the Apostle's escape routes became mission routes,

which accelerated the propagation of the name of Christ to an almost miraculous degree. So the fall of Israel became the salvation of the Gentiles. "How unsearchable are God's judgments!"[36]

a. By going to the Gentiles with the gospel and furnishing their table with the riches of God's grace, Paul hopes that he may somehow "make . . . [his] fellow Jews jealous, and thus save some of them" (14, RSV). It was still a personal sorrow to the apostle that so few of his fellow Jews were coming to the Saviour. However gratified he was with his mission to the Gentiles, he could never forget his Jewish brother. Nor can we, if we are genuinely Christian. "There is an empty chair among us, the chair of our absent brother from Israel," Luthi reminds us; "and that empty chair should be a source of sorrow to us. The joy in the House of the Father at the return of the prodigal son will always be tempered as long as the elder brother refuses to come in."

b. Even so, Paul sees a rainbow of promise for Israel. "For if their rejection is the reconciliation of the world, what will their acceptance be, but life from the dead?" (15, NIV). The apostle clearly foresees the day when Israel is converted to Christ. This is what he means by *their acceptance.* If the hardening of Israel *(their rejection)* has brought such a blessing to the world, he writes, their national turning to the Redeemer *(their acceptance)* will be *life from the dead.* Does Paul simply mean that Israel's conversion will be a miracle like dead persons rising from their graves? Or that the conversion of Israel will occur in connection with Christ's return, when the righteous dead will be raised? The context favors the latter view. "It is clear," Johannes Munck says, that the meaning of this phrase "is to be sought among the last events before or during the Second Coming."[37]

c. Paul proceeds to describe the judgment of hardheartedness on Israel with its beneficial effects upon the Gentiles, in the form of a parable. God planted Israel as a cultivated olive tree, tending and caring for it. But Israel was stubborn; the tree proved unfruitful. Men would pull up such a tree; but God's judgments are merciful. He did not uproot the olive tree; He simply cut off the branches and left the root and trunk standing. Then He went out and found branches from wild olive trees and grafted them into the cultivated trunk. Of course no man could do this successfully; but God can do it, even though it is contrary to nature. In nature it is possible only to graft a cultivated branch into a wild stock. God, however, is capable of doing what man cannot do; He can insert the shoot of a wild olive tree into the trunk of a cultivated one, so that it will bear the fruit of righteousness.

d. Paul's meaning is clear. We Gentiles have been saved only because we have been grafted into Israel. We did not deserve to be grafted in, but we have been ennobled by the boundless mercy and kindness of God. So Paul warns us against boasting of our position in the Church. If the natural branches were broken off because of their unbelief, we stand fast only through persevering faith. "So do not become proud, but stand in awe. For if God did not spare the natural branches, neither will he spare you" (20-21, RSV). This is Paul's word to those of us who are Gentiles, but it offers him the opportunity also of introducing the promise of Israel's ultimate conversion. If we Gentiles have been cut from what is by nature a wild olive tree and grafted, contrary to nature, into a cultivated olive tree, "how much more readily will these, the natural branches, be grafted into their own olive tree?" (24-25, NIV). God is able to effect Israel's conversion!

3. *The Salvation of All Israel.* Paul now shares with us a secret which his lips have been burning to speak. He calls it a *mystery,* which in the New Testament means "a revealed secret" (cf. 16:26; Col. 1:26-27; Eph. 3:3-6; 6:19): "Israel has experienced a hardening in part until the full number of Gentiles has come in" (25, NIV). This hardening of hearts of which he has been speaking is neither total nor permanent. It is serving a purpose, and when

that purpose is achieved it will be taken away. It was brought about to open the way for Gentiles to become a part of God's people, and when *the full number of the Gentiles has come in,* it will be removed.

a. What does the apostle mean by "the full number of Gentiles"? Goppelt says, "Not 'all Gentiles, without exception,' nor the Gentiles predestined to be saved, but rather that multitude of Gentiles comparable to the richness of God's grace." *And so*—after the partial hardening of Israel and the salvation of the Gentiles—*all Israel shall be saved* (26). "'All Israel,' analogous to the full number of Gentiles," to quote Goppelt again, "does not mean the sum of all the members of the Jewish people, nor the host of the predestinated in Israel, but Israel as a whole people."[38]

As in all genuine prophecy, Paul does not spell out the precise details of how this prediction shall be fulfilled. It appears to be "a miraculous event coming just before the impending Parousia of Christ (Rom 13.11 f.) and following the conversion of the nations, perhaps even caused by this conversion; for according to Rom 11.15 Israel's conversion means the days of the final fulfillment."[39]

b. The connection of this event with the Parousia is indicated by the next verse,

The Deliverer will come from Zion,
he will banish ungodliness from Jacob (26, RSV).

In their hardness the Jews may still be *enemies of God,* Paul continues; *but for the sake of their forefathers* (28, RSV), and for the sake of the promises made to their ancestors, they are and always will be *beloved* of God. "For the gifts and the call of God are irrevocable" (29, RSV). We heard earlier that the faithfulness of God is greater than the unfaithfulness of Israel (3:3-4), and "it is not as though the word of God had failed" (9:6, RSV). God's great mercy still embraces Israel. He has not revoked His call of His ancient people. *And so all Israel shall be saved,* believing Jews as well as believing Gentiles.

Such is the inexpressible mystery which was revealed to the Apostle Paul.

c. This is genuine prophecy, and it is given to encourage the new, predominantly Gentile Church to persevere in its witness to the riches of God's grace in Christ Jesus. "Just as you were once disobedient to God but now have received mercy because of their disobedience," he reminds us who are Gentile Christians, "so they have now been disobedient in order that by the mercy shown to you they also may receive mercy" (30-31, RSV). In the end Israel must come in. At the present, it is by their disobedience that we Gentiles have received the offer of Christ and have found mercy, but in the end they too will enter that same mercy! "For God has consigned all men to disobedience, that he may have mercy upon all" (32, RSV). Israel will be saved on the same terms as we Gentiles, through the mercy of God, found at the foot of Jesus' cross (cf. 3:29-30).

d. God's majestic purpose moves onward, and that purpose is the salvation of all men through Christ. Our Christian hope is the salvation of *the world!* But the world is not to be saved by being spared God's judgments; it will be saved by undergoing the judgments of God, even the most terrible. What all this may mean we do not know, but the gospel does give us hope for the salvation of our sinning, sorrowing, stumbling world. "O the depth of the riches and wisdom and knowledge of God! How unsearchable are his judgments and how inscrutable his ways! 'For who has known the mind of the Lord, or who has been his counselor?'" (33-34, RSV). The vision is sure, but the details are presently hidden in the mind of God. "For from him and through him and to him are all things. To him be glory for ever. Amen" (36, RSV).

Practical Applications
Rom. 12:1—16:27

ROMANS 12

Your Spiritual Worship

Romans 12:1-2

> 1 I beseech you therefore, brethren, by the mercies of God, that ye present your bodies a living sacrifice, holy, acceptable unto God, which is your reasonable service.
> 2 And be not conformed to this world: but be ye transformed by the renewing of your mind, that ye may prove what is that good, and acceptable, and perfect, will of God.

We can imagine that, after listening intently to the apostle's tireless argument which had come to such a sublime conclusion at the end of chapter 11, many in the Roman congregation expected to hear some personal greetings from Paul and then his apostolic benediction. But not those who knew him—and a number of these persons were in Rome (cf. c. 16). To them the apostle's emphatic *therefore* would be expected. They knew Paul never stopped with doctrine, that he always hastened to apply the truth of the gospel to the specific details of life.

Tertius, to whom Paul was dictating this Epistle, also knew more was to come. So, after pausing a few moments in the afterglow of the ecstasy which had accompanied the disclosure of the mystery of God's ineffable mercy, Paul began to dictate again: *I appeal to you therefore* (RSV). In view of what he is about to say in the remaining part of the Epistle about their behavior as Christians, he feels the need of establishing a closer bond with them. So he addresses them as *brethren,* reminding them of the *mercies of God,* and refers to "the grace given unto me" (3). "I appeal to you therefore, brethren, by the mercies of God" (1, RSV). He is now talking to the Romans as his brothers, men who like himself have been brought from the death of sin to the life of grace and righteousness through Christ; they too were lost, and now they are saved *by the mercies of God.*

The kind of conduct to which Paul is calling these Romans—and us—is not possible for just anybody. If the apostle had *begun* this Roman Epistle with the twelfth chapter, it would have been just another piece of ethical writing—beautiful but ineffectual. The only people who are ready to hear this appeal to consecration, holiness, and Christlike love are those who have heard and found the gospel as "the power of God unto salvation."

1. As the redeemed of Christ, we are called to put ourselves unreservedly at the disposal of God. "I appeal to you therefore, brethren, by the mercies of God, to present your bodies as a living sacrifice, holy and acceptable to God, which is your spiritual worship" (1, RSV).

In 1725, after reading Bishop Taylor's *Rule and Exercises of Holy Living and Dying,* John Wesley resolved to make his entire life "a sacrifice to God." For the next dozen years he applied himself, with a single-minded devotion which has had few equals in Christian history, to this noble task of being *a living sacrifice . . . to God.* Yet, as we know, he utterly failed. Then, upon returning from his abortive ministry in America, he met Peter Bohler, a Moravian missionary, whom God had prepared for Wesley to show him why his life had been such a spiritual failure. Bohler patiently explained to Mr. Wesley that he was trying to be sanctified without ever having been justified, and that faith in *Christ's* sacrifice, simple trust in the blood of Jesus as shed for us, is the one single condition of acceptance with God. Before we can make *our* lives a sacrifice to God we must receive the benefits of *His* sacrifice. Finally, this truth became clear to Wesley; at the little society gathering on Aldersgate Street in London he put his trust in "Christ, Christ alone, for salvation" and his heart was "strangely warmed."

Years later Wesley makes reference to this "Copernican revolution" in his thinking. Speaking of his brother Charles and himself he wrote: "In 1729, two young men reading the Bible, saw that they could not be saved without holiness, followed after it, and incited others to do so [an allusion to the Holy Club]. In 1737 they saw holiness comes by faith. They saw likewise, that men are justified before they are sanctified; but still holiness was their point. . . ."

a. "Men are justified before they are sanctified." This means that we cannot devote ourselves to God as a living sacrifice as long as we are under the guilt and power of sin. It is not until we have been absolved from the *guilt* of sin through faith in Christ's sacrifice that the *power* of sin is broken. Then, and only then, can we truly consecrate ourselves to God and make our bodies a living sacrifice. "Yield yourselves unto God, *as those that are alive from the dead,* and your members as instruments of righteousness unto God" (6:13). Only the redeemed can consecrate. First, we experience *the mercies of God* in a genuine conversion to Christ; then we can, and must, present our bodies a living sacrifice.

b. I beg of you, brethren, who have experienced the benefits of Christ's atonement, to put yourselves absolutely at God's disposal. This is the meaning of the verb *present.* In view of Christ's redemptive sacrifice for us, such a consecration is our *reasonable service,* our *spiritual* (or *rational,* mg.) *service of worship* (NASB). Our bodies (our entire persons) which were once sin's tools must now become God's weapons! This is only logical and reasonable.

All our powers—of mind and spirit as well as body—must be yielded to God, put in His hands for His holy purposes. All of life then becomes a holy partnership with

Christ. Chester Warren Quimby tells of seeing this sign on the entrance of a farm near Sulphur Springs, Tenn.:

PARTNERSHIP FARM
Christ, Owner
Charles A. Keys, Tenant

"This may seem to some too dramatic, even artificial. But it expresses the essence of the matter. Haying and plowing, milking and hoeing must all express one's glad devotion for Christ's salvation."[1]

Is your all on the altar of sacrifice laid?
Your heart does the Spirit control?
You can only be blest and have peace and sweet rest
As you yield Him your body and soul.

—E. A. HOFFMAN

This total consecration to God is both a crisis and a process, an act and a life. It is like the vows we take in marriage; we say one "I will" that includes *a whole life* of commitment and love. For this reason Paul spells out the "how" of such living.

2. As the redeemed of Christ in the school of salvation, we must heed Paul's second admonition here: "Be not conformed to this world" (2). J. B. Phillips' paraphrase has become almost classic: "Don't let the world around you squeeze you into its own mold."

a. Paul's word for *world* here is literally "age" or "aeon." The Jewish rabbis divided all history into two aeons. The old aeon they regarded as the time before the Messiah and the new aeon as beginning with His appearance. Paul and the New Testament writers modify this; they see the two aeons, or ages, as overlapping between the first and second appearances of Christ.

The new age has dawned with Christ, but the old will continue until He returns in glory to judge the world and consummate the Kingdom. As new men and women in Christ, we have already "tasted . . . the powers of the age to come" (Heb. 6:5, RSV); but since we await "the resurrection of the dead" (Phil. 3:11), we are still under the pressure of "the present evil age" (Gal. 1:4, RSV). Spiritually, we are already living in the new age; temporally, we are still in the old. So we are tempted constantly to conformity to the old age from which we have been delivered by Christ.

The New Testament is faithful to warn us of the threat posed by this world, the culture-pattern which characterizes those who still live under the sway of Satan and sin. The world has been defined correctly as "society organized apart from God." This society has its system of thought and values which is in direct opposition to the faith and values of God's kingdom. The world impinges upon us every moment of our existence. "Love not the world," John warns, "neither the things that are in the world. If any man love the world, the love of the Father is not in him" (1 John 2:15). James writes, "Ye adulterers and adulteresses, know ye not that the friendship of the world is enmity with God? whosoever therefore will be a friend of the world is the enemy of God" (Jas. 4:4). And Paul records one of the saddest biographies of the Bible in one tragic sentence: "Demas hath forsaken me, having loved this present world" (2 Tim. 4:10).

b. To be *conformed* suggests the gradual process by which we are squeezed into the world's mold. As the captors try to brainwash the prisoners of war, so Satan seeks to brainwash the children of God. Paul speaks of the devil as "the prince of the power of the air," and of "the spirit that now worketh in the children of disobedience" (Eph. 2:2). The magazines and books we read; the music, TV, and radio programs which come into our homes—these often become potent agencies of the present evil age.

The world demands conformity. It cajoles and belittles us, sometimes even threatens us, if we do not acquiesce to its wishes and ways. Its godless culture is the very atmosphere of our daily life; its Christless philosophy is sung to us, is shouted at us, seeps in upon us, until sometimes before we realize it we have accepted its characteristic ways of thinking. The corrosives of worldliness would eat away the imprint of grace upon our minds and hearts. In such spiritual weakness it becomes fatally easy to follow Demas—and forsake Christ and His Church!

How do we avoid this tragic world-conformity? Paul leaves us in no doubt: "Adapt yourselves no longer to the pattern of this present world, but let your minds be remade and your whole nature thus transformed" (2, NEB). Nonconformity is demanded, but it is not enough; we must be transformed.

3. The secret of a life of spiritual worship, then, is a day-by-day transformation in which Christ's mind becomes ours. When nonconformity becomes the end, the result is not Christian holiness but legalism—legality rather than spirituality. Simply reacting against the world we become negative, critical, and self-righteous. Whereas we once got our kicks from the world, we now derive our satisfaction from parading our saintliness! Self rather than God is still running the show. This phony holiness fools nobody but its victim!

a. Christian nonconformity is something quite different from all this; it is a Christlike way of life which flows from a daily *metamorphosis* (Paul's actual word here). As the caterpillar undergoes the change which transforms it into a beautiful butterfly, so we are changed from within by the power of Christ's love. With our minds thus remade, we see the emptiness and futility of the present world and its way of life. We shed the world's philosophy and value system just as the butterfly sheds its cocoon. Then we sing,

All of the glory and glamor of earth
To me have grown strangely dim.
The world's fleeting joys seem like poor broken toys
In the radiance that shines from Him.

b. In the final stage of biological *metamorphosis* the cocoon splits open, and the fully developed butterfly, called the *imago,* emerges. In that moment the "predestined" form of the insect is realized. You and I were created in the *Imago Dei,* the image of God. Lost in the

Fall, this *imago* is restored in Christ. The transformation by which we are changed from a mere worldling to a Christian is all to one end, that the *Imago Dei* may emerge, that "Christ, who is the image of God" (2 Cor. 4:4), may truly live and be seen in us. This is what God is intent on, working faithfully within us by His Spirit until we are "conformed to the image of his Son" (9:29).

c. "But all of us who are Christians . . . reflect like mirrors the glory of the Lord. We are transfigured in ever-increasing splendor into his own image, and the transformation comes from the Lord who is the Spirit" (2 Cor. 3:18, Phillips). Paul here uses the same verb again; the metamorphosis by which we are transfigured into Christlikeness is a lifelong process. It is going on every moment as we live openly exposed to "the glory of the Lord," in the honesty and obedience that keeps walking in the light of divine holiness. Then, on that great and final day when Christ appears, we shall stand resplendent in His heavenly glory, transfigured in His complete likeness. You see, our citizenship is not in this world. "For our citizenship is in heaven, from which also we eagerly wait for a Savior, the Lord Jesus Christ; who will transform the body of our humble state into conformity with the body of His glory, by the exertion of the power that He has even to subject all things to Himself" (Phil. 3:20-21, NASB).

"We are called to a process, not a crisis; '*grow* transfigured,'" Bishop Moule reminds us. The *origin* of the process, however, is critical: "Give over your bodies." Moule continues:

> That precept is conveyed, in its Greek form (*parastesai,* aorist), so as to suggest precisely the thought of a critical surrender. The Roman Christian, and his English younger brother, are called here, as they were above (vi.13, 19), to a transaction with the Lord quite definite. . . . They are called, as if once for all, to look their Lord in the face, and to clasp His gifts in their hands, and then to put themselves and His gifts altogether in *His* hands, for perpetual use and service.

So the Christian is called to a "hallowing of himself" decisive, crucial, instantaneous. But its outcome is to be a perpetual progression, a growth . . . in which the surrender in purpose becomes a long series of deepening surrenders in habit and action; and a larger discovery of self, and of the Lord, and of His will, takes effect in the "shining" of the transfigured life "more and more, unto the perfect day" (Prov. iv.18).[2]

Being the Body of Christ

Romans 12:3-8

3 For I say, through the grace given unto me, to every man that is among you, not to think of himself more highly than he ought to think; but to think soberly, according as God hath dealt to every man the measure of faith.
4 For as we have many members in one body, and all members have not the same office:
5 So we, being many, are one body in Christ, and every one members one of another.
6 Having then gifts differing according to the grace that is given to us, whether prophecy, let us prophesy according to the proportion of faith;
7 Or ministry, let us wait on our ministering: or he that teacheth, on teaching;
8 Or he that exhorteth, on exhortation: he that giveth, let him do it with simplicity; he that ruleth, with diligence; he that sheweth mercy, with cheerfulness.

One of the surest signs that we are really being transformed by the mind of Christ is that we are devoid of the haughty individualism which makes us think more highly of ourselves than we ought. As worldlings we tend to be so many rival, competitive individuals, each out to get all he can for himself. In Christ this sinful individualism is broken. Now Spirit-filled, we begin to be loving persons whose concern is to find our place of service in Christ's body and to outdo others in love. In the community of the Spirit which we call the Church, we learn to "think soberly, according as God hath dealt to every man the measure of faith" (3), or according to the measure of responsibility God has given us within the body of Christ.

The spirit of the world is the spirit of self-exaltation and vainglory, with resultant competition, discord, and strife. The Spirit of Christ is the spirit of love and humility, with peace, cooperation, and mutual well-being following as its natural fruit. "Be not conformed to this world: but be ye transformed by the renewing of your mind, that ye may prove what is that good, and acceptable, and perfect, will of God."

1. The single most distinctive mark of our new creaturehood is the fact that "we, being many, are one body in Christ" (5). In the deepest reality, we are *one* in the very body of Christ.

In a parallel passage in Ephesians (4:1-16), where he spells out the unity we have in Christ, Paul leaves no doubt about the meaning of Christian perfection. There, as here in Romans 12, all the gifts of Christ are bestowed for one grand end, "for the edifying of the body of Christ: till we all come in the unity of the faith, and of the knowledge of the Son of God, *unto a perfect man, unto the measure of the stature of the fulness of Christ*" (12-13). The "perfect man" is not a single individual or a composite of individuals, but Christ and His body, the Church, with all its members adjusted perfectly to one another in love. As John Wesley so aptly said, "There is no holiness but social holiness."

You see, we are not supposed to go about competing with one another to see which one of us is the most like Jesus! Comparing ourselves among ourselves *even in this* is carnal, for self is still at the center of such striving. We aren't beginning to be like Christ until we have forgotten all such spiritual individualism. The truly Christlike person is probably the last one to consider himself so; he has "lost" himself in love for others.

"For by one Spirit we were all baptized into one body" (1 Cor. 12:13, RSV). To become a New Testament Christian is to be incorporated by the Holy Spirit into the one undivided body of Christ. Walter Luthi says, "The man who believes in Christ has once and for all ceased to be an only child!" To be a born-again believer is to be a member of the *family* of God, to be a part of the *commun-*

ity of the Spirit. But alas, there are still too many "only children" in the Church! This is a contradiction of our profession that we are in Christ; in Him we are brothers and sisters (cf. 8:15-17).

We have been *baptized,* Paul reminds us, into Christ's very body (1 Cor. 12:13). For Christ, baptism meant death. As He emerged from the waters of Jordan, He saw the shadow of the Cross; from that very moment His face was set like a flint toward Jerusalem, and His death. Speaking of His passion, He said, "I have a baptism to be baptized with; and how am I straitened till it be accomplished!" (Luke 12:50; cf. Mark 10:35-39). This is what baptism by the Spirit must mean for us also—*death.* "Except a corn of wheat fall into the ground and die, it abideth alone: but if it die, it bringeth forth much fruit" (John 12:24). In so saying Jesus is speaking of both His death and ours with Him. Only when the kernel of our individual will dies and we are revivified by the power of the Resurrection is the Spirit released through us.

"Sanctify them through thy truth: thy word is truth," the Saviour prays for His Church; ". . . that they all may be one; as thou, Father, art in me, and I in thee, that they also may be one in us: that the world may believe that thou hast sent me. . . . that the love wherewith thou hast loved me may be in them, and I in them" (John 17:17, 21, 26).

2. However, we are not only one body in Christ; we are also *members one of another* (5). "Looking at Christ," says Luthi, "we see our oneness in Him; looking at His community, however, we see our plurality."

In love we are bound together under the authority of Christ, our sanctifying Head. While this destroys our sinful *individualism,* it enhances our Christian *individuality.* Individualism is sinful; individuality is the mark of Christ's body. "For as in one body we have many members, and all the members do not have the same function, so we, though many, are one body in Christ, and individually members one of another. Having gifts that differ according to the grace given to us . . ." (4-6, RSV).

a. As a member of Christ's body *you* have a gift, a special endowment of the Spirit which equips you for unique service to Christ's body. It is your responsibility, with the help of your fellow Christians, to discover your gift (or gifts). We have recognized this all along with respect to the gift of preaching. We have steadfastly maintained, and quite correctly, that God calls certain persons to preach the gospel. God's call to the individual is confirmed by the Church, which then ordains him to preach. We are now beginning to see, however, that *every* Christian has some gift which is as clearly a divine bestowment as preaching. The several lists of spiritual gifts in the New Testament are certainly not exhaustive; they are more suggestive of the *various* functions individual members perform within the body; the gifts are widely diverse. So, discover your gift. "Know thyself." Ask God to show you what function He has given you within Christ's body.

b. Secondly, accept and use the gift God has bestowed upon you. Do not envy someone else's gift. We are not to complain because some other gift has not been given us. This often means we must accept some humble task, even if we find the contribution we have to offer will be unseen and unknown, without praise or prominence. See 1 Cor. 12:14-27 for Paul's full discussion of this important truth, where he says:

> *Those parts of the body which we think less honorable we invest with the greater honor, and our unpresentable parts are treated with greater modesty, which our more presentable parts do not require. But God has so adjusted the body, giving the greater honor to the inferior part, that there may be no discord in the body, but that the members may have the same care for one another* (23-25, RSV).

When God distributes the final rewards, He will pass by many whom we have thought great and will bestow His highest awards on unknown men and women who in selfless love have poured out their lives for others. The highest gift apart from love is nothing; the humblest gift exercised in Christlike caring is everything. Even the cup of cold water given in His name cannot go unnoticed!

3. Finally, whatever gift we may have, the motive of use must be the building up of Christ's body in love. "Having gifts that differ according to the grace given to us, let us use them: if prophecy, in proportion to our faith; if service, in our serving; he who teaches, in teaching; he who exhorts, in his exhortation; he who contributes, in liberality; he who gives aid, with zeal; he who does acts of mercy, with cheerfulness" (6-8, RSV).

a. Clearly, no gift is a sign of special spiritual attainment. The very thought that I am a superior Christian because I have received a certain manifestation of the Spirit completely misses Paul's teaching concerning the purpose of gifts. When discussing the same issue with the Corinthian converts, he made it clear that he had no sympathy with a spectacular display of religious gifts which calls attention to oneself and leaves the hearers puzzled and uninstructed. "To each is given the manifestation of the Spirit *for the common good*" (1 Cor. 12:7, RSV, italics added).

Here in this Epistle he is saying the same thing differently. Each of us has been apportioned a measure of responsibility in Christ's body. The higher the gift, the greater the responsibility. To become spiritually snobbish because of *any* gift is sheer worldliness, the mark of sinful individualism. The only proof that a gift is a manifestation of the *Holy* Spirit is that it is in the employ of the love of Christ.

Paul's meaning is unmistakable: Spiritual gifts are not for one's private benefit and enjoyment but must be *used* to "edify" the Christian community. "Whatever our special role may be, our service will be marked by concentration on the task committed to us, by zeal in discharging it adequately, and by the gladness of spirit which comes from accepting our proper place in the service of God."[3]

b. Each person, then, has his special gift, and each gift its special quality. *Prophecy,* when exercised *in proportion to our faith,* greatly strengthens the Christian fellowship; but when it is not the expression of Christ's love, the gift of speech, however eloquently employed, is "sounding brass, or a tinkling cymbal" (1 Cor. 13:1). The same thing is true of the other gifts Paul mentions—*ministering, teaching, exhortation.* Each of these has its distinctive marks and must be exercised in such a way as to actually achieve the purpose for which it was intended.

Those gifts which express themselves in practical helpfulness may easily degenerate into routine functions. For this reason those who have these roles must carefully examine the spirit in which they discharge their offices. *He who contributes* (RSV) may do so in such a way as to make a mockery of his gifts. The person who *gives aid* (RSV) (as an "administrator," Paul apparently means) can easily become perfunctory and lose all the interest and urgency which makes this a service of love. Even *acts of mercy* (RSV) can be performed in a spirit which suggests a disagreeable duty, and when so done they lose all their power to comfort and encourage the human soul.

We are to serve one another *in love,* as individual members of Christ's body. Every act must be performed in His Spirit, for the upbuilding of the fellowship. When this is so, Christ himself is present in His gifts, ministering through us. Alexander Irving, in his book *My Lady of the Chimney Corner,* tells of his sainted little Scottish mother, Anna. One day a neighbor lady came to see her, in deep distress of spirit.

"I can't make it through the day, Anna, unless I receive a fresh touch of God."

"Let's go into the bedroom and pray," Anna suggested.

As they entered the room Anna said, "Now kneel down and pray, and ask Him to touch you." They prayed together, and as they did so, Anna reached out a trembling hand, placed it on the woman's head, then withdrew it. At the conclusion of their petition, Anna asked, "Did He touch you?"

"Oh, yes, Anna, I felt His hand—but it felt strangely like *your* hand!"

Whereupon Anna responded, "It was my hand, but it was His hand too. Sometimes He takes the hand of a bishop; sometimes He takes the hand of a surgeon; and sometimes He takes the hand of a poor old creature like me. It was my hand, but it was His hand, too! Christ takes a hand wherever He can find it."

The Power of Christian Love

Romans 12:9-21

> 9 Let love be without dissimulation. Abhor that which is evil; cleave to that which is good.
> 10 Be kindly affectioned one to another with brotherly love; in honour preferring one another;
> 11 Not slothful in business; fervent in spirit; serving the Lord;
> 12 Rejoicing in hope; patient in tribulation; continuing instant in prayer;
> 13 Distributing to the necessity of saints; given to hospitality.
> 14 Bless them which persecute you: bless, and curse not.
> 15 Rejoice with them that do rejoice, and weep with them that weep.
> 16 Be of the same mind one toward another. Mind not high things, but condescend to men of low estate. Be not wise in your own conceits.
> 17 Recompense to no man evil for evil. Provide things honest in the sight of all men.
> 18 If it be possible, as much as lieth in you, live peaceably with all men.
> 19 Dearly beloved, avenge not yourselves, but rather give place unto wrath: for it is written, Vengeance is mine; I will repay, saith the Lord.
> 20 Therefore if thine enemy hunger, feed him; if he thirst, give him drink: for in so doing thou shalt heap coals of fire on his head.
> 21 Be not overcome with evil, but overcome evil with good.

Love came to earth at Bethlehem, taking human expression in Jesus of Nazareth. In Him love was defined in God's own terms. Before Christ, Greek philosophers had tried to explain what love is. But natural man, no matter how brilliant or wise, can never define love. Even in its noblest forms human love is inevitably corrupted by self-interest; and the finest definition the human mind could give—the soul's desire for God—is the exact opposite of the love defined by Christ's life and death. Christ defined love, not in man's but in God's terms: "Herein is love, *not that we loved God, but that he loved us,* and sent his Son to be the propitiation for our sins" (1 John 4:10, italics added).

Human love is love conditioned by the goodness or lovableness of its object; divine love is the spontaneous manifestation of goodwill, even toward those who are its enemies (5:8, 10).

Human love is self-oriented; it desires to possess its object for its own fulfillment. Divine love is others-oriented; it freely spends and sacrifices itself for others, that *they* may find fulfillment.

Human love *seeks* goodness and value in those it would love; divine love *creates* goodness and value.

Human love is man's love for God; divine love is God's love for man. But, "if God so loved us, we ought also to love one another" (1 John 4:11). This is what we mean when we say Christ is the true definition of love.

When Paul writes the Romans and says, "Let love be genuine" (9, RSV), he is using God's definition of love; he is thinking of love solely in terms of its perfect expression in Christ.

1. *Love's Basic Quality: Genuineness*

a. Because by nature we tend to be self-centered, self-loving individuals, we need this admonition to "let love be genuine." Our selfishness so easily blinds us! We may think we love another when in reality we may be trying to *use* that person. Without genuine love parents may thus use their children; married persons, their spouses; even pastors, their people. *Let love be genuine.* Let the Spirit of God reveal to you the falsity and pretense and sentimentality which often mar and debase love.

Love is not genuine unless it is unselfish concern for the well-being of the other person. Love is other-concern. It is not simply a feeling; it is sincere goodwill seeking to understand and identify with another. Love listens. Love is honest. Love quickly surrenders its own opinions and prejudices when truth becomes apparent. Love reaches out the hand and opens the heart to the other. It says, "I see you; I hear you; I am here." Love does not play games; it really cares and stands ready to sacrifice self for the other's welfare and happiness.

b. Love, moreover, is a *moral* quality. It hates evil and loves good. Thus when it encountered human sin, it crimsoned into the sacrifice of Calvary. God loves sinners but He hates and judges our sin. God forgives and accepts us, but only because He has first permitted sin to break His own heart. Love takes the initiative; it suffers for the sake of those it would redeem; it thereby transforms all who respond to it. Love is a divine force which transmutes evil into good. Love accepts us as we are. It does not wait until we change; it says, "Thou art . . . thou shalt be" (John 1:42). This is how God's love operates *toward* us—and it is also the way it transforms others *through* us.

2. *Love's Base of Operation: the Christian fellowship.*

Since love is goodwill in action, it exists only in persons. As we have seen, love found its truest expression in Christ: "This is how we know what love is: Jesus Christ laid down his life for us" (1 John 3:16, NIV). But the love of God is not "perfected" until we "walk as Jesus did" (1 John 2:6, NIV). That is, God's love does not attain its goal until it has re-created *us* as Christlike persons.

a. The Church, the redeemed Christian fellowship, must be the *continuing* manifestation of Christ's love. "A new commandment I give to you," the Master says to us, "that you love one another; even as I have loved you, that you also love one another. By this all men will know that you are my disciples, if you have love one for another" (John 13:34-35, RSV). The Church, as Christ's Spirit-filled body, is the continuing incarnation of His love. On the Day of Pentecost the love which had been incarnate in Jesus was poured out in the hearts of the 120 by the Holy Spirit, who molded these people into a loving fellowship where "all the believers . . . had everything in common. Selling their possessions and goods, they gave to anyone as he had need" (Acts 2:44-45, NIV).

b. Notice Luke's further account of the infant Spirit-filled fellowship: "Every day they continued to meet together in the temple courts. They broke bread in their homes and ate together with glad and sincere hearts, praising God and enjoying the favor of all the people. And the Lord added to their number daily those who were being saved" (Acts 2:46-47, NIV). Here is what God would make of every Christian congregation: A Spirit-embued fellowship, sharing, caring, worshipping, rejoicing, making all of life a sacrament of praise. Such a Christian community cannot help but grow.

So Paul admonishes: "Love one another with brotherly affection; outdo one another in showing honor. Never flag in zeal, be aglow with the Spirit, serve the Lord. Rejoice in your hope; be patient in tribulation, be constant in prayer. Contribute to the needs of the saints, practice hospitality. . . . Rejoice with those who rejoice, weep with those who weep. Live in harmony with one another" (12:10-13, 15-16, RSV).

"Behold, how they love one another!" should be the amazed comment of those who come into the midst of a Christian fellowship. Our generation is suffering from a tragic "cosmic loneliness." Men and women everywhere are searching for life's meaning, yearning for love. When they come into our churches, they should be moved to say, "This is what we've been looking for!" In the words of the popular chorus: "They'll know we are Christians by our love."

3. *Love's Undefeatable Power.*

Although we may recognize that the Spirit-filled Church is the base of love's operations, love cannot possibly be confined to the Christian community. By its very nature it reaches both downward and outward. As Walter Luthi has observed, God's love has "an inherent downward force. It is inclined toward the unimportant, the insignificant, the downtrodden. And conversely . . . it becomes silent in the face of boasting, and it shuns conceited exaggeration." "Live in harmony with one another," Paul therefore admonishes. "Don't be proud, but be willing to associate with people of low position. Don't be conceited" (16, NIV). It is doubtful if God is particularly impressed with our fine churches and our high church steeples; He longs to see His people seeking "the lost, the last, and the least."

But if the first movement of God's love is downward, its direction next turns outward. It refuses to be confined. It cannot stop with embracing brothers in faith; it reaches out to take in the stranger. Even the adversary, our assailant, our enemy is to experience God's love through us. "Bless those who persecute you; bless and do not curse" (14, NIV). Paul is echoing his Master, who said, "If you love those who love you . . . what are you doing more than others? Do not even pagans do that? Be perfect, therefore [in love for enemy as well as friend], as your heavenly Father is perfect [in His love for all]" (see Matt. 5:43-48, NIV).

So, "Do not repay anyone evil for evil. Be careful to do what is right in the sight of everybody" (17, NIV). Even the man outside the Church knows that to be "Christian" is to be forgiving and Christlike. "If it is possible, as far as it depends on you, live at peace with everyone" (18, NIV). "If possible," Paul says reasonably. He knows that, if it takes two to make a quarrel, it also takes two to make peace. But if there is to be a quarrel, let the other person start it. And as a Christian let me be the first to extend the hand in peace.

Nor must I be concerned about justice for myself; God will take care of vengeance. *Love* is my responsibility. It must be my faith that God—who knows all about my adversary as well as about me—is the only One who knows how to make true judgment. Faith in Him who says, "I will repay," relieves me of all anxiety about justice. So

Paul says to you and me, "If your enemy is hungry, feed him; if he is thirsty, give him something to drink. In doing this, you will heap burning coals on his head" (20, NIV). Heaping coals of fire on my enemy's head is the only act of aggression Christian love permits or commands. I must love my enemy in the faith that the fire of God's love can win a victory over all evil. "Do not be overcome by evil," Paul commands me, "but overcome evil with good" (21, NIV). By God's love I must make a friend out of my enemy.

This is God's last word to us: Love! Love, in the confidence that good is stronger than evil. Love, with the conviction that love alone is the one undefeatable power in the universe. Love, because "God is love, and he who abides in love abides in God, and God abides in him" (1 John 4:16, RSV).

ROMANS 13

The Power of Christian Hope

Romans 13:1-14

1 Let every soul be subject unto the higher powers. For there is no power but of God: the powers that be are ordained of God.
2 Whosoever therefore resisteth the power, resisteth the ordinance of God: and they that resist shall receive to themselves damnation.
3 For rulers are not a terror to good works, but to the evil. Wilt thou then not be afraid of the power? do that which is good, and thou shalt have praise of the same:
4 For he is the minister of God to thee for good. But if thou do that which is evil, be afraid; for he beareth not the sword in vain: for he is the minister of God, a revenger to execute wrath upon him that doeth evil.
5 Wherefore ye must needs be subject, not only for wrath, but also for conscience sake.
6 For for this cause pay ye tribute also: for they are God's ministers, attending continually upon this very thing.
7 Render therefore to all their dues: tribute to whom tribute is due; custom to whom custom; fear to whom fear; honour to whom honour.
8 Owe no man any thing, but to love one another: for he that loveth another hath fulfilled the law.
9 For this, Thou shalt not commit adultery, Thou shalt not kill, Thou shalt not steal, Thou shalt not bear false witness, Thou shalt not covet;

and if there be any other commandment, it is briefly comprehended in this saying, namely, Thou shalt love thy neighbor as thyself.
10 Love worketh no ill to his neighbour: therefore love is the fulfilling of the law.
11 And that, knowing the time, that now it is high time to awake out of sleep: for now is our salvation nearer than when we believed.
12 The night is far spent, the day is at hand: let us therefore cast off the works of darkness, and let us put on the armour of light.
13 Let us walk honestly, as in the day; not in rioting and drunkenness, not in chambering and wantonness, not in strife and envying.
14 But put ye on the Lord Jesus Christ, and make not provision for the flesh, to fulfil the lusts thereof.

Christian hope is a badly misunderstood subject. Many both without and within the Church regard it as mere wishful thinking, a pious longing for "pie in the sky, by and by."

But Christian hope is no such wish-fulfillment, no mere projection of thwarted human desires. It is a confident expectation of the future based upon Christ's resurrection. It is the robust conviction that God, who raised His Son from the dead, is the Lord of the future who will bring history to its goal. It is Christian faith saying confidently with Paul, "We know that the one who raised the Lord Jesus from the dead will also raise us with Jesus and present us with you in his presence" (2 Cor. 4:14, NIV). It is the heart-filled certainty that "our salvation is nearer now than when we first believed" (11, NIV).

Walter Luthi tells of seeing a house in Germany which we may call a parable of Christian hope. From a distance you can see written on its roof in bold letters, "Time flies, the end is near; soon the Lord shall appear. Hallelujah!" But the house and the rhyme are kept freshly painted. The owner is expecting the return of Christ and is waiting for the end, yet—strange reasoning indeed!—instead of letting his house fall to pieces he keeps it immaculately neat and clean and even gives it an occasional fresh coat of paint! Such is the divine logic of Christian hope.

Instead of relaxing our faith, works, and holy endeavor, our Christian hope causes us to reinforce and intensify them. Christian hope transforms earth into a vestibule of heaven and suffuses all our earthly duties with the light of God's love and joy.

1. In the first place, Paul reminds us, Christian hope *makes good citizens* (1-7). Confident that God is the sovereign Lord of history and that "the kingdoms of this world" shall yet "become the kingdoms of our Lord, and of his Christ" (Rev. 11:15), Christians are harbingers of God's coming reign of righteousness and peace. The present kingdom of Christ, though "not of this world," has been inaugurated *in* the world and it is destined to grow like a mustard seed into a great tree that shall fill the earth. Like yeast in a loaf, it will permeate society (Matt. 13:31-33). As prophetic of God's future, the Church is the seed of the Kingdom (see Matt. 13:36-43). Yet the final triumph of the Kingdom awaits the return of Christ. "Then the end will come, when he hands over the kingdom to God the Father after he has destroyed all dominion, authority and power" (1 Cor. 15:24, NIV).

As we noted in the exposition of 12:1-2, between the two appearances of Christ the present and the future aeons overlap. The new age has dawned with the kingdom of Christ, but the old continues until He returns. Christ's kingdom has invaded "the present evil age" (Gal. 1:4, NIV), but it has not yet destroyed it. "The mystery of iniquity" still works like evil leaven, and this is where Paul's doctrine of human government comes in. God has ordained the human state as a restraining force upon evil in society until evil is destroyed by Christ's second coming.

Civil government, therefore, is God's order for the present time. Paul lays down three principles to guide the Christian attitude toward temporal authority:

a. There is no authority except from God, and those that exist have been instituted by God (1, RSV). Civil government is more than a human compact; it expresses the divine intention for society.

b. Civil authority is *the "servant" of God* (4, RSV) because it promotes the good of mankind. It preserves a measure of peace and tranquility in human affairs; it protects life and property by restraining and punishing criminals. By the same token it presents no problem to those who seek the good (2-4).

c. Therefore, *everyone must submit himself to the governing authorities* (1, NIV). Christians must be law-abiding citizens who *respect* and *honor* civil rulers. We must also pay *taxes* and *revenue* to support government. All these things we do "for conscience sake" (5-7).

Commentators on this passage sometimes note that Paul does not take into account that human government is often tyrannical, that laws are frequently unjust, that even revolution may be necessary to overthrow a corrupt regime. But nothing Paul says can be made to mean Christians must never object to any law, never agitate for repeal or change, never seek reforms, never revolt. What Paul means is: Never flout decent public order, for along that path lie anarchy and social chaos. Anarchy is anti-God, for God is the Author of decency, law, and order. Moreover, Paul's eye is on the future. To the Philippians he wrote, "We are a colony of heaven" (Phil. 3:20, Moffatt). He saw the Christian community as an outpost of heaven on earth. The Church bears within itself the seed of the future kingdom of God. Let us live like it! Let us embody the peace and goodwill which shall cover the earth "as the waters cover the sea" when Christ has won His final victory.

Early Christians knew themselves to be a "third race." They believed themselves to be God's new breed. This is why they turned the world upside down. They were the advance guard of the coming King of Righteousness. They lived like it, and they died like it. So must we. Is this not what Christ meant when He commanded, "Occupy till I come"?

2. Furthermore, Christian hope *makes us good neighbors* (8-10). This is true because the Christ whose return we await is already present in our hearts by the indwelling

Holy Spirit. "We realize that our life in this world is actually his life lived in us" (1 John 4:17, Phillips).

a. Christ now lives His life of love in us. When He was in the flesh He fulfilled the law *for* us by His obedience unto death. He now fulfills the law *in* us by the Spirit, through whom He is reproduced in our experience and life. We may return for a moment to the great declaration the apostle has already made in chapter 8: "God has done what the law, weakened by the flesh, could not do; sending his own Son in the likeness of sinful flesh and for sin, he condemned sin in the flesh, in order that *the just requirement of the law* might be fulfilled in us, who walk not according to the flesh but according to the Spirit" (8:3-4), RSV, italics added). Here in chapter 13, Paul spells out what that "just requirement of the law" is: *love.* "Let no debt remain outstanding," he admonishes us, "except the continuing debt to love one another, for he who loves his fellow man has fulfilled the law. The commandments . . . are summed up in this one rule: 'Love your neighbor as yourself.' Love does no harm to its neighbor. Therefore love is the fulfillment of the law" (8-10, NIV). The heart of Christian experience is to have Christ in one's heart. And the fruit of that relationship is love.

b. The fruits of Christian faith are love and hope—not love *or* hope, but love *and* hope. Because of the tension between Christ living in us and Christ coming for us, the balance between these two fruits is not always maintained. A church member who did not think his pastor was properly emphasizing the Second Coming asked, "Pastor, don't you know that Christ is coming back?" A bit defensively the preacher replied, "I didn't realize He had been away!" Both men were right, but insofar as they destroyed the balance between these two truths they were wrong. Faith, hope, and love are a trinity in Christian experience. "Therefore, since we have been justified through *faith,* we have peace with God through our Lord Jesus Christ, through whom we have gained access by faith into this grace in which we now stand. And we rejoice in the *hope* of the glory of God. . . . And hope does not disappoint us, because God has poured out his *love* into our hearts by the Holy Spirit" (5:1-2, 5, NIV, italics added). This love which reinforces hope is not mere sentiment; it is the positive goodwill which forms the cement of all human relations. Christian hope, indeed, makes good neighbors.

3. Finally, Christian hope *sanctifies the whole of life* (11-13). "Understanding the present time [we know that] our salvation is nearer now than when we first believed. . . . So let us put aside the deeds of darkness and put on the armor of light" (11-12, NIV).

If we are tempted to think Paul was mistaken in his expectation of Christ's imminent return, we must remember that even Jesus did not know the day or the hour the Father has reserved in His own authority. "But, beloved, be not ignorant of this one thing," Peter writes, "that one day is with the Lord as a thousand years, and a thousand years as one day. The Lord is not slack concerning his promise, as some men count slackness; but is longsuffering to us-ward, not willing that any should perish, but that all should come to repentance. But the day of the Lord will come as a thief in the night; in the which the heavens shall pass away with a great noise, and the elements shall melt with fervent heat, the earth also and the works therein shall be burned up. Seeing then that all these things shall be dissolved, what manner of persons ought ye to be in all holy conversation and godliness?" (2 Pet. 3:8-11).

Eschatology no longer seems to be "an antique from the lumber room of theology." It has instead become a living issue of tremendous urgency. Nuclear physicists have just (August, 1974) moved the minute hand of the Doomsday Clock from 12 minutes to 9 minutes before midnight. Irving A. Lerch, staff physicist of the International Atomic Energy Agency, says he would have advanced the clock to 3 minutes before midnight. When it has ceased to be a figure of speech to write of the elements melting in fervent heat, New Testament eschatology becomes unexpectedly relevant in our times.

We who believe, however, are not cast into despair by the world's prophecy of doom. "And when these things come to pass," Jesus said, "then look up, and lift up your heads; for your redemption draweth nigh" (Luke 21:28). For us, the coming of the Lord is not doomsday; it is our "blessed hope"! "Everyone who has this hope in him purifies himself, just as he is pure" (1 John 3:3, NIV).

"The night is far gone, the day is at hand. Let us then cast off the works of darkness and put on the armor of light; let us conduct ourselves becomingly as in the day, not in reveling and drunkenness, not in debauchery and licentiousness, not in quarreling and jealousy. But put on the Lord Jesus Christ, and make no provision for the flesh, to gratify its desires" (12-14, RSV). Before he became a father in the Church, Augustine, as he himself tells us, lived a life of riotous excess. One summer day in the year A.D. 386, the brilliant young rhetorician sat weeping in the garden of his friend Alypius. Having fled the prayers of his godly mother, Monica, he had come under the influence of Bishop Ambrose's ministry in Milan. As he sat that day in the garden, almost persuaded to break with his old life of sin, he heard the voices of children at play. He thought he caught the words, "Take and read, take and read!" Taking up the New Testament scroll which lay at his friend's side, his eyes fell on the above verses. "No further would I read," he tells us, "nor needed I; for instantly . . . by a light as it were of serenity infused into my heart, all the darkness of doubt vanished away." The illumination of Augustine's mind and heart from this word of God in Romans completely transformed him. Augustine the sinner, by the power of this word of saving hope, became Augustine the saint.

"Put on the Lord Jesus Christ," God says to you and

me, "and make no provision for the flesh, to gratify its desires."

When He shall come with trumpet sound,
Oh, may I then in Him be found,
Dressed in His righteousness alone,
Faultless to stand before His throne!

—EDWARD MOTE

ROMANS 14

Weak and Strong Christians

Romans 14:1—15:13

1 Him that is weak in the faith receive ye, but not to doubtful disputations.
2 For one believeth that he may eat all things: another, who is weak, eateth herbs.
3 Let not him that eateth despise him that eateth not; and let not him which eateth not judge him that eateth: for God hath received him.
4 Who art thou that judgest another man's servant? to his own master he standeth or falleth. Yea, he shall be holden up: for God is able to make him stand.
5 One man esteemeth one day above another: another esteemeth every day alike. Let every man be fully persuaded in his own mind.
6 He that regardeth the day, regardeth it unto the Lord; and he that regardeth not the day, to the Lord he doth not regard it. He that eateth, eateth to the Lord, for he giveth God thanks; and he that eateth not, to the Lord he eateth not, and giveth God thanks.
7 For none of us liveth to himself, and no man dieth to himself.
8 For whether we live, we live unto the Lord; and whether we die, we die unto the Lord: whether we live therefore, or die, we are the Lord's.
9 For to this end Christ both died, and rose, and revived, that he might be Lord both of the dead and living.
10 But why dost thou judge thy brother? or why dost thou set at nought thy brother? for we shall all stand before the judgment seat of Christ.
11 For it is written, As I live, saith the Lord, every knee shall bow to me, and every tongue shall confess to God.
12 So then every one of us shall give account of himself to God.
13 Let us not therefore judge one another any more: but judge this rather, that no man put a stumblingblock or an occasion to fall in his brother's way.
14 I know, and am persuaded by the Lord Jesus, that there is nothing unclean of itself: but to him that esteemeth any thing to be unclean, to him it is unclean.
15 But if thy brother be grieved with thy meat, now walkest thou not charitably. Destroy not him with thy meat, for whom Christ died.

16 Let not then your good be evil spoken of:
17 For the kingdom of God is not meat and drink; but righteousness,
and peace, and joy in the Holy Ghost.
18 For he that in these things serveth Christ is acceptable to God, and
approved of men.
19 Let us therefore follow after the things which make for peace, and
things wherewith one may edify another.
20 For meat destroy not the work of God. All things indeed are pure;
but it is evil for that man who eateth with offence.
21 It is good neither to eat flesh, nor to drink wine, nor any thing
whereby thy brother stumbleth, or is offended, or is made weak.
22 Hast thou faith? have it to thyself before God. Happy is he that
condemneth not himself in that thing which he alloweth.
23 And he that doubteth is damned if he eat, because he eateth not of
faith: for whatsoever is not of faith is sin.
15:1 We then that are strong ought to bear the infirmities of the weak,
and not to please ourselves.
2 Let every one of us please his neighbour for his good to edification.
3 For even Christ pleased not himself: but, as it is written, The re-
proaches of them that reproached thee fell on me.
4 For whatsoever things were written aforetime were written for our
learning, that we through patience and comfort of the scriptures might
have hope.
5 Now the God of patience and consolation grant you to be like-
minded one toward another according to Christ Jesus:
6 That ye may with one mind and one mouth glorify God, even the
Father of our Lord Jesus Christ.
7 Wherefore receive ye one another, as Christ also received us to the
glory of God.
8 Now I say that Jesus Christ was a minister of the circumcision for
the truth of God, to confirm the promises made unto the fathers:
9 And that the Gentiles might glorify God for his mercy; as it is
written, For this cause I will confess to thee among the Gentiles, and
sing unto thy name.
10 And again he saith, Rejoice, ye Gentiles, with his people.
11 And again, Praise the Lord, all ye Gentiles; and laud him, all ye
people.
12 And again, Esaias saith, There shall be a root of Jesse, and he
that shall rise to reign over the Gentiles; in him shall the Gentiles trust.
13 Now the God of hope fill you with all joy and peace in believing,
that ye may abound in hope, through the power of the Holy Ghost.

The Christians in Rome were not divided in their faith like Christendom today, where some are "evangelical" and base their hope solely on Christ while others are "liberal" and do not accept the historic Christian faith. No, these first recipients of the Epistle to the Romans gladly confessed their hope of salvation on Christ alone, who "died and returned to life so that he might be the Lord of both the dead and the living" (9, NIV). It would never have occurred to these early Christians to attribute their salvation and hope of life eternal to any other than Jesus Christ, the Son of God. He was the One who had suffered under Pontius Pilate; was crucified, dead, and buried; who on the third day rose again from the dead and ascended to heaven, from whence He shall come to judge the quick and the dead.

But in spite of their common Christian faith, the Roman Christians were experiencing real difficulties in living that faith out within their own fellowship. They were one family in Christ, but they were divided among themselves on many details of the Christian life. At the bottom of their problem was the fact that the congregation had begun as a Jewish Christian fellowship, but over the years had become predominantly Gentile. Questions over matters of the ceremonial law had become burning issues. Besides that, some of the Gentile Christians still had scruples about eating meat offered in sacrifice to pagan deities.

Many of the Romans probably had a clear understanding of the gospel of the grace of God and knew that Christ had set them free from mere taboos. They knew that "the kingdom of God is not a matter of eating and drinking, but of righteousness, peace and joy in the Holy Spirit" (17, NIV). Consequently, they enjoyed true spiritual freedom in Christ. These persons Paul calls the "strong" in faith.

Others in the fellowship, evidently a minority, failed to grasp the full meaning of the gospel. They were in bondage to religious taboos out of their past. They felt the need of rules to insulate them from both their pre-Christian background and from their pagan environment. They seem to have put emphasis on fasting and abstinence. They felt it was wrong to eat meat. Some found it difficult to make the transition from the Old Testament sabbath to the Christian Lord's day. These Paul describes as "weak in the faith." That is, their faith lacked full knowledge. They made superficial distinctions. Their lives were surrounded with scruples. Their faith was made up largely of prohibitions.

The problem arose when these two groups began to criticize each other. The stricter group began to *judge* the others for being too "liberal," while the majority were tempted to *look down on* the weak as being "narrow-minded" (see 3-4, NIV). The Roman problem suddenly becomes familiar!

In helping the Romans find a solution to their disunity, Paul addresses both groups, but characteristically he makes his chief appeal to the strong, with whom he himself identifies. His plea is for consideration of the weak: "We who are strong ought to bear with the failings of the weak, and not to please ourselves" (15:1, NIV).

As the apostle comes to grips with this problem, he illustrates the meaning of the ancient Christian maxim: "In essentials unity, in nonessentials liberty, in all things charity." His opening admonition is—

1. *Accept One Another* (14:1-12). In essence Paul is here saying, As each of us has been accepted by God on the basis of Christ's death and resurrection, so we should accept one another, remembering always that "each of us will give an account of *himself* to God" (12, NIV, italics added). Let us see if we can summarize the apostle's directions:

a. The church must "accept him whose faith is weak, without passing judgment on disputable matters" (1, NIV). We must not enter into disputes with the weak Christians, but receive him with respect for his scruples. Arguments about freedom must not be allowed to jeopardize the brotherly relationship of love.

b. Both strong and weak must refrain from judging each other. The temptation of the weak is to unchristianize those who do not share their scruples; the strong are tempted to pride and superiority feelings. Resist both temptations!

c. Matters of conscience must be settled in relationship to God. God alone has the prerogative of judgment. "Judge not," Jesus himself said, "that ye be not judged"

(Matt. 7:1). Each of us must decide right and wrong in nonessential matters on the basis of his personal accountability to God.

d. Let every man be fully persuaded in his own mind (5). This does not mean a Christian has the right to do as he pleases without regard to what others think or that he is his own standard of right or wrong. But it does mean each of us must be convinced in his own mind *for himself,* irrespective of the scruples of others and without being critical of them.

e. Finally, every one of us is accountable to Christ and answerable only to Him. Whatever one does he must do it *to the Lord* (6-7, NIV). "For none of us lives to himself alone and none of us dies to himself alone" (7, NIV). The Christian belongs to the Lord, not to himself. We have no right to judge others; we acknowledge Christ as Lord and prepare to give account to Him for ourselves alone.

2. *Guard Your Influence* (14:13-23). Paul is now speaking directly to the strong. We must never exercise our freedom in such a way as to damage a weaker brother or sister in Christ. We are responsible for our influence over others. Many moral choices will be determined by this principle. Some courses of action may not be inherently wrong for us, but if it will do injury to another, love dictates self-denial. Paul's teaching can be summed up in three admonitions:

a. Do not exercise your freedom in Christ to the hurt of others. It is a sin to put a stumbling block in a weak person's way. Is this not what Jesus meant when He said it is better to have a millstone hung around one's neck and to be drowned in the sea than to "offend one of these little ones who believe in me" (Matt. 18:6)? Some choices are not to be decided on whether or not *I* can do a certain thing but on the basis of my influence on others. If someone who lacks insight for proper Christian evaluation will be hurt, then I do wrong in offending his conscience.

Of course this principle is not absolute. Paul immediately qualifies it: "Do not destroy . . . your brother for whom Christ died" (15, NIV). We cannot avoid every offense of conscience; such endeavor would destroy *us*. But we must avoid doing anything which would *destroy the work of God* (20, NIV) in a person's life. We must do nothing which would cause a weak Christian to give up his faith in Christ and turn back to the world. We must watch lest the exercise of our freedom causes another to stumble (20, NIV). "It is better not to eat meat or drink wine or to do anything else that will cause your brother to fall" (21, NIV). The welfare of my brother in Christ is more important than my own rights (cf. 1 Corinthians 9).

b. Remember, the kingdom of God requires real righteousness. It is not a system prohibiting the eating of flesh or approving vegetables, or anything external or ceremonial. It is a matter of inner righteousness and peace and joy in the Holy Spirit. But this does not give license to self-indulgence or yielding to the flesh at any point. The Kingdom rather requires personal uprightness and loving relationships with others. It calls for moral influence of the highest and strongest quality. We must follow practices which make for peace. Our influence must contribute to harmony and to the moral strength and spiritual growth of others. "Anyone who serves Christ in this way is pleasing to God and approved by men" (18, NIV).

c. Practice self-denial for the good of others. The sum of what Paul is saying is that the Christian of mature faith will never flaunt it before others or insist that he can do as he pleases without moral injury to himself and damage to others. To insist on one's rights to the harm of one's brother is a sign of original sin: *self-centeredness*. To practice self-denial for the upbuilding of the work of God in others and the Christian community is the sign of God's grace: *self-sacrificing agape*. "Knowledge puffs up, but love builds up" (1 Cor. 8:1, NIV). Personal liberty is secondary to the spiritual welfare of others.

Paul adds a word in verse 23 for the person whose faith wavers regarding taboos. The doing of anything, such as eating nonkosher food, is sinful if it does not proceed from the Christian conviction that "all things are clean," since such a person is doing what he is still inwardly convinced is wrong. To go against a conscience unenlightened by faith is sin.

ROMANS 15

3. *Imitate Christ* (15:1-13). This passage continues the preceding exhortation but holds up Christ as our perfect Example. He did not insist on His own rights; He considered the needs of others. "For even Christ did not please himself but, as it is written: 'The insults of those who insult you have fallen on me'" (3, NIV). Those who are strong in faith must bear with the failings and infirmities of the weak. They must help those whose faith is feeble, help those with conscientious scruples, help the fainthearted who are struggling with temptations and doubts. Our purpose should be not to please ourselves but to help our brothers and sisters in Christ become strong and victorious in faith. This will sometimes call for bearing the reproaches of others, just as Christ did.

God has given us the Scriptures, Paul tells us, in order to enable us to maintain our Christian hope with Christlike patience. "May the God of steadfastness and encouragement grant you to live in such harmony with one another, in accord with Christ Jesus, that together you may with one voice glorify the God and Father of our Lord Jesus Christ" (5-6, RSV). Let all barriers be removed, Paul is praying. Let the mind which was in Christ Jesus so remold you that differences of opinion cannot divide you. With one voice glorify the Father of our Lord Jesus. "Accept one another, then, just as Christ accepted you, in order to bring praise to God" (7, NIV). As Christ has accepted you, the unacceptable, even dying for sinners and then receiving them into His body, the Church (5:6-8; Eph. 2:13), so accept one another. In this way we permit Christ to break down the human walls of partition which divide us. Then we truly sing, "We are one in the bond of love." But the burden is upon us who are strong, to be even like Jesus.

Oh, to be like Thee! full of compassion,
Loving, forgiving, tender, and kind,
Helping the helpless, cheering the fainting,
Seeking the wand'ring sinner to find!

Oh, to be like Thee! Oh, to be like Thee,
Blessed Redeemer, pure as Thou art!
Come in Thy sweetness, come in Thy fullness;
Stamp Thine own image deep on my heart.

—T. O. CHISHOLM

The Christian Mission

Romans 15:14-33

14 And I myself also am persuaded of you, my brethren, that ye also
are full of goodness, filled with all knowledge, able also to admonish
one another.
15 Nevertheless, brethren, I have written the more boldly unto you
in some sort, as putting you in mind, because of the grace that is given
to me of God,
16 That I should be the minister of Jesus Christ to the Gentiles, min-
istering the gospel of God, that the offering up of the Gentiles might
be acceptable, being sanctified by the Holy Ghost.
17 I have therefore whereof I may glory through Jesus Christ in those
things which pertain to God.
18 For I will not dare to speak of any of those things which Christ hath
not wrought by me, to make the Gentiles obedient, by word and deed,
19 Through mighty signs and wonders, by the power of the Spirit of
God; so that from Jerusalem, and round about unto Illyricum, I have
fully preached the gospel of Christ.
20 Yea, so have I strived to preach the gospel, not where Christ was
named, lest I should build upon another man's foundation:
21 But as it is written, To whom he was not spoken of, they shall see:
and they that have not heard shall understand.
22 For which cause also I have been much hindered from coming to
you.
23 But now having no more place in these parts, and having a great
desire these many years to come unto you;
24 Whensoever I take my journey into Spain, I will come to you: for I
trust to see you in my journey, and to be brought on my way thither-
ward by you, if first I be somewhat filled with your company.
25 But now I go unto Jerusalem to minister unto the saints.
26 For it hath pleased them of Macedonia and Achaia to make a
certain contribution for the poor saints which are at Jerusalem.

27 It hath pleased them verily; and their debtors they are. For if the Gentiles have been made partakers of their spiritual things, their duty is also to minister unto them in carnal things.
28 When therefore I have performed this, and have sealed to them this fruit, I will come by you into Spain.
29 And I am sure that, when I come unto you, I shall come in the fulness of the blessing of the gospel of Christ.
30 Now I beseech you, brethren, for the Lord Jesus Christ's sake, and for the love of the Spirit, that ye strive together with me in your prayers to God for me;
31 That I may be delivered from them that do not believe in Judaea; and that my service which I have for Jerusalem may be accepted of the saints;
32 That I may come unto you with joy by the will of God, and may with you be refreshed.
33 Now the God of peace be with you all. Amen.

"I will not venture to speak of anything except what Christ has accomplished through me" (18, NIV). Here we see again what Paul will not let us forget: that God, through Christ, loved us while we were yet ungodly, while we were still sinners, while we were even enemies. Christ is the Saviour of the whole world, of the Gentiles as well as the Jews. This is what made Paul an apostle—the gospel of Christ. As certainly as Christ is the Saviour of mankind, so surely has Paul been entrusted with the gospel as an apostle. "Paul, a servant of Christ Jesus, called to be an apostle and set apart for the gospel of God" (1:1, NIV). These were the words with which he opened this Epistle, and now he is back to them. Through the proclamation of Christ, Gentiles everywhere—people like you and me—were being led to obey God.

Paul is long since gone from the scene, but God still has His gospel ministers. It is not the human instruments who are important; it is Christ. It is not their sermons that are significant; it is the gospel. It is not the human strategy which the Church works out which accomplishes the divine will; it is the stream of the Spirit which ceaselessly flows on. Because these things are so, we can easily relate to what Paul is saying here. Names of preachers and places change, but the thrilling story of missions goes on because God is still not willing that any should perish, but that all should come to repentance and life through Christ.

1. *The Power of Christ at Work.* Christ! Christ through me! "I will not venture to speak of anything except what Christ has accomplished through me" (18, NIV). In order to get what Paul is trying to say, we must fix our eyes exclusively on Christ. To read this superficially is to get the false impression that Paul is talking about himself and his own accomplishments. But it would be unfortunate simply to talk about "Paul's missionary plan" when preaching from this passage. "Not I, but Christ," Paul would surely correct us.

Such an awareness of Christ's working, however, does not reduce Paul to a nobody. He knows he is someone. He has what we would call ego-strength, in abundance. At least 20 times in this very passage he uses the personal pronoun "I." But we misunderstand Paul's egoism, unless we remember what he says later when writing to his Philippian friends, "I can do all things *through Christ*" (Phil. 4:13, italics added). He understood perfectly that apart from Christ he could do nothing (cf. John 15:5). His ego was "hidden with Christ in God" (Col. 3:3, NIV). So when he shares with us what he has achieved he is really telling us what *Christ* has accomplished through him; yet he is so confident in Christ's working through him that he is willing to face any challenge and undertake any assignment.

Remembering, therefore, that it is Christ and not Paul, let's notice a few statements he makes. "From Jerusalem all the way around to Illyricum, I have fully proclaimed the gospel of Christ" (19, NIV). Obviously he is aware he has covered a wide circle in his proclamation of Christ, setting a record no other apostle could touch. "It has always been my ambition to preach the gospel where Christ was not known" (20, NIV). "Ambition"? Yes, to pioneer for Christ, hoping that others and still others will follow his example until the whole world has been reached. "I hope to see you . . . as I go to Spain" (24, RSV). He will not be satisfied until he has reached the outpost of the empire for Christ! And he is sure of his relationship to God: "I know that when I come to you I shall come in the fulness of the blessing of Christ" (29, RSV). He is joyously confident in the fullness of the Spirit. Right here is the secret of his life. At the very outset of his ministry he was filled with the Spirit (Acts 9:17); this fullness is still his strength as a veteran apostle and missionary.

2. *The Ministry of the Gospel*

a. Paul is well aware that he is taking a risk in writing such a letter as this Epistle to a church he has never visited; he may appear to be imposing *his* teaching upon them. He knows that fundamentally he cannot write anything to them that they may not already understand and that they are themselves capable of teaching one another. So he writes tactfully, "I myself am convinced, my brothers, that you yourselves are full of goodness, complete in knowledge and competent to instruct one another" (14, NIV). This is a heartwarming example of Pauline courtesy, but it is more. Paul is affirming what Nels F. S. Ferrè would sometimes say to a theology class: "My only confidence as a teacher is that the Holy Spirit is the only Teacher." You see, the gospel we believe is not from man but from God. And since the humblest believer has received the anointing and illumination of the Spirit, apostles and theologians have no corner on the truth (cf. 1 John 2:27).

b. Nevertheless, Paul continues by saying, "I have written you quite boldly on some points, as if to remind you of them again, because of the grace God gave me" (15, NIV). He has been reminding the Romans of truths they already knew, but with a measure of authority which requires justification. To some churches he could speak *quite boldly* because he had founded them and was their spiritual father. Here he falls back on the more general fact that God has called him to be an apostle to the Gentiles. He has been commissioned *a minister of Christ Jesus to the Gentiles with the priestly duty of proclaiming the gospel of God, so that the Gentiles might become an offering acceptable to God, sanctified by the Holy Spirit* (15-

16, NIV). It was this divine commission which gave him the authority to write as he has to the Romans.

Paul's language here calls for comment. He uses expressions which have very close associations with sacrificial customs, and some of the words are technical phrases in the religious vocabulary of the Greek version of the Old Testament, with which the Romans would be familiar. As a *minister of Christ Jesus* he is a priest at God's altar. Preaching the gospel is his *priestly service* (16, RSV). As John Knox puts it, "He is the mediator of the love of God in Christ to the Gentiles and the one through whom the Gentile church offers itself to God as a sacrifice (cf. 12:1-2)." But it was not Paul; it was the gospel proclaimed *by the power of the Holy Spirit* (19, RSV) which saved persons and called upon them to become living sacrifices to God.

It was Bishop Gore who said that "the true Christian idea of sacrifice makes the substance of it to be always persons returning to God the life He gave them." All other offerings are but outward symbols of this central truth. It is the *priestly duty* of every minister of Jesus Christ to proclaim the gospel in the power of the Spirit and to make plain to all that each of us is called to offer himself to God as a living sacrifice. As gospel priests, Gerald Cragg says,

> We do not so much call down God's blessing on others as we lift them up into his presence. Then every heart should be an altar, and every needy soul an offering set before God that his quickening fire may fall upon the sacrifice. And it is Paul's conviction that this is precisely what will happen. God will receive the sacrifice because it will be *sanctified by the Holy Spirit.*[4]

c. Because God has signally used him as this kind of minister, Paul can say, "In Christ Jesus, then, I have reason to be proud of my work for God" (17, RSV). The crucial words here, as we have already seen, are *in Christ Jesus.* A man does not serve God in the spirit Paul exemplifies except through intimacy with and dependency upon Christ. But when he does serve God in this way he has reason to be proud of his work. Transformed lives will accompany his ministry. Churches will be born and flourish in the Spirit. God calls His ministers to succeed on these terms. When we are caught up in this divine enterprise we know we are serving a great purpose, and there is no comparable source of dignity and courage.

3. *The Stream of the Spirit.* Through His servant and "minister . . . to the Gentiles" Christ accomplished more than we can imagine, after He encountered Paul on the Damascus Road and then filled him with the Spirit. At that moment something powerful began, comparable to one of nature's great phenomena. Those who swim in the ocean know that they must watch against the undertow of the sea, that current which carries away irresistibly anyone who is caught in it. It is as if one is being sucked away and swallowed up by the deep. This is Walter Luthi's figure for what happened to Paul as he ventured out on the sea of nations as a pardoned servant entrusted with the gospel message. "He was caught in a current; not a current of destruction, but of salvation. It was not a current of death, but a saving stream."

a. So as Paul launched out as an apostle to the Gentiles he found himself drawn into a mysterious current: the love of Christ for the whole world. "For the love of Christ controls us," he writes to the Corinthians, "because we are convinced that one has died for all; therefore all have died. And he died for all, that those who live might live no longer for themselves but for him who for their sake died and was raised" (2 Cor. 5:14-15, RSV). This is the strong current which swept him "from Jerusalem all the way around to Illyricum" (19, NIV). It was this current which moved him westward to Rome and then to Spain. The current of the Lord had been pulling the apostle towards Rome for years. However, now he realizes his stay in Rome will be only short and that the Lord will be drawing him on westward to Spain, so that "those who were not told about him will see, and those who have not heard will understand" (21, NIV). Paul's mission can be understood in no other way than the movement of God's Spirit.

b. For the time being, however, the pull was toward Jerusalem. His Gentile converts in Macedonia and Achaia had given liberally out of their poverty to help the poor among the saints in Jerusalem. "They were pleased to do it," Paul explains, "and indeed they owe it to them. For if the Gentiles have shared in the Jews' spiritual blessings, they owe it to the Jews to share with them their material blessings. So after I have completed this task and have made sure that they have received this fruit, I will go to Spain and visit you on the way" (27-28, NIV). Although he was the apostle to the Gentiles, Paul never forgot that the gospel came to the Jews first. He undoubtedly felt that the thank offering he had raised among his Gentile converts was a kind of sacramental gift which would seal the unity of Jews and Gentiles in the true Israel of God. Nothing could deter him, therefore, from going to Jerusalem, even the threat of death at the hands of hostile Jews there (21).

We know that Paul's fears were justified. He was seized in Jerusalem and would have been killed by the fanatical devotees of the law in the very Temple area, except for the intervention of Roman soldiers. After two years of imprisonment in Jerusalem and Caesarea, Paul did make his trip to Rome, as an imperial prisoner. The account of his entry into Rome and the ministry he found there is beautifully told in the last chapter of Acts. God's way of leading the apostle to the center of the empire was not the way Paul had envisioned it. Whether he ever got to Spain is still debated. We have no New Testament account of any such visit, but some scholars believe he was released after his first imprisonment and that he did eventually present Christ on the Iberian peninsula before being arrested again and finally executed for Christ.

c. The important lesson the Church must learn from this, however, is not simply factual history. We need to realize that God has His own sovereign plan for spreading His gospel among men. We do not know why the gospel tide flowed westward toward Rome instead of eastward toward Benares and Peking. But we do know that the current of God's salvation in Christ is still moving in history. It is our responsibility and privilege to be drawn on by that current. The Church must live and witness in the stream of the Spirit.

The important truth enshrined in this passage is that the Church *is* mission. "The church exists by mission," says Emil Brunner, "as fire exists by burning." From the very beginning, when God called Abram that through him all families of the earth should be blessed, down to this very moment, God has been seeking to reveal himself to all people as the Redeemer. The stream of the Spirit would carry us into all the world. And, thank God, we have a promise: "You will receive power when the Holy Spirit comes on you; and you will be my witnesses in Jerusalem, and in all Judea and Samaria, and to the ends of the earth" (Acts 1:8, NIV).

Blest river of salvation,
Pursue thine onward way;
Flow thou to every nation,
Nor in thy richness stay.
Stay not till all the lowly,
Triumphant, reach their home.
Stay not till all the holy
Proclaim, "The Lord is come!"

—S. F. Smith

ROMANS 16

A Glimpse of a Real Church

Romans 16:1-27

1 I commend unto you Phebe our sister, which is a servant of the church which is at Cenchrea:
2 That ye receive her in the Lord, as becometh saints, and that ye

assist her in whatsoever business she hath need of you: for she hath been a succourer of many, and of myself also.
3 Greet Priscilla and Aquila my helpers in Christ Jesus:
4 Who have for my life laid down their own necks: unto whom not only I give thanks, but also all the churches of the Gentiles.
5 Likewise greet the church that is in their house. Salute my well beloved Epaenetus, who is the firstfruits of Achaia unto Christ.
6 Greet Mary, who bestowed much labour on us.
7 Salute Andronicus and Junia, my kinsmen, and my fellowprisoners, who are of note among the apostles, who also were in Christ before me.
8 Greet Amplias my beloved in the Lord.
9 Salute Urbane, our helper in Christ, and Stachys my beloved.
10 Salute Apelles approved in Christ. Salute them which are of Aristobulus' household.
11 Salute Herodion my kinsman. Greet them that be of the household of Narcissus, which are in the Lord.
12 Salute Tryphena and Tryphosa, who labour in the Lord. Salute the beloved Persis, which laboured much in the Lord.
13 Salute Rufus chosen in the Lord, and his mother and mine.
14 Salute Asyncritus, Phlegon, Hermas, Patrobas, Hermes, and the brethren which are with them.
15 Salute Philologus, and Julia, Nereus, and his sister, and Olympas, and all the saints which are with them.
16 Salute one another with an holy kiss. The churches of Christ salute you.
17 Now I beseech you, brethren, mark them which cause divisions and offences contrary to the doctrine which ye have learned; and avoid them.
18 For they that are such serve not our Lord Jesus Christ, but their own belly; and by good words and fair speeches deceive the hearts of the simple.
19 For your obedience is come abroad unto all men. I am glad therefore on your behalf: but yet I would have you wise unto that which is good, and simple concerning evil.
20 And the God of peace shall bruise Satan under your feet shortly. The grace of our Lord Jesus Christ be with you. Amen.
21 Timotheus my workfellow, and Lucius, and Jason, and Sosipater, my kinsmen, salute you.
22 I Tertius, who wrote this epistle, salute you in the Lord.
23 Gaius mine host, and of the whole church, saluteth you. Erastus the chamberlain of the city saluteth you, and Quartus a brother.
24 The grace of our Lord Jesus Christ be with you all. Amen.
25 Now to him that is of power to stablish you according to my gospel, and the preaching of Jesus Christ, according to the revelation of the mystery, which was kept secret since the world began,
26 But now is made manifest, and by the scriptures of the prophets, according to the commandment of the everlasting God, made known to all nations for the obedience of faith:
27 To God only wise, be glory through Jesus Christ for ever. Amen.

Throughout this Epistle, Paul has been talking to us about life-and-death issues of Christian faith and practice.

He has led us through the foundational doctrines of sin, the atonement, justification, sanctification, and glorification. He has given us an overview of holy history from the call of Abraham to the final salvation of Israel. In the process he has given us a glimpse into the meaning of divine sovereignty, predestination, and election. He has outlined for us the meaning of Christian ethics both in the Christian community and in society in general. He has held up before us the Christian hope with its transforming power and suggested the Christian mission in which the Church must ever be engaged. These tremendous themes come alive in the 15 chapters which comprise the body of the Epistle to the Romans.

Abruptly, all this changes. Enter Phoebe, the deaconess of the church at Cenchraea, a few miles from Corinth where the Epistle was written. Paul had chosen her to deliver the Epistle and she probably read it to the Roman church. Think of it—Paul entrusted this greatest of Christian writings to a woman, and gave her the unspeakable privilege of becoming his personal emissary! What does this say about the apostle's alleged antifeminism?

In this final chapter we also meet Tertius, Paul's amanuensis (or secretary) to whom he dictated the Book of Romans. Yes, shorthand was in vogue in A.D. 58. Tertius faithfully wrote as Paul paced back and forth in his private quarters in Corinth and composed this theological treatise. "I, Tertius, who wrote down this letter, greet you in the Lord" (22, NIV).

But above all, Paul gives us the unspeakable privilege of glimpsing the real Church of Jesus Christ in the imperial city, about 25 years after its origin. It is a church of house-congregations. One of the groups, the church which met in the house of Priscilla and Aquila, is mentioned specifically (3-5), but there were certainly a number of such small fellowships which gathered throughout the city in the homes of the more prominent members. There were no church buildings such as we have until 200 years later.

The body of Christ in the city of seven hills on the Tiber lived and witnessed long before there were any magnificent edifices.

1. *The Fellowship of Saints* (3-16). Here is the longest list of names given in any of Paul's letters. Priscilla and Aquila had originally lived in Rome, but had fled to Corinth when the Emperor Claudius evicted all Jews from Rome in A.D. 52. They accompanied Paul from Corinth to Ephesus, where they had a residence like the one they had left in Rome, in which the local congregation met (1 Cor. 16:19). Now they are back in Rome, and many of their Asian Christian friends have apparently moved with them to the capital. Priscilla was a wealthy Jewish Christian from a highborn Roman family, an influential matron in her own right. This is probably why her name precedes that of her husband. The site of their house-church is still pointed out to visitors in Rome, but the identification is dubious.

Some scholars think the rest of the names in these verses are of the members of the house-congregation of Priscilla and Aquila. Epaenetus was the *firstfruits* of the Christian mission in Asia, perhaps conferring on him a position of special honor in the community (5). Andronicus and Junia possibly belonged originally to the congregation in Antioch, Syria; their conversion, Paul says, preceded his. They were distinguished missionaries of Christ (the meaning of *apostles* in v. 7). Bishop Lightfoot thinks that Ampliatus and Urbanus (8-9, RSV) were members of "Caesar's household" (cf. Phil. 4:22), since their names are found in the imperial household lists of that time. Aristobulus mentioned in v. 10 was quite likely the person of this name who was the grandson of Herod the Great and brother of Agrippa I. He ended his life, as a private individual, in Rome. Aristobulus' household, which Paul greets, would be mainly Jews. In v. 11, Paul calls Herodion his "relative" (NIV), and he may have been part of Aristobulus' household. Rufus (in v. 13) is thought to be the Rufus of Mark 15:21, the son of Simon of Cyrene. At least this is early Christian tradition.

We know nothing about the rest of the people mentioned here, apart from their names and what Paul says about them. Why then are they in our Bibles? Because in scripture no name is ever mentioned without good reason. These people embody the Lord's words through the prophet Isaiah: "Fear not, for I have redeemed you; I have called you by name, you are mine" (Isa. 43:1, RSV). This is the purpose for the list of names: Paul is singling out people who have been redeemed by Christ. Names both Eastern and Western, Jewish and Gentile, Latin and Greek are mentioned. Christ found some of these people in Palestine, others in Syria; in the Balkans or in Asia Minor. Some were from cities, others from the country. But all of them Christ had lifted up and saved, and He says to them, "You are mine."

The Roman Epistle proclaims with great conviction that the gospel is "the power of God unto salvation to every one that believeth; to the Jew first, and also to the Greek." Every one of the names mentioned here bears eloquent witness to the truth of Christ's gospel. And since their names were written, myriads of others have been added, that "multitude which no man could number, from every nation, from all tribes and peoples and tongues" (Rev. 7:9, RSV). And someday, by His grace, your name and mine will be added to this list; for Paul tells us that God "desires all men to be saved and to come to the knowledge of the truth" (1 Tim. 2:4, RSV). There is not a name of one man in the whole world which could not someday be written in the book of life.

2. *Sinners in the Congregation* (17-20). It is a sad but eloquent fact that right in the midst of these beautiful saints were "those who cause divisions and put obstacles" in their way, contrary to the teaching of Christ, people who were "not serving our Lord Christ, but their own appetites" (NIV).

Think of it! Less than 30 years after Jesus' death there were people in the church who were bent on doing Satan's rather than God's will, hypocrites, subverters of the faith of others. This is both distressing and encouraging. It reminds us that what Jesus himself said has been true from the beginning, that along with the good seed of the Kingdom, in the Church we will always find Satan's tares (Matt. 13:36-43).

Just what variety of false Christians these were, scholars do not agree upon. But it does not matter as far as we are concerned. They seem to have been libertines of some sort, who thought Christian freedom means the right to indulge all your appetites as you please. They were smooth talkers who by their flattery deceived the naive. Up to this time Paul has been writing in a general way about errors of doctrine. Now he takes off his gloves, here at the end of the Epistle, and uses strong language in denouncing those who were perpetrating error and leading simple Christians astray.

Christian discipline is an essential element in ministry. Paul never shrank from this responsibility. He did not expect the church to be perfect, but he was careful to preserve Christian faith and practice from perversions which destroy the reality of the gospel and undermine holiness.

But Paul is not negative. He has a good word for the majority of the church. "Everyone has heard about your obedience, so I am full of joy over you," he writes; "but I want you to be wise about what is good, and innocent about what is evil" (19, NIV). He is not only positive; he is confident that "the God of peace will soon crush Satan under your feet" (20, NIV). We must never let the false blind us to the true or destroy our faith in the power of Christ and His gospel. We can be realistic without becoming negative and pessimistic.

3. *The Circle of Christ* (21-27). We now find a list of Paul's companions, who send greetings to the Roman church.

Timothy heads the roll as Paul's "fellow worker" (21, NIV). He is the apostle's inseparable aide-de-camp and is usually mentioned at the beginning of letters (2 Cor. 1:1; Phil. 1:1; Col. 1:1; 2 Thess. 1:1; Philem. 1).

The three following names (Lucius, Jason, Sosipater) are clearly Jewish Christians whom Paul calls "my relatives" (21, NIV). Lucius, a Roman name, recalls Lucius of Cyrene (Acts 13:1), but it may be "Luke, the beloved physician." The other two are also Greek names. Tertius and Quartus are both familiar Roman names.

"Gaius, whose hospitality I and the whole church here enjoy," as Paul puts it (23, NIV), must be a wealthy Christian. Erastus in the same verse is "city treasurer" (RSV) or perhaps "the city's director of public works" (NIV), in Corinth. Evidently Christianity was penetrating all strata of society by this time.

All the personal names listed in this chapter give us an insight into Paul the man. The apostle was a great man, but he was also a great friend. He recalled with glowing words of gratitude the favors he had received. He watched with solicitude over his converts' growth in grace. He remembered his friends by name and lifted them often to God in prayer.

Having read through this Epistle to the Romans, we might view with alarm the prospect of spending an evening in Paul's company. We might study this letter with profit to our souls, but we probably would shrink from choosing the apostle as our friend. He sets a high standard which we would have difficulty measuring up to. However, the evidence is here, as throughout his writings, to prove that Paul not only felt a great affection for his converts, but elicited from them an answering love. He reminds the Galatians that one time they would have plucked out their eyes for him (Gal. 4:15), and the whole tenor of the Philippian letter suggests a relationship of warmest mutual regard. Here the picture is of a man surrounded by those who cherish his friendship and count themselves blessed to be associated with him.

The Church of Jesus Christ is a family. In Christ we are brothers and sisters. There is no place for "great" men and women who condescend to "ordinary laymen." Apostle and slave, city treasurer and some unknown Mary, highborn Priscilla and humble Persis, are all one in Christ.

> *Now to him who is able to establish you by my gospel and the proclamation of Jesus Christ, according to the revelation of the mystery hidden for long ages past, but now revealed and made known through the prophetic writings by the command of the eternal God, so that all nations might believe and obey him—to the only wise God be glory forever through Jesus Christ! Amen* (25-27, NIV).

Reference Notes

INTRODUCTION

1. Anders Nygren, *Commentary on Romans,* trans. Carl C. Rasmussen (Philadelphia: The Fortress Press, 1949), p. 3.

2. Quoted by Hans J. Hillerbrand, *The Reformation* (New York: Harper and Row, 1964), p. 27.

3. *The Works of the Rev. John Wesley* (Kansas City: Nazarene Publishing House, n.d.), 1:103.

4. P. T. Forsyth, *The Person and Place of Jesus Christ* (London: Independent Press, 1948), p. 60.

5. See *Beacon Bible Commentary* (Kansas City: Beacon Hill Press of Kansas City, 1968), 8:41-46. (Hereafter referred to as *BBC*.)

6. A. M. Hunter, *Romans* (London: SCM Press, Ltd., 1955), p. 19.

INTRODUCTION AND THEME

1. Sydney Martin, *The Gospel of Power* (Kansas City: Beacon Hill Press of Kansas City, 1973), p. 11.

2. P. T. Forsyth, *Positive Preaching and the Modern Mind* (London: Hodder and Stoughton, 1907), p. 6.

3. *The Works of John Wesley,* 6:509.

4. *Luther's Works,* Weimar edition, 54:179-80.

5. Frank Staggs, *Polarities of Man's Existence in Biblical Perspective* (Philadelphia: The Westminster Press, 1973), p. 152.

6. *Ibid.*

7. *The Works of John Wesley,* 5:9.

THE WRATH AND THE RIGHTEOUSNESS OF GOD

1. A. M. Hunter, *Interpreting Paul's Gospel* (Philadelphia: The Westminster Press, 1954), pp. 69-70.

2. Burton Throckmorton, *Romans for the Layman* (Philadelphia: The Westminster Press, 1961), p. 24.

3. John Macquarrie, *The Problem of God Today,* Drawbridge Memorial Lecture (London: Christian Evidence Society, 1972), p. 6.

4. D. R. Davies, *Down Peacock's Feathers* (New York: The Macmillan Co., 1944), p. 70.

5. Staggs, *Polarities of Man's Existence,* p. 33.

6. *The Works of John Wesley,* 11:446.

7. *Ibid.,* 9:456.

8. Richard V. Spivey, *The Gospel According to St. Paul* (London: Epworth Press, 1949), pp. 13-14.

9. *Ibid.,* p. 12.

10. Matthew Black, *Romans, New Century Bible* (London: Oliphants, 1973), p. 63.

11. W. H. Fitchett, *Wesley and His Century* (New York: Eaton and Mains, 1808), pp. 510-11.

12. John Wesley, *Explanatory Notes upon the New Testament* (London: The Epworth Press, n.d.), p. 532.

13. C. Anderson Scott, *Romans, The Abingdon Bible Commentary* (New York: The Abingdon Press, 1929), p. 1145. (Hereafter referred to as *ABC.*)

14. Martin Luther, *Lectures on Romans,* trans. Wilhelm Pauck (Philadelphia: The Westminster Press, 1961), p. 4.

15. *The Works of John Wesley, loc. cit.*

16. Cited by William R. Cannon, *The Theology of John Wesley* (New York: The Abingdon Press, 1946), p. 81.

17. *The Works of John Wesley,* 6:48.

18. John Calvin, *Institutes of the Christian Religion,* III, 18, 8.

19. Fitchett, *Wesley and His Century,* p. 383.

20. *Works of Martin Luther, Translated with Introductions and Notes* (Philadelphia: Muhlenberg Press, 1932), 6:449 f. and 451 f.

21. *The Works of John Wesley,* 11:417-19.

22. F. F. Bruce, "The Epistle of Paul to the Romans," *The Tyndale New Testament Commentaries* (Grand Rapids, Mich.: Wm. B. Eerdmans Publishing Co., 1963), pp. 116-17.

God's Eternal Purpose in Christ

1. *Ibid.,* p. 127.

2. *Ibid.,* pp. 125-26.

3. Keith Miller, *The Becomers* (Waco, Tex.: Word Books, Publishers, 1973), pp. 63-87.

4. See Thomas A. Harris, *I'm OK—You're OK* (New York: Avon Books, 1973).

5. Gerald Cragg, *Interpreter's Bible* (Exposition) (Nashville: The Abingdon-Cokesbury Press, 1954), 9:469-70.

6. Wesley, *Explanatory Notes, loc. cit.*

7. Bill Bright, *How to Walk in the Spirit* (San Bernardino, Calif.: Campus Crusade for Christ, Inc., 1971), pp. 47-48.

8. H. C. G. Moule, *The Epistle of Paul to the Romans* (Cincinnati: Jennings and Graham, n.d.), p. 169.

9. E. Stanley Jones, *Victorious Living* (New York: The Abingdon Press, 1936), p. 120.

10. Moule, *Romans,* p. 173.

11. Oswald Chambers, *My utmost for His Highest* (New York: Dodd, Mead and Company, 1935), p. 81.

12. Moule, *Romans,* pp. 176-77.

13. Hunter, *Romans,* pp. 66-67.

14. Greathouse, *BBC,* 8:146.

15. C. H. Dodd, *The Epistle of Paul to the Romans* (New York: Harper and Brothers, 1932), p. 108.

16. See William M. Greathouse, *Romans, Search the Scriptures* (Kansas City: Nazarene Publishing House, 1955), NT 6:30-31.

17. J. A. T. Robinson, *The Body* (London: SCM Press, Ltd., 1952), p. 19.

18. I am indebted to Prof. R. E. Howard for this analysis.

19. Scott, *ABC,* p. 1153.

20. Dodd, *Romans,* p. 93.

21. Moule, *Romans,* p. 211.

22. H. C. G. Moule, *Ephesian Studies* (London: Pickering and Inglis, Ltd., n.d.), p. 128; cited by W. H. Taylor in *Beacon Bible Commentary,* 9:195.

23. Moule, *Romans,* pp. 215-16.

24. *Ibid.,* p. 220.

25. Robinson, *The Body,* p. 28.

26. W. E. Sangster, *The Pure in Heart* (New York and Nashville: The Abingdon Press, 1954), pp. 235-36.

27. *The Works of John Wesley,* 5:127.

28. Greathouse, *BBC,* 8:181.

29. Paul Stromberg Rees, *If God Be for Us* (Grand Rapids, Mich.: Wm. B. Eerdmans Publishing Co., 1940), pp. 112-20. Sermon used by permission of author and publisher.

30. Chester Warren Quimby, *The Great Redemption* (New York: The Macmillan Co., 1950), p. 160.

31. *Ibid.,* p. 161.

32. *Ibid.,* pp. 163-64.

33. Walter Luthi, *The Letter to the Romans* (Richmond, Va.: John Knox Press, 1961), pp. 141-42.

34. *Ibid.*, p. 143.

35. Leonard Goppelt, *Jesus, Paul and Judaism* (New York: Thomas Nelson and Sons, 1964), p. 158.

36. Luthi, *Romans,* p. 152.

37. Johannes Munck, *Christ and Israel, an Interpretation of Romans 9—11* (Philadelphia: The Fortress Press, 1967), p. 127.

38. Goppelt, *Jesus, Paul and Judaism,* p. 160.

39. *Ibid.*, p. 161.

PRACTICAL APPLICATIONS

1. Quimby, *Great Redemption,* p. 174.
2. Moule, *Romans,* pp. 328-29.
3. Cragg, *Interpreter's Bible,* 9:585.
4. *Ibid.*, 9:644.

Bibliography

(An expanded book list for study purposes)

Barclay, William. *The Letter to the Romans.* "The Daily Study Bible." Philadelphia: The Westminster Press, 1957.

Barrett, Charles Kingsley. *The Epistle to the Romans.* "Harper's New Testament Commentaries." New York: Harper and Brothers, 1957.

Barth, Karl. *The Epistle to the Romans.* Translated from the 6th edition by Edwin C. Hoskyns. London: Oxford University Press, 1933.

———. *A Shorter Commentary on Romans.* Richmond, Va.: John Knox Press, 1959.

Beet, Joseph Agar. *St. Paul's Epistle to the Romans.* London: Hodder and Stoughton, 1885.

Black, Matthew. *Romans.* "New Century Bible." London: Oliphants, 1973.

Brokke, Harold J. *Saved by His Life, An Exposition of Paul's Epistle to the Romans.* Minneapolis: Bethany Fellowship, Inc., 1964.

Bruce, F. F. *The Epistle of Paul to the Romans.* "The Tyndale New Testament Commentaries." Grand Rapids, Mich.: Wm. B. Eerdmans Publishing Co., 1963.

Brunner, Emil. *The Letter to the Romans.* Translated by H. A. Kennedy. Philadelphia: The Westminster Press, 1959.

Cragg, Gerald. "The Epistle to the Romans" (Exposition). *The Interpreter's Bible.* Edited by George A. Buttrick, *et al.*, Vol. IX. New York: Abingdon-Cokesbury Press, 1951.

Davies, D. R. *Down Peacock's Feathers.* New York: The Macmillan Co., 1944.

Denney, James. "St. Paul's Epistle to the Romans." *The Expositor's Greek Testament.* Edited by W. Robertson Nicoll, Vol. II. Grand Rapids, Mich.: Wm. B. Eerdmans Publishing Company, n.d.

Dodd, C. H. *The Epistle to the Romans.* "The Moffatt New Testament Commentary." New York: Harper and Brothers Publishers, 1932.

Earle, Ralph. *Word Meanings in the New Testament,* Vol. 3, Kansas City: Beacon Hill Press of Kansas City, 1974.

Eerdman, Charles R. *The Epistle of Paul to the Romans.* Philadelphia: The Westminster Press, 1925.

Fitchett, W. H. *Wesley and His Century.* New York: Eaton and Mains, 1808.

Godet, F. *St. Paul's Epistle to the Romans.* Translated by A. Cusin. New York: Funk and Wagnalls, 1883.

Goppelt, Leonard. *Jesus, Paul and Judaism.* Translated by Edward Shroeder. New York: Thomas Nelson and Sons, 1964.

Greathouse, William M. "Romans." *Beacon Bible Commentary.* Kansas City: Beacon Hill Press of Kansas City, 1968.

———. "Romans." *Search the Scriptures,* New Testament Vol. 6. Edited by Norman R. Oke. Kansas City: Nazarene Publishing House, 1955.

Hunter, A. M. *Interpreting Paul's Gospel.* Philadelphia: The Westminster Press, 1954.

———. *Romans.* London: SCM Press, Ltd., 1955.

Leonhardt, Franz J. *The Epistle to the Romans.* Cleveland and New York: The World Publishing Company, 1957.

Luther, Martin. *Lectures on Romans.* Translated by Wilhelm Pauck. Philadelphia: The Westminster Press, 1961.

Luthi, Walter. *The Letter to the Romans.* Richmond, Va.: John Knox Press, 1961.

Martin, Sydney. *The Gospel of Power.* Kansas City: Beacon Hill Press of Kansas City, 1973.

Moule, H. C. G. *The Epistle of Paul to the Romans.* Cincinnati, Ohio: Jennings and Graham, n.d.

Munck, Johannes. *Christ and Israel, an Interpretation of Romans.* Philadelphia: The Fortress Press, 1967.

Murray, John. *The Epistle to the Romans.* Grand Rapids, Mich.: Wm. B. Eerdmans Publishing Company, 1959.

Nygren, Anders. *Commentary on Romans.* Translated by Carl C. Rasmussen. Philadelphia: The Fortress Press, 1949.

Quimby, Chester Warren. *The Great Redemption.* New York: The Macmillan Company, 1950.

Rees, Paul Stromberg. *If God Be for Us.* Grand Rapids, Mich.: Wm. B. Eerdmans Publishing Co., 1940.

Richardson, John R., and Chamblin, Knox. "The Epistle to the Romans." *Proclaiming the New Testament.* Grand Rapids, Mich.: Baker Book House, 1963.

Robinson, J. A. T. *The Body.* London: SCM Press, Ltd., 1952.

Sanday, W., and Headlam, A. C. *The Epistle to the Romans.* "The International Critical Commentary." New York: Charles Scribner's Sons, 1929.

Sangster, W. E. *The Pure in Heart.* New York and Nashville: The Abingdon Press, 1954.

Scott, C. Anderson. *Romans. The Abingdon Bible Commentary.* Edited by David C. Downey. New York: The Abingdon Press, 1929.

Spivey, Richard V. *The Gospel According to St. Paul.* London: Epworth Press, 1949.

Staggs, Frank. *Polarities of Man's Existence in Biblical Perspective.* Philadelphia: The Westminster Press, 1973.

Thomas, E. Griffith. *St. Paul's Epistle to the Romans.* Grand Rapids, Mich.: Wm. B. Eerdmans Publishing Co., 1947.

Throckmorton, Burton H., Jr. *Romans for the Layman.* Philadelphia: The Westminster Press, 1961.

Wesley, John. *Explanatory Notes upon the New Testament.* London: Epworth Press, 1950 (reprint).

———. *The Works of the Rev. John Wesley.* 14 vols. Kansas City: Nazarene Publishing House, n.d.

Wood, A. Skevington. *Life by the Spirit.* Grand Rapids, Mich.: Wm. B. Eerdmans Publishing Co., 1963.